POLICING AND CRIME CONTROL IN POST-APARTHEID SOUTH AFRICA

Interdisciplinary Research Series in Ethnic, Gender and Class Relations

Series Editor: Biko Agozino, Cheyney University of Pennsylvania, USA

This series brings together research from a range of disciplines including criminology, cultural studies and applied social studies, focusing on experiences of ethnic, gender and class relations. In particular, the series examines the treatment of marginalized groups within the social systems for criminal justice, education, health, employment and welfare.

Also published in this series

W.E.B. Du Bois on Crime and Justice
Shaun L. Gabbidon
ISBN 978-0-7546-4956-4

Democratic Policing in Transitional and Developing Countries
Edited by Nathan Pino and Michael D. Wiatrowski
ISBN 978-0-7546-4719-5

Modernization and the Crisis of Development in Africa:
The Nigerian Experience
Jeremiah I. Dibua
ISBN 978-0-7546-4228-2

Africa Beyond the Post-Colonial: Political and Socio-Cultural Identities
Edited by Ola Uduku and Alfred B. Zack-Williams
ISBN 978-0-7546-3171-2

Pan-African Issues in Crime and Justice
Edited by Anita Kalunta-Crumpton and Biko Agozino
ISBN 978-0-7546-1882-9

Main Issues in Mental Health and Race
Edited by David Ndegwa and Dele Olajide
ISBN 978-1-84014-812-1

Policing and Crime Control in Post-apartheid South Africa

ANNE-MARIE SINGH
Ryerson University, Toronto, Canada

ASHGATE

Published by
Ashgate Publishing Limited
Gower House
Croft Road
Aldershot
Hampshire GU11 3HR
England

Ashgate Publishing Company
Suite 420
101 Cherry Street
Burlington, VT 05401-4405
USA

Ashgate website: http://www.ashgate.com

British Library Cataloguing in Publication Data
Singh, Anne-Marie
Policing and crime control in post-apartheid South Africa. - (Interdisciplinary research series in ethnic, gender and class relations)
1. Crime prevention - South Africa 2. Private security services - South Africa 3. Police, Private - South Africa 4. Community policing - South Africa 5. South Africa - Politics and government - 1994-
I. Title
363.2'3'0968

Library of Congress Cataloging-in-Publication Data
Singh, Anne-Marie.
Policing and crime control in post-apartheid South Africa / by Anne-Marie Singh.
p. cm. -- (Interdisciplinary research series in ethnic, gender and class relations)
Includes bibliographical references and index.
ISBN 978-0-7546-4457-6
1. Crime prevention--South Africa. 2. Private security services--South Africa. 3. Police, Private--South Africa. 4. Community policing--South Africa 5. South Africa--Politics and government--1994- I. Title.

HV7150.5.S59 2008
363.2'30968--dc22

2007042383

ISBN: 978-0-7546-4457-6

Printed and bound in Great Britain by MPG Books Ltd, Bodmin, Cornwall.

Contents

For Mathilda who survived by dreaming

Series Editor's Preface

Biko Agozino
The University of the West Indies, St. Augustine

The Ashgate Publishers' Interdisciplinary Research Series in Ethnic, Gender and Class Relations was launched ten years ago with my book on *Black Women and the Criminal Justice System* (1997). After a decade, more than two dozen books have appeared in the series and this one about policing in the democratic South Africa will prove to be yet another major contribution to the series.

The introductory chapter and the second chapter simply frame the analysis and present a background to the discourse of the real focus of the author, the booming private security industry in South Africa. After reading Chapter 3 and realizing that this business is worth billions of Rands annually, a reader would be forgiven to wonder if he or she is in the right business when there is serious money to be made in the private security business. But more importantly, hardly any university is offering courses in the field of private security business in South Africa while scholars who specialize on policing tend to focus on the state police force rather than the private security firms. This book tries to fill this gap in knowledge by offering a Foucauldian analysis of governmentality with reference to private policing powers under the guidance of market forces.

Chapter 4 contributes to the discourse by reminding readers that the private sector does not start where the state sector ends but that the two are inextricably intertwined given that some police officials establish their own security firms before retirement or moonlight as security guards when they are off duty while big firms make donations to the police force to help with the war on crime. The irony here is that private policing as a business designed for profit is also expected to help to reduce the very substance on which its profitability is based – crime. This leads to a Durkheimian discourse that sees crime as a normal part of development and sees policing as a mechanism for the management of the problem and not necessarily for its reduction as we are made to believe by public officials.

In addition, Chapter 5 goes beyond the public police and private police personnel to focus on self-policing by members of the community as illustrated by cases that the author was made aware of during her fieldwork. This again goes along with Foucault's excavation of bio-power or the ability of individuals to exercise power over their own body even while they are also subject to the powers exercised by the dominant authorities. In the case of South Africa, the role of community justice is often presented as an opposition to state justice especially when the condemned individuals were seen as agents of a hostile state structure especially under apartheid. Such community activism continued in the new South Africa as individuals sometimes preferred the more instant results and often more punitive orientation of popular justice to the often long delays and sometimes less severe outcomes that they see in courts. The extent to which such authoritarian populism, as Stuart Hall would put it following Gramsci, makes the study of policing more complex than a simple matter of observing the state police and private security forces as is predominantly the case in the literature on policing.

The book concludes by outlining its contributions to the literature on policing as something that goes beyond the police and the discourse of governmentality or the philosophy of government which always goes beyond the formal structures of governance to encompass the many ways that political sociology enable us to understand the relationships between politics and society, security and the market, state and civil society. Readers will find this as a useful introduction to some of the relevant literature in political science, sociology, history and business administration.

Acknowledgements

A great many people have influenced me in my professional journeys. The late Kevin Carriere introduced me to the work of Michel Foucault and encouraged me to pursue post-graduate studies. Clifford Shearing sparked my interest in policing transformations in South Africa and provided me with the opportunity to work there in the mid-1990s. I am grateful for his continued encouragement and friendship. Mariana Valverde's advice and support over the years has been tremendous and is deeply valued.

I also owe a debt of gratitude to many individuals in South Africa without whom this project would not have been possible. Special thanks go out to David Africa, Sipho Citabatwa, Sarah Henkeman, Charlotte McClain, Mbali Mncadi, Daniel Nina, Wilfried Schärf and the rest of the crowd at the University of Cape Town, and all those who freely gave of their time to be interviewed.

I am thankful to those who have commented on various versions of the arguments presented in this book, including Nikolas Rose, James Sheptycki and Kevin Stenson. I am especially grateful for the criticisms, suggestions and encouragement from Kevin Haggerty and Michael Kempa. Janet MacMillan has provided excellent copy-editing and has become a good friend along the way. Kamara Jeffrey's assistance in compiling the bibliography is gratefully acknowledged. This book is much improved because of their input – though the usual caveat applies.

Biko Agozino deserves special mention for his enduring patience and his belief in this project.

Financial support for the early stages of this research came from the Social Sciences and Humanities Research Council of Canada. Without such assistance it is doubtful that the project would have been completed.

An earlier version of Chapter Three first appeared as A.-M. Singh (2005), 'Private Security and Crime Control', *Theoretical Criminology* 9(2), 153-174. I would like to thank Sage Publications Ltd. for permission to publish this material. Chapter Four is an extended version of A.-M. Singh (2005), 'Some Critical Reflections on the Governance of Crime in Post-Apartheid South Africa', in J. Sheptycki and A. Wardak (eds) *Transnational Criminology* (Great Britain: Glasshouse Press), 135–155. I am grateful to Routledge-Cavendish for permission to publish this material.

I also gratefully acknowledge the emotional support of Shaamela Cassiem, Kelly Hannah-Moffat, friends and colleagues at Laurie Grove Baths, and especially Andrea Joyce and my family.

List of Abbreviations

ANC	African National Congress
BAC	Business Against Crime
BIACC	Business Initiative Against Crime and Corruption
BIDs	Business Improvement Districts
BSA	Business South Africa
CBD	City Centre's Business District
COSAB	Council of South African Banks
DoCS	Department of Correctional Services
DoJC	Department of Justice and Constitutional Development
DoSS	Department of Safety and Security
DP	Democratic Party
DPSA	Department of Public Service and Administration
GEAR	Growth, Employment and Redistribution plan
ISS	Institute for Security Studies
NBI	National Business Initiative
NCPS	National Crime Prevention Strategy
NIM	Network of Independent Monitors
NP	National Party
PSIRA	Private Security Industry Regulatory Authority
RDP	Reconstruction and Development Programme
SANSEA	South African National Security Employers' Association
SAP	South African Police
SAPS	South African Police Service
SASA	Security Association of South Africa
SOA	*Security Officers Act*
SOB	Security Officers Board
SPPS	Support Partnership with Police Stations Project
TBVC	Transkei, Bophuthatswana, Venda and Ciskei
TRC	Truth and Reconciliation Commission

Chapter 1

Introduction

> In a sense, we do not know the meaning of peace, except in the imagination. But because we have not known true peace in its real meaning, because for centuries generations have had to bury the victims of state violence, we have fought for the right to experience peace.
>
> Nelson Mandela (address to US Congress, 26 June 1990)

> The season for violence is over. The time for reconstruction and reconciliation has arrived.
>
> F.W. De Klerk (State President's parliamentary address, 2 February 1990)

South Africa's transition from apartheid rule to liberal democracy has been marked by a type of (not unreasonable) national anxiety about violence. One can detect a visible shift from a concern with political violence (in the early 1990s) to a concern with violent crime (post-1994). From the African National Congress (ANC) to the National Party (NP), political bodies spanning the spectrum vigorously campaigned for a 'war on crime'. Conferences and workshops involving diverse participants (academics, practitioners, politicians, business leaders, community activists, etc.) proliferated, with the management of crime in the new South Africa as their central theme. Local dailies kept a running tally of crime in the 'Crime Count' sections on their front pages. National crime surveys identified a growing consensus, across the racial divide, that prioritized crime and violence as a, if not the most, significant threat to liberalization (Mattes 2006; Nedcor April 1996; Nedcor/ISS 1998).[1] At the private sector level, businesses invested considerable resources in high-profile initiatives against crime; for example, money from the sale of 'crimebuster combos' at a popular national restaurant chain went towards supporting local police station projects. Within South Africa's poor black townships, civic structures such as street committees refocused their energies and organized anti-crime drives at the local level (Schärf 1991; Seekings 2001). Crime was not, and still is not, merely a background feature of daily existence in post-apartheid South Africa. It became – and it remains – a central object and target of the regulatory schemes of state, market and community authorities alike.

Perhaps the political cartoonist, Zapiro, best captured public opinion when he sketched a David and Goliath scenario of Nelson Mandela who, having slain the

---

1 These and similar surveys classify the South African population using the categorizations of 'black', 'Indian', 'coloured' and 'white'. In this book I adopt this approach and note that such designations continue to influence how South Africans think of themselves and others.

apartheid ogre with his slingshot, remained unaware of the danger looming large behind him – the gigantic figure of crime. In one key sense, though, Zapiro missed a significant aspect of contemporary experiences of the 'crime problem', an aspect that this book inquires into. Across diverse sites, a multitude of groupings of various persuasions – politicians on the left and the right, police officials, small businesses and multinationals, community activists, civic associations, churches, academics, newspaper editors and so forth – *simultaneously* stressed the importance of government commitment to fighting crime and highlighted a civil responsibility for security on the part of each and every citizen. From then on, the battle against crime was to be waged in terms of a new politics of control coupled with a new politics of ethicalization.

What was at stake was no longer the security of the state (which was the key problematic under apartheid rule); nor was it simply a matter of defending society against criminal elements. Rather, the issue increasingly turned on the question of the routine exercise of freedom, autonomy and choice as central practices of democracy. Under the banner of crime control, efforts were mounted to form the kinds of self-regulating citizens that liberal democracy expects: a form of 'democratization through crime'. Strategies emerged to train individuals, either singly or collectively, in the capacities, sensibilities and habits required to actively and successfully participate in contemporary economic, political and social reality. The training involved a form of civics education that included instruction on the importance of human rights, rule of law, process and procedure – precisely those traditions widely acknowledged as lacking in post-apartheid South Africa. The lack of those traditions was seen as restricting the prospects of political transformation. The training should not be understood negatively as marking out the limits of acceptable behaviour. Instead, such strategies acquired a more positive value linked to the articulation of new styles of individual conduct. Citizens were taught to see law less as an external force bearing down on them and more as a crucial resource to their self-fashioning and self-ordering projects. This was an attempt to cultivate a new morality wherein law, far from existing only on the margins as a code of rules commanding fear and obedience, actually constituted a core set of ethical values for understanding and acting on oneself and others. In this way, self-conduct became linked up with the political objectives and interests of governing authorities.

Crucially, freedom does not consist in the absence of rules, but is itself regulated (Foucault 1997; Rose 1992, 1999). This expresses a key tension in liberal democratic rule: citizens are recognized as operating their own internal logics and mechanisms of self-governance which can not be interdicted yet must be rendered acceptable to a range of authorities (Barry, Osborne and Rose 1996; Burchell, G. 1993; Burchell, Gordon and Miller 1991). South Africans were not simply liberated from the tyranny of the apartheid regime; they had to be made free. And increasingly, crime control came to assume an important and distinctive role as a citizen-forming mechanism. What I term 'democratization through crime' represents a significant and innovative development in contemporary politics of rule, yet one that remains little researched. Crime control provides an expansive opportunity for the creation of self-regulating, free, morally responsible individuals. It therefore constitutes a productive and positive exercise of power; it is perhaps best seen as a governmental practice, broadly understood as the more or less rational attempts to shape human subjectivity and conduct (O'Malley 1992; Stenson 1993). Foucault (1979) used the term government not in the conventional sense to refer to the state. Instead, the concept encompasses all those strategies to conduct one's own conduct and that of others.

Democratization strategies emanate not only, or even mainly, from within the state apparatus. Market- and community-based authorities, as routine performers in crime control practices, also initiate and engage in projects to 'make up' citizens and reshape the state along liberal democratic lines.

In the field of crime control, as in several others, citizens – whether at the individual or collective level – are expected to assume an active role in resolving their own problems, seeking out approved ways of securing themselves against crime and associated risks. This involves, in part, the voluntary engagement of the security services provided by commercial and community sectors. But unlike the other fields – for example, health – state and non-state crime control practices have become complementary, not competing, purposes. This stands in some contrast to existing accounts which suggest that, in the context of an increasingly marketized (neo-liberal) political economy, the interventionist state begins to give way to an enabling state as primary responsibility for crime prevention shifts onto the market and individuals (see Garland 1996; O'Malley 1992; Rose 1999). However, in post-apartheid South Africa, not only is there a great deal of state, market and community support (though for different reasons) for coercive solutions to the 'crime problem', solutions that impact disproportionately on the poor, largely black underclass, but privatized security arrangements (which focus as much on controlling as preventing crime) are adjuncts to, not replacements for, state services (see Hudson 2001 for a similar discussion on the relationship between privatization and state penal provision in the UK and US). The failings and inefficiencies of state provision of crime control were not met by demands that individuals, families and communities claim primary responsibility for their own welfare. Instead, these were met by demands that the South African state refigure itself and become a predictable and effective source of order and security (Nedcor/ISS 1998, 2000; also DoSS 1998). This book sheds light on the roles and responsibilities that are to be uploaded back onto state agents and agencies and in so doing seeks to build on the accounts of Garland, O'Malley, Rose and others who draw on and engage with Foucault's work 'on governmentality' (see Foucault 1979).

Since the onset of the transition to liberal democracy, there has been growing and widespread insistence – among the South African public, the civic leaders, the business community, the politicians, etc. – that the state and the criminal justice system reorient themselves towards the policing of crime and away from (more) expressly political functions such as the suppression of dissent and dissidence.[2] Indeed, today it is generally accepted that a key priority of the government must be to guarantee at least basic levels of safety and security, primarily through applications

2 Shaw (2002, 1) observes that '[t]he South African Police's (SAP) official historian concedes that, during the apartheid era, only one in ten members of the force was engaged in crime detection and investigation.'

On the criminalization of politics and the politicization of crime under apartheid rule, see: Brewer (1994a and b); Brogden and Shearing (1993); Cawthra (1992, 1993); Haysom (nd); Steytler (1993); and van der Spuy (1989).

of law and coercive technologies; a legitimate, professional and competent criminal justice system, in particular, is seen to provide the necessary foundation for the free play of market and interpersonal relations. Certainly, there was a more limited sense of the transformative powers of the state, and a growing belief in the market as the organizing principle of contemporary reality (Taylor and Vale 2000). Consequently, the state increasingly moved away from forceful interventions in every aspect of people's lives. Correlatively, it adopted a more enabling role, delivering programmes to mobilize, encourage, advise and educate citizens in the exercise of their self-regulatory capacities; but more than this, the state also sought to increase its *routine* provision of punitive controls on crime, thereby securing minimum conditions of existence. The liberal democratic state was thus interventionist at the same time as it was enabling; both in the sense that it sought to manage crime directly through its command and control structures, as well as indirectly by activating the self-governing capacities of individuals, and in the sense that freedom of individual choice and market responses required for their guarantee a strong sovereign authority armed with considerable coercive powers.

The Post-apartheid Context

'Post-apartheid' does not so much refer to the end of apartheid and the beginning of a new liberal democratic era. It did not begin with the release of Nelson Mandela from prison in February 1990 or with the first democratic elections in April 1994. Instead, 'post-apartheid' is conceived in this book in terms of the emergence of new ways of thinking about how to organize and administer political, economic and everyday life. This highlights the shifting perceptions of the proper sphere of state action and what was seen as within the competence of other agencies and agents. These 'new' reflections on rule – conceived broadly as the attempts to act on the actions of individuals so as to shape, modify and guide their self-conduct in desired directions and towards particular ends (Foucault 1979; Gordon 1991; Rose and Miller 1992) – probably surfaced in the 1980s, but were clearly articulated by the 1990s.

President De Klerk, in a speech in early 1990, firmly placed the question of the proper role for a police force within the context of a reconfiguration of political power. In his address, in Pretoria, to the country's 500 highest-ranking police officers, De Klerk said:

> Up to now the police have been required to perform two types of functions. The one is to handle typical crime situations – murder, rape, theft, etc. – the task of a police force all over the world. But you also had other tasks to fulfil, and that was a control function connected to a specific political party and the execution of laws …
>
> You will no longer be required to prevent people from gathering to canvas support for their views. This is the political arena and we want to take the police out of it. We don't want to use you any more as instruments to reach certain political goals. We as politicians must take full responsibility for politics … This is the direction we are taking and I want you to make peace with this new line.
>
> (in Cawthra 1992, 3)

De Klerk's agenda for police reform was inseparable from the broader project to re-evaluate the nature, targets, objectives, techniques, authorities and limits of political rule. The partial establishment of a new liberal diagram of power was seen in parliamentary debates throughout 1990. In his State Presidential Address on 2 February 1990, De Klerk argued that the institution of a system to recognize and protect individual, collective, minority and national rights was justifiable from both the 'security' and the 'political' point of view (Hansard, Joint Sitting, 2 February 1990, 3–18). Not just the NP government and the South African Police (SAP), but parliamentary representatives from all sides of the floor agreed that national and individual security and prosperity demanded that the police accord the highest priority to the investigation and prevention of crime; that this law and order function be undertaken in partnership with the public, for ultimately the solutions to crime and violence lay within local communities; and that every citizen within a community assume some responsibility for their own safety and for the protection of private property (Hansard, Chamber of Parliament 23 April 1990, cols. 6903–6938). Crime control thus appeared as a matrix for acting to foster and increase individual and collective security, economic growth and social development *and* for specifying and activating a particular notion of citizenship – ethically reflective, active, morally responsible.

Outside parliamentary corridors, the newly unbanned ANC began, in the same year, the journey from a politics of liberation to a politics of governing and within this context posed itself the question of how to rule. ANC interviewees[3] suggested that perhaps for the first time a policy on policing began to take shape, which aimed to set out and clarify the mutual responsibilities of the SAP, citizens and civic structures (for example, ANC linked Self-Defence Units in some townships) in managing crime.

By the middle of the 1990s, a multiplicity of practical strategies and projects to mobilize and responsibilize the active participation of individuals and organizations in crime control came to dominate the political landscape (see Schärf and Nina 2001). Although they emanated largely from outside the state – in the business, NGO (non-governmental organization) and informal/community sectors – these 'private' interventions nonetheless linked up with government structures in strange and interesting ways, thus forming delicate and mobile alliances. While the governmentality literature tends to focus on how the specific interests and goals of local actors become articulated to the objectives of state agencies and professional bodies, Stenson (1999, 2005) reminds us of the need to examine the ways in which local actors could also enrol political authorities in their micro-level governing schemes to secure local territory, regulate economic activity and manage perceived risks of victimization and criminal offending (see also O'Malley, Weir and Shearing 1997).

Mechanisms of crime control remained heterogeneous and fragmented. Policing thus consists of a wide array of institutional forms for managing crime and disorder, involving myriad state and non-state agents and agencies in varied

3 Interviews conducted in 1996 and 1997 with key ANC activists then working in the Department of Safety and Security.

relations. This book makes no attempt to capture all the transformations in crime control and security practices in post-apartheid South Africa. Nor is the concern to map out the connections or linkages between state, market and voluntary initiatives. Rather, I want to give some sense of the heterogeneity of this field, to highlight the persistent struggles over the exercise and regulation of crime control authority and responsibility. The debates and disputes over the distribution of crime control and other governmental tasks did not only occur in legal and policy circles. Individual citizens, communities, NGOs and businesses also participated in such discussions as much as, and perhaps even more than, politicians and state officials.

Crime control was debated and divided up in new ways among political, economic and social authorities. Chapters 2 through 5 examine, respectively, certain state, private security, big business and local (township) community strategies to rethink the 'crime problem' and its resolution, in which they claimed specific and specialized crime control roles and powers. Each chapter's topic is interesting in its own right and each can be read as a stand-alone chapter. Together, they point up some 'new' models of liberal democratic citizenship that were elaborated under the banner of crime control. As already indicated, subjectification did not end with the demise of authoritarian rule. People today continue to be made subjects. This is not a matter of dominance, and even less so a loss of freedom. It is instead about constituting individuals as subjects in and through practices of crime control. This book also explores how knowledge and truths about citizen-subjects, and crime and the state were produced and defended – through what means, towards what ends and with what effects?

The concluding chapter addresses the place of coercion in contemporary practices for the government of conduct. State and non-state agents and organizations *routinely* operate punitive measures to manage crime and associated risks. This has important implications for governmentality approaches – which tend to underestimate sovereign controls operating through applications of law and other coercive technologies – and for the sociology of policing approaches – which tend to overestimate the significance of techniques of compulsion.

Chapter 2

Crime Control and Political Authorities

> South Africa shall be a society where its inhabitants can pursue their daily lives in peace and safety free from undue fear of crime and violence. It shall be a society in which the fundamental rights of the individual are effectively protected with the support and co-operation of fellow citizens. Economic development amongst all sectors shall be unhindered by fear and South Africa shall attract the confidence of investors and the interest of tourists.
>
> Vision for the National Crime Prevention Strategy (DoSS 1996b, 5)

Introduction

Post-apartheid criminal justice policy exhibited a marked optimism in the fight against crime. Indeed, by the mid-1990s the ANC-led government had committed itself to reducing crime rates and maintaining social order. This was to be achieved, ideally, through three interrelated, state-initiated mechanisms, each of which prioritized and promoted an image of the individual as a reflective, self-governing agent: (1) sovereign command strategies emphasizing the prevention and control of crime; (2) active partnerships between criminal justice agencies, other state departments and civil society; and (3) techniques of moral regeneration stressing 'responsibility', 'prosperity', 'self-reliance' and 'self-worth' (<http://www.mrm.org.za> accessed 1 June 2007). Increasingly, the fight against crime was waged in terms of a new politics of control and a new politics of ethicalization. At the same time as the state imposed coercive controls on crime, it also acted 'at-a-distance', encouraging students, communities, retailers and others to assume an active role in managing crime and associated risks in accordance with certain political interests and objectives. These twin concerns – with the exercise of state sovereignty and with relations involving free, autonomous, enterprising individuals – were not competing rationalities of rule (though in certain instances they may very well have been). Indeed, effective law enforcement came to be seen as providing the necessary basis on which strategies to activate the self-regulating capacities of the individual and collectivity rested.

This chapter draws on South Africa's National Crime Prevention Strategy (NCPS) (DoSS 1996b) to examine the intersection of direct and indirect mechanisms for governing human conduct and subjectivity. Existing studies of policing typically view crime control and crime prevention as competing objectives and as a result have left largely unexplored the extent to which these have become complementary purposes in the context of an increasingly marketized (neo-liberal) political economy.

Observers of post-apartheid transformations in public policing claim that the state's initial – and in the view of such commentators, altogether too brief – interest in crime prevention quickly shifted to an emphasis on controlling crimes after they occurred (see Dixon 2004; Samara 2003; Shaw 2002; van Zyl Smit and van der Spuy 2004). This chapter argues, in contrast, that from the outset the liberal democratic state sought to prevent crime through deterrence and law enforcement, coupled with strategies to foster moral and practical responsibility among citizens for their own security. While the view of crime control and crime prevention as mutually reinforcing security functions was explicitly detailed in the Safety and Security White Paper (1998), this was already evident, albeit implicitly and somewhat inconsistently, in the earlier NCPS, one of the first anti-crime policies following the 1994 democratic elections.

The NCPS was the product of a major initiative by the ANC-led government to recalibrate the crime management roles and responsibilities of state, market and community agents and agencies. Launched in May 1996, this inter-ministerial document entailed a reconfiguration in the official discourse on crime and, therefore, requires closer examination even if few of its proposals were ever implemented. This is not, however, to suggest that the NCPS had no effect; all government departments had to align their priorities, programmes and budgets with the NCPS objectives. Further, the NCPS represented a key site for the strategic partnership that developed in the mid-1990s between government and Business Against Crime (BAC), a high-profile corporate-sponsored anti-crime initiative (see the discussion in Chapter 4).

Analyses of the NCPS – mostly of the policy studies type – tend to focus on the difficulties of translating policy into practice, and rehearse the textbook standard of locating programmatic failure at the level of either conceptual design or implementation (see, for example, Naudé 2000). Such accounts often fail to consider that it is precisely through the *language* of policy, rather than in its application, that crime is rendered as an object to be known, calculated and administered. Language, as Judith Butler reminds us, is not simply descriptive, but is also performative: words and things, rhetoric and reality are not opposed, but are mutually constitutive (see also Valverde 1990). Language is perhaps best seen as an intellectual technique for inscribing reality, rendering it intelligent, calculable, manageable and practicable (Miller and Rose 1990; Rose 1993; Ericson and Haggerty 1997).

While critics charge that the NCPS was 'another paper strategy' (Shaw 2002), it is better understood by reference to new ways of problematizing crime and criminal justice in an increasingly marketized political economy. The NCPS sought to liberalize crime-management and in so doing it brought into existence new sites for governmental intervention. In other words, it brought into play a series of different ways of thinking and acting in relation to crime. Reframing crime as a preventable problem involved various technologies and devices to regularize crime, to render it predicable and thus amenable to administration. Crime emerged as a particular problem in relation to an identifiable set of practices.

The remainder of this chapter addresses the truth claims that circulated in and through the NCPS. I explore the specific problem that crime posed to political authorities; the vocabularies for formulating and at the same time, for constituting these problems; the various techniques and strategies advanced as solutions to the crime problem; and the models of citizenship that emerged and to which authorities appealed. This chapter thus points to a type of political rationalization at work in regard to the government of crime.

The next section provides some background detail on the formulation of the NCPS. The section thereafter demonstrates that crime was reframed as a social issue, rather than a threat to the political sovereignty of the state, and was articulated in the language of growth and development. The crime problem was regarded as most effectively governed by acting through and in terms of individuals as morally self-regulating citizens, as active partners of state agencies, and as rational choice offenders who bear the consequences of freely made decisions. Moreover, in seeking to secure the conditions necessary for civil society and the market to function optimally, the state increasingly relied on coercive strategies to prevent and control crime and disorder.

A striking feature of contemporary crime control policy is the emphasis on governing not only crime, but also criminal justice (Garland 1999; Haggerty 2001; Hudson 2001; McLaughlin and Murji 2001). The fourth section of this chapter investigates the strategies, techniques and devices that enabled an integrated criminal justice system to emerge – a system that was more attuned to issues of economy, effectiveness and efficiency than to the achievement of justice. The fifth section analyzes the crucial role of statistical knowledges in governing crime and criminal justice. Contemporary developments in criminal justice policy do not necessarily display a high degree of consistency and the sixth section specifies multiple constructions of both the offender and the victim. In the context of changing forms of governance, crime management practices come to embody different assumptions of the subjects of government.

Policy Development

Crime and its control came to be problematized in new ways, partly under the influence of widespread political and social transformations in post-apartheid South Africa. These transformations involved a significant reshaping of the authority, objectives, tasks and limits of state rule; that is, a reconceptualization of what was properly a state concern and what was best left to other agents and agencies. The emergence of new ways to understand and manage crime was also linked to recent shifts in criminological discourses and practices (van Zyl Smit 1999), which were themselves tied to a refiguring of governmental rationalities (O'Malley 1996a; O'Malley and Palmer 1996; Stenson 1993). Although academics did not author the NCPS, both local and international criminologists exerted considerable influence on policy development and in the transformation period more generally.[1]

Policing scholars have demonstrated that crime control is no longer a monopoly practice of the state – if indeed it ever was – and have drawn particular attention to private security (South 1988, 1997; Rigakos 2002), the insurance industry (Ericson and Haggerty 1997), as well as other bodies not readily comprehended in terms

1 See Brogden and Shearing (1993) for a critical view of the international marketization of police expertise in South Africa.

of the public/private divide (for example, railway police, park wardens) (Johnston 1992, 2000). The decentring of the state was not limited to policing, however, but occurred across the criminal justice field more generally, as well as in other areas of contemporary existence such as health and education (Miller and Rose 1990; Rose 1999; Rose and Miller 1992). Across diverse sites, the state divested itself of the primary responsibility for meeting all of the population's needs, concentrating instead on delivering particular forms of expertise and resources. At the same time, it took on the ambitious role of coordinating and managing the resultant network of competing service providers (Lacey 1994; Garland 1996). In many ways, then, the state did not wither away, but expanded and extended its reach considerably.

These themes were evident in the NCPS. The composition of the policy development team, for example, was reflective of the emergent multi-sectoral approach to the problem of crime. The NCPS was a centrally-driven and centrally-controlled project drafted by an interdepartmental team composed largely of civilian officials. Six national ministries comprised the interdepartmental committee: the Ministries of Safety and Security, Defence, and Intelligence, together forming the State Security Services, historically dominated the political landscape especially in the 1980s with the rise to power of the 'securocrats' (military strategists drawn from the police, army and intelligence sectors) (Cawthra 1992); and the Ministries of Justice, Correctional Services, and Welfare, each with a criminal justice function though traditionally occupying a less privileged position in the security apparatus of the state. The functional remit of these ministries in regard to crime was as follows:

- Safety and Security: preservation of public order and internal security – the police service;
- Defence: defence of national security against external threats and to a lesser extent, maintenance of internal law and order – the army;
- Intelligence – promotion and defence of national security interests by gathering, evaluating and coordinating domestic, departmental and foreign intelligence;
- Justice:[2] administration of justice – courts and legislation;
- Correctional Services:[3] penal policy – prisons and parole;
- Welfare: social welfare and population development – probation.

Other national government departments (Education, Transport, Trade and Industry), civil society, the business community and domestic and international experts also helped formulate the strategy: a few as consultants, others as workshop participants and still others through oral and written submissions. The corporate sector in particular was a key driving force and was represented on the drafting team (see the discussion in Chapter 4). The multiplicity of voices authorized to speak on the crime problem makes clear that the discourse on crime control was no longer police, or even state, property. As the then Minister of Safety and Security proclaimed during the planning stage: 'the NCPS … should be owned by the broadest possible cross-

2 During the NCPS formulation period and well after, the Minister of Intelligence was also the Minister of Justice.

3 Prior to 1990, Prison Services fell under the Department of Justice.

section of South Africa's population and should go beyond a mere police response to crime … ' (Mufamadi, May 1995 in Rauch 2001, 1).

Governing Crime

The management of crime and associated risks and the reframing of other social problems under the banner of 'crime control' (Dixon 2006) came to occupy, in the late twentieth century and the early twenty-first century, a central place on the political and public agendas (on 'governing through crime' in the more advanced liberal democracies of the West see: Simon 1997; Stenson and Sullivan 2001). Beginning perhaps with the NCPS, crime came to be understood as 'one of the primary problems confronting the new democracy in South Africa' (DoSS 1996b, 4). Notwithstanding methodological concerns about counting practices – for example, under-reporting, recording inconsistencies, changing policing tactics, an altering population base[4] – widespread agreement does exist that crime levels remain indeed very high (Comaroff and Comaroff 2006; ISS 2004; Shaw 1997, 2002).

Crime rates have been rising steadily since at the least the 1980s, with dramatic increases recorded in the latter part of that decade and the early 1990s. Police statistics for the period of 1990 to 1995 – the onset of the negotiated political transition through to Cabinet's decision to develop the NCPS – confirm an upward trend in serious crimes, with increases in violent offences outstripping those of property-related crimes (Nedcor April 1996). Since 1998, crime levels have in fact stabilized or decreased though it remains the case that violent offences are high by international standards and public expectations. Moreover, overall victimization rates – for both personal and property related crimes – are still heavily concentrated in poor, black communities (Comaroff and Comaroff 2006; Schönteich 2002).

It is certainly not inevitable that elevated crime levels will be seen as an abnormal state of affairs. Shaw (2002) observed that the newly elected ANC-led government was reluctant to attach, prior to 1995, any great significance to crime and resisted placing it on the political agenda – and this despite the already heightened crime rates noted above. In more established Western democracies, according to Garland (1996), high crime levels have become a 'normal social fact', a standard feature of daily existence. For Garland, it is not so much that criminal activities *per se* pose problems for politics as it is the contemporary crises of sovereignty, the very real limitations on the state's crime control monopoly. 'The predicament for governments today, then, is that they (i.e. ministers, officials, agency executives etc.) see the need to withdraw or at least qualify their claim to be the primary and effective provider of security and crime control, but they also see, just as clearly, that the political costs

4 To illustrate further, self-governing black homelands or Bantustans were historically excluded from urban and regional crime counts of the police (Shaw 2002). Subsequent calculations that include these neglected areas thus manifest an altered population base making difficult any time–trend analysis of crime. The NCPS also noted that 'a pre-disposition to interpret violence as political in the pre-election period may have been replaced by a pre-disposition to interpret such violence as criminal in the post-election phase … we may simply be re-labeling essentially consistent trends in social conflict … ' (DoSS 1996b, 11).

of such a move are likely to be disastrous' (*ibid.*, p. 449). According to Garland, the contradictory character of governmental policy – its punitive strategies, as well as strategies to enlist all state actors and agencies in crime control measures – should be read within this problem space.

In contrast to the Anglo liberal crime control situation discussed by Garland, it was precisely the routinization of crime and the prospect of high crime levels being seen as *the* defining feature of the new South Africa that most troubled political authorities. They accordingly sought to re-present elevated crime rates as a temporary condition and to establish what 'normal' levels *should* be. This involved comparisons with Eastern European states (for example Russia) and Namibia, as these countries underwent rapid transition to democracy (DoSS 1996b, 13; DoSS 1998; Gastrow 1997; Glantz 1995; Grant 1989; Shaw 1997). Comparative analyses seemed to reveal an association between rising crime and political and economic liberalization; in this way, increases in crime were constituted as an expected, but nonetheless intolerable, accompaniment to democratic transformation. These analyses also provided international crime averages against which the South African rates were measured and judged. Notions of normality thus arose out of, rather than provided the basis for, the governance of crime (cf. Canguilhem 1978; Foucault 1977; also Comaroff and Comaroff 2006).

Ideas of normality – of order, the state and citizenship – were conditioned by an emergent neo-liberal rationality of rule. Indeed, as market-based reforms[5] took root, crime came to be seen as one of the most – if not the most – significant challenges to South Africa's socio-economic future. The problem of crime was that it raised concerns about the ability of elected officials to govern the fledgling liberal market society.

> Crime in South Africa presents a major threat to the government's strategic and policy objectives. It presents a major constraint on development initiatives, undermines the process of reconciliation, impacts negatively on public confidence in government and on investment in the country, threatens the building of a human rights culture and compromises the very process of transformation to democracy.
>
> (DoSS 1996b, 43)

In the post-apartheid context, crime was linked to socio-economic and political restructuring, that is to projects for liberal democratization. Moreover, national (for example, public and corporate sector) and international (for example, foreign investor) support for democratic change, as much as 'the governmental will' of South African political authorities, became crucial resources in managing crime. The parameters of a liberal democratic society were set out in the NCPS 'vision' quoted at the outset of this chapter. It is a society where crime and violence do not pose a significant threat to daily life; where the actualization of individual rights depends on the existence of mutuality and cooperation; and it is an economically viable enterprise.

---

5 In 1996, the government published its market-driven macro-reform strategy GEAR (Growth, Employment and Redistribution Programme). This effectively replaced the more welfarist RDP (Reconstruction and Development Programme).

Crime and crime control were increasingly regarded as a public concern, an issue of public safety rather than regime security. The NCPS framed this as 'a shift in emphasis on crime as a *security* issue – towards crime as a *social* issue' (DoSS 1996b, 6). The problem of crime was posed less in terms of territorial integrity or state sovereignty – as it was under the apartheid project (Brewer 1994b; Frankel, Pines and Swilling 1988; Nathan 1992; Price 1991) – and more as a question of the prosperity, well-being and happiness of the population. In large part, liberal democratic rule in crime control came to depend on strategies to mobilize and shape the conduct of the population taken either collectively or singly: that is, an emphasis on population management. Crime now presented a problem of freedom and liberty as practices of democracy. Rather than seeking to eliminate crime altogether by completely dominating human subjects and quashing their capacity for self-directed action, crime was to be brought down to acceptable ('normal') levels by maximizing and regulating those freedoms that have come to be invested in active citizens. Crime was thus rendered manageable through techniques and strategies for persuading individuals to freely take on certain forms of liberal citizenship: a type of 'democratization through crime'.

Under the crime control banner, the population was to be trained in the capacities required for active participation in contemporary social, economic and political life. With the market as the key organizing principle for the 'new' South Africa (Taylor and Vale 2000), individuals were increasingly understood by reference to an 'enterprise model' of action that was extended beyond the economy to encompass the conduct of individuals themselves (Burchell D. 1995; Burchell G. 1996). Subsequently, attention centred on personal choice, rationality, autonomy, innovation and self-fulfilment in all spheres of existence. As subjects of governance, individuals were not, however, only self-interested rational calculators. They were also and equally responsible beings with strong moral ties to community networks.

The moral agency of rational individuals constituted a crucial governmental concern. Strategies were introduced that aimed to effect ethical transformations across the population, activating the self-regulatory capacities of community networks understood as voluntary alignments of agentive, expert and morally interdependent individuals. In some ways this was a type of crime prevention through community development, a concern with enhancing the informal social controls that inhibit crime. Consider, for example, the third NCPS 'Pillar' or focal area for governmental intervention – 'Public Values and Education'. This emphasized the development of 'responsible and empowered citizenship' (DoSS 1996b, 76). The proposed national programmes – *Public Education* and *School Education* – entailed a kind of civics training involving instruction on the importance of rule of law, human rights and legislative process and procedure, precisely those traditions that the NCPS recognized as lacking and as crucial to successful democratization. Crime, at least within certain categories, was to be reduced by strengthening habits and values at individual (common sense) and collective (culture) levels that were discouraging of criminal activity (see also NCPS News 1997). As the then Minister of Safety and Security insisted in his foreword to the *Annual Plan of the South African Police Service 1996/97*, crime was to be deterred by 'inculcating an anti-crime consciousness in the minds of all our citizens'. A new morality thus began to take shape that structured and transformed how crime was thought about – no longer as a preferred solution to interpersonal or political conflict but as an infringement of human rights which link individuals together in community – and how crime was acted upon – within the boundaries of the law, through criminal justice agencies (DoSS 1996b, 73–7).

Such developments formed part of a moral renewal campaign, which achieved prominence at the close of the twentieth century. A regime of moral regeneration extended across all public sectors, focusing attention on individual 'responsibility', 'prosperity', 'self-reliance' and 'participation', along with 'partnerships' (<http://www.mrm.org.za> accessed 1 June 2007). As self-regulating, enterprising decision-makers, individuals did not exist in a relationship of obligation with the state and its officials. Individuals became the partners of political authorities, not their dependants. A new contractual image of 'partnerships' emerged both as a way to visualize and administer contemporary relations between statutory agencies, civil society, NGOs and the corporate sector, and as a key mechanism of crime control. The NCPS pursued a 'multi-agency approach', which saw crime as the 'shared responsibility and collective priority' of state and non-state organizations and individuals (p. 80). Without exception, each of its 17 national programmes for action assembled together a range of experts and expertise – criminal justice departments and other government authorities (at local, provincial and national levels), community groups, NGOs, the private sector – promoting inter-agency collaboration and coordination in the governing of crime. Similarly, popular participation and involvement in crime prevention featured significantly in the Safety and Security White Paper (1998), with community policing held out as the most appropriate model for police-public partnerships. The partnerships thus established went beyond the mere cooperation envisioned by political officials in 1990: '[A public-police partnership] can only exist if the public, as the *passive* partner, supports the police … ' [emphasis added] (Hansard, Extended Committee, 23 April 1990, cols. 6906). Instead, the public now appeared as an *active* partner, with the requisite expertise and knowledge to participate in the shaping and delivery of anti-crime programmes and, moreover, competent to conduct 'independent initiatives' especially at local levels (DoSS 1996b, 47–8; on passive and active forms of community policing see O'Malley and Palmer 1996).

The state took on the role of managing and coordinating the emergent anti-crime partnerships and of providing the knowledge and skills necessary to mobilize the self-regulating capacities of individuals and organizations (on the state's new managerial role see Lacey 1994). But more than this, the state also claimed to be a primary and reliable guarantor of safety and security. The 'Criminal Justice Process Pillar' – the most prominent of the four NCPS focal areas – concentrated on bolstering the deterrent impact of the state's legal controls by increasing their severity, swiftness and certainty. Analysts tend to treat this emphasis on law enforcement as detracting from the importance of crime prevention (see Dixon 2004; Shaw 2002). However, preventative and reactive tactics operated in tandem. Crime prevention strategies were tied into a reactive agenda where concern rested with detecting and punishing offenders who were understood primarily as rational choice actors and who respond to opportunities to commit crime. Programmes to create a new moral climate resistant to crime also regarded civic activism as including full participation in the criminal justice process – reporting crime, assisting in police investigations, testifying in court. 'Environmental Design' (Pillar 2) was expected to simultaneously reduce criminal opportunity through situational crime prevention and 'facilitate law enforcement' by ensuring easy detection of offenders (DoSS 1996b, 68). Through such programmes, government acted on the public/private divide, effectively reframing the responsibilities of the state and citizens alike. Citizens were to prevent crime in the home, schools, workplace and commercial and recreational centres, *and* facilitate criminal justice response when crime did occur in these spaces. The primary responsibility of the state was to control crime and maintain public order through applications of the law and punitive technologies.

Governing Criminal Justice

The criminal justice process represented, in the NCPS, one of the four focal areas or 'Pillars' for governmental intervention. Although a multi-agency approach involving all government departments and civil society was advocated, it was an integrated and coordinated criminal justice *system* that was promoted as 'central to the development of the NCPS' (DoSS 1996b, 46). This was echoed in the Safety and Security White Paper (1998) and in subsequent government documents. Thus, the most recent draft White Paper on Corrections (2004) stressed:

> The South African correctional system is an integral part of the country's criminal justice system and requires an effective integrated justice system for service delivery on the DCS's core mandate.

The criminal justice *system* emerged as a new governmental object, which could be known and administered.[6] Increasingly, the problematization and management of criminal justice came to be coded in the language of systematization.

High recorded rates of crime, the lack of skilled criminal justice personnel and a critical public have given rise to new governmental problems such as integration and coordination in criminal justice, and economy, efficiency and effectiveness (the '3Es') in the use of resources and service delivery. System or 'enterprise' planning and information management have emerged as key practices for understanding and addressing these problems. Once understood to comprise 'entirely separate departments' (DoSS 1996b) – each with its 'own sphere of autonomous action' and 'its own objectives and working ideologies' (Garland 1999), though loosely linked through a shared commitment to apartheid – criminal justice has now been recast as an integrated and coherent *system* composed of interdependent agencies. These agencies include Safety and Security, Justice, Correctional Services and Welfare

6 The Ministry of Safety and Security has increasingly laid claim to this governmental role (Director, Crime Prevention Co-Ordination, NCPS National Secretariat, interview 17 December 1996). Safety and Security assumed primary responsibility for the implementation of the NCPS. The most recent White Paper (1998) sought to extend this mandate, proposing the establishment of a National Crime Prevention Strategy Centre that has, as one of it main functions, the 'achievement of an integrated justice system'.

– the four 'core' criminal justice departments – as well as Defence and Intelligence for which crime constitutes, far more than in Western liberal democracies, a key operational concern. The NCPS identified the South African National Defence Force (SANDF) (including the Air Force and Defence Intelligence), the National Intelligence Agency (NIA) and the South African Secret Service (SASS)) as part of the criminal justice system, mainly because of the collaborative anti-crime projects undertaken with the SAPS.

> The SANDF has formulated a comprehensive internal security strategy which includes a crime prevention component. Crime prevention activities currently entail more operational energy than any other SANDF secondary function. These activities involve all arms of the SANDF, and provide for joint planning and execution with the SAPS ... Crime is one of the current national priorities of the intelligence community and the National Intelligence Co-Ordinating Committee (NICOC) is the statutory body empowered to co-ordinate the national intelligence effort [of the National Crime Investigation Service of the SAPS, the NIA, the SASS and Defence Intelligence].
>
> (DoSS 1996b, 24–5)

In a speech to the National Conference on Criminal Justice and Democracy in Cape Town, the Minister for Safety and Security included Home Affairs as yet a further component of an 'integrated justice system' (Nqakula, 17 March 2004 <http://www.gov.za/speeches/2004/04031912461003.htm>, accessed 01 June 2007)). Thus, the composition of the criminal justice system includes, at times, up to seven different government departments.

An exclusive focus on one of these agencies, rather than on the intimate connections between them, is seen to have little, if any, impact on crime. Moreover, it can result in conflict over, and poor utilization of, scarce resources and lead to legitimacy concerns. As the Chief Director Court Services Branch (Department of Justice) stressed in a conference presentation, 'Towards an Integrated Justice System':

> ... the various links cannot operate in silos ... the criminal justice system has to be made to function well across its entire value chain – investigations; arrests; prosecution; finalisation of cases in time; and aspects related to awaiting trial (AWT) detainees and sentenced persons ... If the chain is weakened or broken anywhere, it leads to justice not to be done or experienced – that in turn leads to legitimacy concerns and the public losing faith in the CJS.
>
> (du Rand 2005)

Thus, proposals that advocated more stringent bail conditions and mandatory sentencing as a deterrent to crime, for example, were criticized for ignoring the knock-on effects such as increased pressure on an already strained prison capacity (Nedcor/ISS 1997). Such proposals were also not in keeping with prominent strands in criminological theory and research, which suggested that it is the certainty of being captured, convicted and punished that presents the greatest deterrent rather than harshness of punishment. As the NCPS notes, 'this [punitive penal] approach is inherently dependent on more effective policing, intelligence, investigation, as well as prosecution' (p. 45; see also Safety and Security White Paper 1998). And while punitive penal sanctions may make sense as a deterrent for those crimes closely approximating the rational choice model of offending, it is argued that they are more difficult to justify, in instrumental and moral terms, for other offence categories such as 'crimes of passion' or 'crimes of economic necessity' (DoSS 1996b). Clearly 'system' imageries of criminal justice (as well as the shift towards a 'dis-aggregated understanding of crime and its varied causation'), pose significant challenges to 'mono-dimensional' or 'single factor' solutions such as more police or longer prison terms (DoSS 1996b). Such 'mono-dimensional' solutions do little to reduce crime and indeed may even lead to an amplification of the problem. In a passage that superficially recalls the 'risk society' analyses of Beck (1992) and Ericson and Haggerty (1997), the NCPS stressed that the exclusive focus, as evident in the National Intelligence Co-Ordination Committee (NICOC), on innovating, enhancing and redeploying criminal intelligence and 'information and analytical technology at the disposal of the SAPS ... often simply gives rise [as in the case of car theft and hijacking] to new forms of crime, which in turn presents a new set of technological and resource allocation problems which have to be solved' (p. 45). Increasingly, the criminal justice process comes to be regarded as most appropriately or effectively administered by working through *system* properties and processes, rather than in terms of the professional autonomy and site-specific expertise of individual departments: 'To reduce crime effectively, to deliver justice and to enhance public confidence, the CJS has to work as a coherent, joined-up system, with all those involved, adopting a common set of values to meet a common set of goals' (du Rand 2005).

System coordination and integration; economy, efficiency and effectiveness (the '3 Es'); and accountability – these are the new objectives in governing criminal justice. The introduction of these objectives is consistent with a managerialist agenda for the market-based reform of criminal justice. Militarization begins to give way to managerialism, marketization and monetarization in criminal justice, as in the public sector more generally (see Batho Pele White Paper 1997) – though this shift is far from complete (on the militarization of public policing organizations see Haggerty and Ericson 2001; Nunn 2003). In the process, criminal justice practices have been restructured 'in the direction of service oriented governance', with an emphasis on 'customer satisfaction' and 'cost-effectiveness' throughout the system (DoSS 1996b). The introduction of business plans within the SAPS, for instance, forced the police to consider principles of cost-effectiveness and efficiency in all aspects of their operation. Both in operation and structure, criminal justice agencies were obliged to become more 'business-like'. Thus, 'the Department of Justice and Constitutional Development has recently been restructured. It now consists of a Board of Directors that manages the Department and advises the Ministry. A Chief Executive Officer and managing directors of eight business units serve as executive members of the Board' (Lue-Dugmore 2003, 11). Consider also the 1997 appointment of Meyer Kahn, head of South African Breweries, as chief executive officer of the SAPS, 'a new civilian position calculated to direct and accelerate the conversion of the SAPS into an effective law-enforcement and crime-prevention agency' (*F&T Weekly* 1997, 43). SAPS organizational charts showed Kahn and the National Police Commissioner to be on the same footing, both reporting directly to the Minister of Safety and Security. As these examples illustrate, private sector authorities and expertise assumed a high profile in criminal justice reform: legitimacy and authority was accorded to business leaders, NGOs and others – specialists in management techniques and who were armed 'with knowledge of the workings of the entire [criminal justice] system' (DoSS 1996b, 54). (A more detailed discussion of private sector involvement in policing transformation is provided in Chapter 3.)

The modernization of criminal justice also involved new techniques and strategies to translate criminal justice objectives into practice. Instead of simply assuming, as critics sometimes claim (see Rauch 2001), that integration and coordination would occur 'naturally' and 'spontaneously', government actively intervened, installing devices and measures to enable a criminal justice *system* to emerge and to function efficiently, effectively and economically. In particular, there have developed 'new strategies of system integration and system monitoring, which seek to implement a level of process and information management which was previously lacking' (Garland 1996, 455). Central government initiatives established a common policy framework and introduced a series of national programmes to coordinate and integrate operational efforts, especially around Cabinet-designated 'priority crimes': firearm-related offences; white-collar crime and corruption; gender violence and crimes against children; violence associated with inter-group conflict; vehicle theft and hijacking; and paramilitary activity (DoSS 1996b; also the 1996 *National Growth and Development Strategy*). The two most widely publicized of these programmes were the *Integrated Management System*, which set detailed output-based quantifiable performance indicators for the criminal justice system, and the *Integrated Information Network*, which provided audit and inspection devices for the ongoing evaluation and monitoring of these performance standards by line function managers (DoSS 1996b). Overlaying all of this was a new regime of financial calculation. The Treasury's recent 'cluster financing' approach was applied to the police, courts and corrections – the 'criminal justice cluster'. The government increasingly promoted budget reform as a major mechanism for transforming public services.

This array of centrally implemented controls sought to render the criminal justice process more unified and homogenized (Garland 1999). The focus of attention shifted to the movement of cases, information, exhibits and resources through the system, from investigation to prosecution and punishment (DoSS 1996b; *F & T Weekly* 1997). The daily activities and decision-making of officials in the various agencies were also subject to greater standardization and regularization and hence made amenable to comparison and evaluation. There is no question here of denying or eliminating the professional autonomy and discretion of criminal justice practitioners; rather, political authorities sought to promote and shape individual agency in particular ways. Government policies and strategies allowed for the retention of police operational autonomy, prosecutorial discretion and judicial independence, but the actions and judgments of criminal justice agents came to be transformed in novel ways. These were increasingly made visible and calculable and, hence, governable. Criminal justice officials were made responsive, for the first time, to 'customers' and 'users' of the system – especially victims – through 'victim complaint and customer satisfaction audits', which provided concrete forms of accountability (DoSS 1996b, 67). Equally, a new relation with the central state machinery also took shape, with state powers increasing as the state sought to govern 'at a distance'. Criminal justice activities were collated, quantified, traced over time, compared and transported to centres of calculation where decisions were taken on budgetary allocation, policy objectives and service deliverables and standards. Criminal justice professionals, however, were not only resources for, and objects of, central government calculations and assessments, but were also required to become the kind of calculating agents that liberal democracy expects. They have now been left with a wide scope of discretionary authority in their day-to-day practices, which they are obliged to exercise in a standardized and systematized manner; hence the proposal to link 'enterprise level' performance monitoring to 'appraisal systems within the realm of human resource management' (DoSS 1996b, 49). Criminal justice functionaries were encouraged to become more self-steering and enterprising, but to do so according to centrally set criteria and performance measures: 'autonomization plus responsibilization' (Rose 1999).

The new performance indicators were results-oriented, focusing on resource use and service delivery. Increasingly, criminal justice came to be evaluated in terms of targeted 'outputs', changes that can be measured using short- to mid-range quantitative tools (SAPS 1996; see also Garland 1996; McLaughlin and Murji 2001; O'Malley 2001).

> … ongoing evaluation … requires the development of Key Performance Indicators. These indicators are vital for three reasons.
>
> Firstly, they ensure that activities are goal oriented and that expenditure is matched by measurable outputs.
>
> Secondly, they assist in transformation of the departments themselves in the direction of service oriented governance.
>
> Thirdly, they ensure that the relative contribution of various activities can be assessed in a meaningful way, hence providing a basis for the allocation of resources through the budget process.
>
> (DoSS 1996b, 51–2)

This emphasis on cost-effectiveness and ongoing evaluation tends to restrict the scope of long-term, social justice projects (cf. O'Malley 2001). Thus, the proposed NCPS national programmes were assessed not in terms of their impact on crime levels, recidivism rates or root causes of crime, but rather by reference to goals over which criminal justice agencies exercised near complete control: for example, the number of prisoners awaiting trial, the number of escapes from custody and prison, the number of case withdrawals and the number of lost case files (Ebrahim 2003; NCPS News July 1997). More generally, criminal justice performance monitoring appeared less concerned with achieving justice *per se* than with 'outputs' such as: the number of multi-agency initiatives on crimes against women and children, and the number of police operations in high crime areas (*SAPS Strategic Plan 2002–5*); the number of new courts and court hours worked (*DoJC Annual Report 2002/3*); the number of custodial beds and renovated correctional facilities (*DoCS Strategic*

Plan 2005/6-2009/10). Increasingly, legitimacy comes to be linked to questions of economy, effectiveness and efficiency, to internal, managerial objectives rather than to a commitment to justice (Hudson 2001).

New Concepts and Practical Knowledges

Accompanying the shift in the content of crime as an object of governance were new mechanisms to record and calculate crime, rendering it amenable to governmental intervention. Significantly, the NCPS noted that its success depended on the development and management of a statistical information database. Managing crime successfully requires knowledge of its internal nature and processes. Effective action can only be undertaken where knowledge of the problem exists. Yet statistics do not simply describe nor capture a pre-existing reality. Instead, they actually bring crime, as a preventable, social problem, into being. Here, knowledge is best understood as practical and performative rather than merely contemplative or descriptive (Miller and Rose 1990).

Statistics

The introductory section of the NCPS made explicit the importance of numericized information to the management of crime. The opening line of the NCPS reads: 'Levels of crime have been of dire concern to the Government of National Unity since 1994. In recognition of this, in 1995 the Cabinet initiated a process for the development of a National Crime Prevention Strategy (NCPS)' (p. 4). And the control of crime rates was identified as the 'ultimate objective of the NCPS' (p. 5). Rose (1991; 1999) has pointed out that while government depends on, and gives rise to, knowledge, such knowledge need not be statisticalized.[7] The fact that numbers hold special significance for the government of crime thus requires closer scrutiny.

A link exists between the political problematization of crime as a predictable, public concern and numericized techniques for inscribing this problem, for rendering it amenable to governmental calculation and intervention. Where crime is seen as a preventable event, or more accurately a mass of events, government and civil society need no longer wait until after an offence has been committed to act. The initiation of action is no longer dependent on the existence of a complainant or complaint, but can proceed without these based on the likelihood that crime *may* occur (cf. Castel 1991). Thus, state agencies and the public must adopt a proactive stance and anticipate criminality. This requires forward-thinking, an orientation to the future and the capacity to predict events (Giddens 1990). It involves going beyond the individual offence looked at in isolation, to the law of large numbers, to seeing an offence in terms of group or aggregate properties. The analysis of crime becomes a technical enterprise with action based on the collation of factors seen as predictive of crime (Ericson and Haggerty 1997; Johnston 1997). The government of crime

7 In this section I draw substantially from Rose's cogent arguments on the link between government and numeracy (Rose 1991, 1999).

thus demands the collection and analysis of significant facts that are in large part numerical.

Statistical knowledge and measurement have come to acquire great importance and are increasingly invested with confidence and assigned positive value. Numerical data, graphs, flow charts, geographical information systems, victimization surveys and crime databases are key mechanisms through which reality can be 'objectively' and 'reliably' captured and plotted. Numbers reveal crime's internal regularities and intrinsic dynamics and they permit the scientific establishment of the harms that crime generates. In a neo-liberal context, particular emphasis centres on the quantification of the costs of crime, elaborated in the language of growth and development:

> ... it is vital that the impact of various forms of crime can be quantitatively measured in their impact on development in South Africa. For this reason it is suggested that further research should be conducted to assess the impact of crime based on – amongst others – the following indicators
>
> - government expenditure on the criminal justice system
> - expenditure on private security
> - costs of community deterioration
> - value of stolen goods
> - victim compensation and aid
> - health costs of treating victims of violent crime
> - economic value of lives ruined (loss of years of life)
> - loss of productivity and revenue due to emigration of taxpayers
> - the costs of white collar crime and other serious economic crimes
> - loss of international investment.
>
> (DoSS 1996b, 8)

Such statistical information no longer serves the 'administrative needs of officials' (*ibid.*, 47), needs historically tied into projects to control the races, and to multiply state control and authority over territory. Rather, liberal governance of crime aims to enhance the socio-economic well-being of the population, and requires stable and combinable knowledge of crime – its cycles, trends, frequency, spatial and temporal patterns and the like.

Practices of quantification not only played an integral role in constituting crime as a governmental object with its own inherent characteristics and regularities, but also helped authorize political authority (Comaroff and Comaroff 2006; Haggerty 2001). In the context of public scepticism about the 'government's ability to counter the crime problem' (DoSS 1996b, 6), of the 'politically-oriented legacy' of 'inherited' state institutions, especially criminal justice agencies and of weakening state authority, government sought to ground its crime control practices in terms of objectivity and increasingly such objectivity assumed a numerical form. The legitimacy of government's crime management efforts depends on the deployment of numbers in the formulation, justification and evaluation of those efforts. Policy documents and other official writings repeatedly stress that 'objective facts' established by statistical calculations form the basis for rational action on crime (see DoSS 1996b). Numbers appear as neutral and technical mechanisms to render criminal justice decisions.

Of course, ignored in such presentations is the fact that numbers are inevitably politicized (Comaroff and Comaroff 2006; Haggerty 2001). In the aftermath of the first democratic elections of 1994, acts and behaviours previously labelled as political violence were often recoded – for policing and measurement purposes – as criminal violence (DoSS 1996b; Shaw 2002). During the same period, national crime counts were expanded to include data from the four former self-governing black homelands or Bantustans, apartheid-created independent states (Shaw 2002). As Alonso and Starr (1987, 3) cogently observe, 'political judgements are implicit in the choice of what to measure, how to measure it, how often to measure it and how to present and interpret the results'. At the same time, however, numbers 'appear to depoliticize whole areas of political judgement. They redraw the boundaries between politics and objectivity by purporting to act as automatic technical mechanisms for making judgements, prioritizing problems and allocating scarce resources' (Rose 1999, 198). That numbers help reconfigure the boundaries of the political and the technical is especially significant given the historical context of the politicization of crime in South Africa (see Brewer 1994b; Brogden and Shearing 1993; Cawthra 1992; Steytler 1993; van der Spuy 1989). Numbers not only make it possible to govern crime, but also to do so objectively, that is to say, better.

Practices of quantification are crucial to the development, justification, implementation and evaluation of liberal democratic crime control. Statistics emerge as technical tools for specifying appropriate spaces for criminal justice action and for regularizing and monitoring such action. Crime-data-gathering is conceived of as an 'analytical enterprise' (DoSS 1996b, 11), with statistics providing the 'objective' grounds on which government can prioritise specific crimes, devise and coordinate appropriate crime prevention programmes and strategies, allocate resources, measure departmental performance and assess efficiency, and inform public opinion and media debates on crime. To elaborate, in the distribution of public policing resources – most contentious in regard to urban townships and former Bantustans – priority was given to the development of a 'scientifically based formula' to be applied to the results of a 'census audit' of the 'actual number and current distribution' of resources (SAPS November 1996). Subjective judgement and political ideology no longer provide an acceptable grounding for criminal justice decision-making. Rather, the statisticalization of managerial techniques (Rose 1991, 1999) becomes evident: a 'criminal justice information network', a statistical data-base, is promoted as:

> the basis for appropriate management information which senior line managers require to monitor the outputs and efficiency of various components of the [justice] system … [and to make] informed decisions on the optimal allocation of resources, human resource development and [to identify] areas which require special attention.
>
> (DoSS 1996b, 12)

Further, it was this very database that enabled the integration of various components – Safety and Security, Justice, Corrections, Welfare – into a coherent criminal justice *system*, establishing 'a relationship between crimes committed, crimes reported, rates of successful investigation and prosecution, sentencing policy, rates of recidivism etc.' (*ibid.*, 12; see also Garland 1996; Haggerty 2001). The creation of the 'criminal justice information network' enabled the NCPS Director-Generals Committee and its Secretariat to operate as central coordinating mechanisms. These national structures sought to integrate, from a distance, the different crime management approaches of various government agencies (at all three tiers) by action on, and in terms of, centrally stored information on diverse and remote settings – police stations, Attorneys General, District Surgeons and provincial government offices.

But coordination also occurs between government and civil society. If political authorities are to engage in calculated action against crime, so too is the public. Successful crime prevention requires the active participation of citizens knowledgeable about the costs of crime (Leighton 1991; O'Malley and Palmer 1996): 'For this reason it is imperative that government develop an effective communications strategy ... to properly inform public opinion ... This enterprise will be significantly enhanced through the development of efficient information gathering and processing [that is, the criminal justice information network]' (DoSS 1996b, 47). A numericized public discourse on crime is thus produced. Government seeks to exert influence from a distance, through regular publications of 'objective' crime indices which individuals are expected and urged to consider in their daily routines. As Rose (1991, 690) observes, 'democratic political rationalities that accord significance to rational and calculative self-steering of independent citizens in their personal and business activities also must sustain a public environment of numbers within which those citizens may calculate' (see also Rose 1999). Thus, in 1994, the police started to regularly publish crime statistics, which were held out as *the* measure against which crime risks were to be calculated. And in 1996, the SAPS made public, for the very first time, its policing priorities and objectives. With the aim of shaping the proper exercise of civilian crime prevention responsibilities and of informing public debate on police policy and performance, the *1996/7 Annual Police Plan* provided detailed statistical data on budgetary allocation and expenditure, regional and national resource distributions (for example, police stations, satellite stations and contact points, police personnel, Community Police Forums) and national and regional demographic profiles (for example, land surface, population size). It is also within the context of concern with maximizing the rational calculating capacities of autonomous and rational citizens that the Department of Safety and Security conducted, in 1998, the first nationwide victimization survey. In their everyday conduct, individuals were to be guided by facts and figures, not by subjective perceptions or anecdotal information on crime.

Crime facts and figures thus entered into the public domain, influencing how citizens thought about and acted on crime. It is also these very facts and figures that enabled citizens to evaluate government's performance. Public scrutiny of state activity – a key feature of liberalism (Gordon 1991) – occurs within the technical and seemingly objective framework offered by numbers. In its delivery of security services, government is subjected to assessments conducted in numerical terms: number of arrests, conviction rates, security budgets etc. In South Africa, as I have argued throughout, crime rates have become the diagnostic index of good governance (see also Comaroff and Comaroff 2006; Shaw 2002). There is a sentiment that quantitative calculations of the costs of crime should not eclipse qualitative ones and that under-reporting, changes in police practice and record-keeping procedures all have an effect on crime rates (DoSS 1996b). But from the mid-90s on, the 'fight against crime' was by and large conducted in the language of statistics. Representations of crime, interventionist measures and assessments of such measures must all be conducted in the language of numbers. The mapping out of crime's peculiar dimensions – its causes, cycles, victims, perpetrators, frequency, costs etc. – provides the basis for evaluating the state's performance of its crime prevention and control function. On the basis of numericized information depicting crime's statistical dynamics, citizens can hold government to account and personally undertake various activities against crime.

Given the importance of numbers to practices of liberal governance, one of the recurrent themes in the numerical discourse on crime concerns the accuracy of the numbers, not only in terms of their reliability and validity, but also how they are interpreted by the public (Pratt 1999; Haggerty 2001; Hudson 2001). These debates came to a head in 2000 when a very public conflict erupted between President Mbeki and women's lobby groups over how best to represent the statistical truths about rape (Shaw 2002, 47). Drawing on victimization surveys, feminist activists argued that official counts drastically under-represented the actual number of rapes and suggested that only 1 in 36 cases was reported to the police – a figure originally given by the SAPS itself and cited in UN and Human Rights Watch reports. The 1 in 36 reporting figure was vigorously challenged by Mbeki who ordered an investigation into the matter. Nonetheless, it featured prominently in an anti-rape television campaign, which portrayed rape as an epidemic of gigantic proportions.

In the wake of this dispute, the then Minister of Safety and Security announced, in July 2000, a moratorium on the public release of all crime statistics, a moratorium that was lifted on 31 March 2001. Throughout this period, government emphasized that responsible action on the part of liberal democratic subjects required not only access to reliable and valid crime statistics, but also that citizens make rational use of such data. Conceding that certain methodological problems existed in relation to the available data,[8] officials nevertheless insisted that the public had 'blow[n] up the levels of crime', negatively impacting pubic confidence in government, the tourism industry and foreign investment, thus threatening to 'blow South Africa out of existence' (*The Star* 17 July 2000, in Comaroff and Comaroff 2006, 221). Crime rates, government maintained, had in fact either levelled off or decreased, a claim supported by independent victimization surveys (ISS 2004; also Schönteich 2002).

In the public discourse, however, officially recorded statistics and the moratorium on their release were both read as political manoeuvres designed to conceal upsurges in crime. While many were suspicious of official data and, in any case, hardly used them in their everyday risk calculations (Shaw 2002), the argument arose that the public had a right to such numbers as without them it was impossible to properly

8 Concerns centred on how the data was gathered and analyzed. A variety of measures were introduced to counter these concerns including: training 3,000 people and recruiting another 600 'to specialize on the issue of crime information' (Presidential State of the Nation Address, 9 February 2001); and the implementation, as of June 2001, of computerized Geographic Information Systems at 340 priority police stations covering 80% of the country (Streek 2001).

evaluate the government's performance (*Independent Online* 7 February 2001). In an effort to persuade the state of its duty to publicize crime statistics, victims produced their own crime counts for publication in local dailies. As Comaroff and Comaroff point out, '[h]ere all parties "argued with numbers", using them to confirm their own assertions and to discount those touted by others' (2006, 223). The problem of crime was thus bound up with the problem of numbers.

To sum up, statistics do not simply reflect reality, but are implicated in how reality is produced and organized. While data analysis proceeds from the assumption that crime is a predictable, routine and systematic phenomenon with identifiable spatial and temporal coordinates, it is the very processes required to produce, stabilize, transmit and interpret these numbers that produces these properties (Garland 1996, 1997). Numbers play a crucial role in constituting criminal justice as a *system* and citizens as active partners of government in crime prevention. And domestic and international confidence in the state's ability to rule is greatly influenced, as suggested in the NCPS, by the recorded rates of crime and by the state's willingness to subject their practices to statistical scrutiny.

Changing the Subject

A striking feature of contemporary criminal justice policy is the prominence now accorded to victims (Garland 1997, 2000; O'Malley 1996a). Indeed, one of the most interesting things about the NCPS is that it addressed not only offenders, but victims (actual and potential) as well, offering diverse specifications of both offenders and victims as governmental subjects. In so doing, an image of the 'good citizen' materialised, which outlined the capacities of individuals, their limitations, their duties and obligations as liberal democratic citizens. As Canguilheim (1978) and Foucault (1977) have emphasized, notions of normality emerge out of, rather than provide the basis for, studies of deviance, madness, pathology and disease. The NCPS articulates the terms in which the population is to both govern itself and be governed within a liberal democracy. It is in this sense that we can speak of 'governing through crime'.

The Offender

Offenders as disadvantaged Two different, though related, constructions of the criminal exist. In the first, offenders are understood in relation to various social forces and are to be governed through disciplinary coercion. This depicts the offender as driven to commit crimes by factors largely beyond his (and to a lesser extent, her) control. These factors are located either in the external, surrounding environment (for example, a culture of political intolerance and violence; social inequalities and inequities) or, less often, within the individual (for example, socio-psychological stress) (DoSS 1996b, 13–23). This marks a notable shift away from group pathology (an atavistic account of black offending that predominated during the apartheid period) towards situating the individual within the wider social-structural context and stressing the negative influence and impact of abnormal social circumstances.

Hereditarian arguments about crime give way to a focus on the social conditions that individuals find themselves in and how these impinge on and structure each individual's actions and decisions. Criminal activity will cease only to the extent that these underlying conditions are attended to – either removed or ameliorated – which is a 'social crime prevention' approach.

The criminal subject characteristic of such accounts appears in a very familiar and even sympathetic light: they are a product of apartheid, an 'innocent victim' of an immoral, unjust, racist practice. The offender is thus no different from the majority of South Africans who have been 'historically disadvantaged by the previous undemocratic era' (DoSS 1996b, 15). What they share are experiences – past and present – of social, economic, political and educational marginalization and the sense of powerlessness and frustration that this engenders.

Attention is thus directed to the rehabilitation of the disadvantaged, to equipping them with the necessary skills and resources for their (re)adjustment to the new socio-economic and political order. For example, the Department of Correctional Services (DoCS) provides basic education and occupational skills training to inmates, which is aimed at 'changing their attitudes, behaviour and social circumstances' (DoCS 2004, 10). Programmes to educate, train, treat and rehabilitate offenders act, in Garland's terms (1997), *on* the individual (see also O'Malley 1992). Offenders are made to submit to disciplinary techniques designed to re-form them: to tame unrealistic material aspirations arising out of the 'culture of entitlement' associated with new-found freedoms (DoSS 1996b, 15); to instil respect for the rule of law and human rights; to cultivate political tolerance; and to inculcate new moral habits resistant to the seductions of crime. A 1998 pamphlet – *The Department of Correctional Services and the Battle Against Crime!* – is illustrative. Commenting on the role of the DoCS in preventing reoffending, the Commissioner at the time promised to '*subject* [convicted prisoners] to an environment which is conducive to positive change' and to prepare inmates 'for appropriate employment or economic independence after release by *subjecting* them to educational, vocational, entrepreneurship and life skills programmes' [emphasis added]. For those offenders who proved too disruptive to this disciplinary regime, 'Closed Maximum Units' (C-Max) were introduced within existing prison facilities. C-Max did not so much operate as a containment option for 'dangerous and problematic' inmates, for these troublesome offenders are nonetheless viewed as 'changeable', instead, the objective of C-Max was to 'subject culprits to intensive supervision, security and control … to assist in changing their disruptive behaviour and facilitate their successful reintegration into 'normal' prison … '. C-Max sought to produce docile and obedient individuals, rendering them more manageable within the carceral context (and hopefully outside, in society). Once returned to 'normal prison', the offenders were made to participate in programmes that targeted the motivational chains of offending. Disciplinary penal strategies, such as those set out above, provided for the detailed inspection, evaluation and management of each inmate by reference to generalizable norms of conduct, productivity and the like (cf. Foucault 1977). This was not to deny or crush the capacity for self-directed action, but to reshape it so that upon release into society offenders would conduct themselves in appropriate and approved ways without the need for direct state interventions. As the most recent DoCS (2004) draft White Paper makes clear, disadvantaged offenders are to guided by a new moral code celebrating 'self-discipline', 'social independence', and societal and familial service.

Offenders as rational The marginalization of social or psychological explanations in the new discourse on crime means that the disadvantaged offender largely disappears from view.[9] Moreover, as Garland (1997) and O'Malley (1992, 1996b) have noted:

> following Foucault – if causal analyses of crime diminish or obliterate individual responsibility then a shift away from social determination should reintroduce personal responsibility. And indeed, the second and preferred model of the criminal emphasizes the offender's autonomy, rationality and responsibility.

Seen in rational choice terms, this opportunistic individual responds to situations and circumstances where there are easy opportunities to commit crime. Crime results from the calculative choices of rational individuals. One can thus dispense with the need for special theories of offender motivation or causal analyses of criminality. Attention centres on the cost–benefit calculation itself, independent of the personal and social history of the calculator. The criminal appears neither as socially inadequate nor as especially different from the average individual. Thus the rational choice model has a democratizing effect: everyone – black and white, ANC and National Party supporter – is a potential offender. Criminality resides not at the level of personality, genetic make-up or institutional identity, but at the level of mere behaviour or action (Cohen 1985). The decision to offend depends on the quite rational exercise of a cost–benefit calculation (see Crawford 1998 for a critical review of rational choice theory in criminology). The regulation of the actions of offenders comes to depend on transforming neither desires nor motivations, but the physical and social settings in which individuals act (Feeley and Simon 1994; Reichman 1986). Manipulations of the environment or the effects of crime aim to raise the costs of criminal activity relative to the anticipated gains. Faced with an excess of costs, the offender's interests shift to 'avoiding the penalty' rather than 'risking the crime' (Foucault 1977, 96).

Governing the rational choice criminal involves altering the balance of the cost–benefit equation that underpins rational conduct, in particular by ensuring the certainty and swiftness of detection, apprehension, prosecution and detention. Whilst there exists little interest in treating the offender, concern centres on the capacity to

---

9 The *negotiated* transition to democracy effectively set limits on (party) political attempts to blame apartheid for all societal ills, including crime. One variant of this reluctance to see apartheid as the source of all problems (crime included) was represented in the Truth and Reconciliation Commission's hearings. Amnesty applicants were instructed that it was not enough to argue that they had committed crimes for political reasons – that is, to maintain or resist apartheid. Instead, they were required to argue that they had engaged in criminal activity in order to further very clear and specific political goals derived from the agenda of a political organisation of which they were members.

On the production of 'truth telling' by the Truth and Reconciliation Commission, see Leman-Langlois and Shearing (2004).

intervene at the level of the individual because as rational and responsible calculators, criminals bear the consequences of their decisions (cf. O'Malley 1994, 1996b). Consider several NCPS projects to address Cabinet-designated 'national priority' crimes – firearms-related offences; organized crime; white-collar crime; gender violence and crimes against children; inter-group conflict; vehicle theft and hijacking; and corruption within the criminal justice system. These projects conceive of crime primarily in terms of opportunities and thus as manageable through situational crime prevention schemes (reducing opportunities and rewards) and punitive legal strategies (increasing costs). The *Crime Information and Intelligence Gathering* programme, under Pillar 1 (the 'Criminal Justice Process'), recommended the introduction of uniform investigative and prosecutorial policies designed to improve the state's capacity to detect and prosecute organized crime, a coordinated approach held out as crucial since crime syndicates typically operated across jurisdictional boundaries. Where crime syndicates recruited young people, the *Secure Care for Juveniles* programme (under Pillar 1) proposed the imposition of 'harsher sentences' to deter the exploitation of juveniles. But youth were not merely dupes and this programme also endorsed the development of secure care facilities for youth accused of 'serious crimes' in order to help to prevent escapes from custody pre- and post-trial, thereby ensuring that the offenders faced the consequences of their actions. The *Motor Vehicle Regulation* programme, under Pillar 2 ('Environmental Design'), comprised a national online registration and licensing system to combat the proliferation of false documents and counselled manufacturers to mark parts, thereby enabling the policing of the motor parts trade and preventing duplication of vehicle identification numbers. The *Corruption and Commercial Crime* programme (curiously under Pillar 2) urged the 'development of a code of conduct for business which requires reporting of cases [of white-collar and economic offences] to the commercial branch [of the police]' (DoSS 1996b, 73) and supported the preparation of legislation on money laundering and asset forfeiture. These enhanced legal and situational controls conveyed to the public that government took seriously organized crime, young offenders, white-collar crime and vehicle theft, and aimed to build much needed confidence in the state's resolve and capacity to manage crime. But more than this, it aimed to reduce crime by increasing the costs of criminal activity, decreasing the expected rewards and increasing the risk of encountering and being processed by the criminal justice system.

Also apparent is a second set of correctional strategies. Different to that directed at the disadvantaged criminal, this penal regime works *through* the autonomy and rationality of the offender (see Garland 1997; also O'Malley 1994). For example, 'personal development programmes', a joint NCPS and DoCS venture, made the inmate 'co-responsible' for rehabilitation: 'The Institutional Committee of each prison, together with each inmate, decide on a rehabilitation programme to meet the needs of the inmate' (DoSS 1996b, 28). The efficacy of rehabilitation programmes, then, depends on the active participation of the offender in partnership with correctional officials and a range of state-aligned, though independent, lifestyle experts such as 'educationists, psychologists, social workers and religious caregivers' (*ibid.*). But there is no assumption here of the offender as 'naturally' responsible or self-reliant etc. Thus, while premised on the admission of responsibility, *Diversion Programmes* (under Pillar 1), as an alternative to prosecution, and *Community-based Sentencing* (under Pillar 1), as an alternative to imprisonment, both focus on 'creat[ing] a sense of responsibility' on the part of offenders by building their 'personal resources', 'self-sufficiency' and 'self-esteem' (pp. 59–61). Within the confines of the prison, 'personal development programmes' emphasize the 'empowerment'[10] of inmates and the 'development' of the individual. In other words, these correctional strategies simultaneously imagine and produce the independent, rationally choosing, responsible individual.

There are two important observations to be made here. First, unlike the account of British crime control strategies provided by Garland (1996), little or no conflict exists between the punitive policies of the South African government and constructions of the offender as a rational choice actor. In the context of abnormally high crime rates, deterrence-based measures such as greater legislative controls and harsher sentences are linked, through the model of the rational choice offender, to crime prevention (cf. O'Malley 1994, 1996b). In contemporary South Africa, expressions of sovereign power are conditioned by the liberal democratic ideal of the autonomous, freely choosing, self-regulating citizen.

The second point is that what is excluded in both depictions of the offender is the 'other', described by Garland as 'the threatening outcast, the fearsome stranger, the excluded and the embittered' (1996, 461). Both the disadvantaged offender and the rational choice criminal appear in a familiar light as not much different from the population in general. Where the 'other' momentarily surfaces it is in the form of the 'illegal immigrant'.

The racialized 'other' The forging of an inclusive South Africa – 'the Rainbow Nation' – involved constituting certain categories of individuals as 'other', the 'receptacles of projected fears and hatreds' (Stenson 1995, 120; also Harris 2002). With Cabinet defining illegal immigration as a 'national priority' crime, the 'other' increasingly comes to assume the form of the foreigner. Despite recognizing the 'urgent' need for 'more accurate' information, the NCPS explicitly constructs the illegal immigrant as: a decisive threat to South Africa's economic development given an already overstretched socio-economic infrastructure; a trigger of inter-group conflict given their inability to 'establish permanent roots in communities'; and as a perpetrator of cross-border crimes involving drugs, firearms, endangered species etc. (DoSS 1996b, 33, 77–80). As in the UK and elsewhere (Stenson 2005), concerns about crime, economic growth, limited resources, inter-ethnic violence, and community cohesion and solidarity become linked to debates on immigration policy.

In South Africa, the demonization of the foreigner is effected by categorizing illegal immigration alongside organized crime, gang-related offences and the trafficking of

10 Hannah-Moffat provides a critical analysis of empowerment projects for federally sentenced women in Canada (1999, 2001). Whereas the category of 'needs' – both at the level of the individual female offender and the offender population – previously served as a critique of state penal policy and practice, it operates, she argues, as an instrument for the governance of prisoners. 'Needs' become a way of calculating criminogenic 'risk' and are entered into the 'security management model' for regulating the prison population.

drugs and endangered species under the general heading of 'Trans-national Crime' (Pillar 4). Such categorization blurs the distinction between foreign nationals who are 'illegal aliens' and those who use South Africa as a base to run drugs or trade arms etc., and links the 'illegal immigrant' to crime and criminal activity. Attention centres on regional borders and regional migration policies, a concern with neighbouring countries – Lesotho, Swaziland, Zimbabwe, Botswana, Zambia, Malawi, Mozambique, Angola, Namibia, Tanzania and Mauritius – indicating that the identity of the illegal immigrant is clearly racialized. The criminal face not only belongs to the foreigner, but it is also black. Here we see the resurgence of a security discourse, one that casts crime as a threat to sovereignty and territorial integrity and demands a militarized response. The interests and needs of illegal immigrants and the South African state are calculated in zero-sum terms: the illegal immigrant has become the new 'enemy of the state'. The strategies contemplated under Pillar 4 do not target the increasingly hostile attitudes and behaviours of South Africans towards foreign nationals. Rather, Safety and Security, Defence, Foreign Affairs, Home Affairs and the Department of Trade and Industry cooperate to control the movement of 'illegals' across South African borders through the application of stringent visa restrictions and repatriation provisions and through the fortification of ports of entry. Techniques of surveillance, repression and exclusion thus predominate. The measures envisaged tend much more towards the defence of South Africa's economic, political and social resources – seemingly threatened by the mere presence of large numbers of illegal immigrants – than towards curbing crime, whether committed by, or directed at, illegal aliens. Rather than manifesting an instrumental rationality, these strategies reveal the morally- and emotionally-charged undercurrents influencing contemporary crime control policy.

This raises important questions about the rights and protections afforded to foreigners in general. The human rights discourse that frames much, if not most, of the NCPS is noticeably absent when it comes to mapping and regulating state interactions with 'illegal immigrants'. How government deals with marginalized groupings constitutes a key test of liberal democracy as practised in South Africa. Disturbingly, in its first term in office the ANC government faced allegations, set out in a Human Rights Watch report, of widespread abuses of refugees and migrants, in particular black African foreigners (*The Mail & Guardian online*, 20 March 1998). The publication of a South African Human Rights Commission survey in 1999, which documented the routine deportation of individuals with legitimate refugee claims (Dempster 2003), revealed that the discriminatory and often violent treatment of 'other' black Africans remained largely unaddressed as the government entered its second term (see also Harris 2002). Concerns about xenophobia have not dissipated and in fact have even escalated, prompting the Commission to launch another, more recent investigation. The subtle, though no less insidious, insertion of the 'race question' into the discourse on crime – for example, through notions such as 'illegal immigrant' and 'regional security' – clearly warrants research.

The Victim

A victim-centred approach constitutes a crucial element within the new discourse on crime. This centring of the victim has much in common with international developments in criminology and criminal justice that shifted focus from offenders towards the effects and costs of crime (Braithwaite 1989). In liberal democratic South Africa, attention shifted to the individual victim, rather than the state, and, in particular, to the victimization of blacks, which was long ignored by previous governments. In the context of high levels of crime, '*everyone*', the NCPS warned, 'is forced to contemplate themselves as potential victims' [emphasis added] (DoSS 1996b, 21). Indeed, as Comaroff and Comaroff (2006) suggest, 'victimhood' emerges as a key defining feature of the 'new' South Africa over and above political affiliation, class and race.

Victims as rational Victims and potential victims are rational choice actors responsible, in certain respects, for their own protection against victimization and for the commission of crime itself (cf. Garland 1996; O'Malley 1992). This view is crystallized in the government's anti-crime strategy. Projects envisaged under Pillar 3 ('Public Values and Education') aimed to mobilize churches, political parties, provincial and local authorities and communities, and emphasized 'active public participation in crime prevention' and, more specifically, the importance of community values and attitudes in the reduction of tolerance of criminal activities (pp. 73–4). The Environmental Design and Maintenance programme (under Pillar 2) addressed the residential and retail sectors and the transport industry, all of which 'can impact on crime through reducing the opportunities for crime' (p. 68). Indeed, the belief underlying the NCPS is that the state can not go it alone, that effective action against crime requires government 'to specifically seek out partnerships and cooperative working relationships with non-governmental, civil society and business sectors, all of which have expertise and vested interests in the elimination of crime' (p. 44). The SAPS 1996/97 Annual Plan, for instance, promoted 'partnerships' to the level of operational strategy to improve the effectiveness of the police in dealing with crime. Thus, a prevailing theme throughout is the 'sharing of responsibilities' for crime prevention and control between a professional police in particular (and other criminal justice agencies) and a skilled, knowledgeable and agentive public.

In exercising this responsibility, the interests and goals of victims and potential victims must be aligned with the objectives of governing authorities. The activities of individuals in respect of crime are to be conducted in an officially approved manner (Crawford 1994; Johnston 1992; Garland 1996; O'Malley and Palmer 1996). Individuals are to be instructed that the preventative or pre-emptive measures they take may in fact constitute more of a threat to, than a defence of, individual and collective freedoms. For example, reliance on firearms – readily accessible through legal and illegal means – is discouraged. It is likely that the arming of the citizenry had repercussions in several areas: the nature of offending – the increased use of violence in the commission of crime as offenders expect a better armed public 'ready to fight back' (*The Mail & Guardian* online 11 September 1996); the levels and types of crime – as the demand for guns escalates, so too do the theft of firearms and the illegal arms trade; and, quality of life issues – loss of life, injury and psychological trauma. Nor does the state authorize the coercive practices of collective forms of self-policing – popular courts (Schärf 1991; Seekings 1991; Nina 1995a and b), gangs (Kinnes 2000) and the politically-aligned Self-Defence Units (ANC) and

Self-Protection Units (Inkatha Freedom Party) (Marks and Mckenzie 1998) – that mushroomed throughout the black urban townships in the early 1990s within the context of profound distrust in, and resistance to, government agencies of criminal justice. (The chapters that follow discuss the policing initiatives of private enterprise and local township inhabitants.) Here the state seeks to (re)define the appropriate spaces for the democratic exercise of coercive power. From now on, victims and potential victims are to act within the confines of democracy, to act without, for instance, violating the emerging culture of human rights. Independent self-policing initiatives threaten democratic rule not so much because of the coercive powers at their disposal, but if they reject the state's authority to *define* the legitimate use of force.

A number of methods are identified through and by means of which government communicates to the public both the 'reality' of the crime situation and the appropriate steps to reduce the risk of victimization. For example, statistical analyses quantify the social and economic costs of crime and offer profiles of those most at risk of victimization and of so-called 'hot spots' (Leighton 1991), those areas likely to be targeted by criminals. These analyses assist in 'properly informing public opinion' and in 'facilitat[ing] public participation in effective crime prevention' (DoSS 1996b, 47). As rational choice actors, individuals are to calculate their crime risks and undertake preventive action based on 'objective' facts not subjective perceptions or anecdotal information on crime. Consider, too, public education campaigns (Pillar 3) to 'enhance public knowledge and information on the effects of crime' (p. 73), to provide a working knowledge of the criminal justice system, to foster a new collective morality discouraging of crime and to endorse non-violent solutions to conflict. A proposed safety and security curriculum, for example, aims to teach school children 'responsible and empowered citizenship' by equipping them with life skills, including confidence building, anger management, conflict resolution and gender education, so that they may 'deal effectively with domestic violence, child abuse and gender-related crime and gang formation' in communities (p. 76).

In most contemporary Western societies this 'responsibilization' strategy is often accompanied by the injunction that victims (actual and potential) seek protection primarily from private sources such as insurance companies and the private security industry as an alternative to reliance on the state provision of security (O'Malley 1992; 1996b). The NCPS clearly recognizes the importance of private sector involvement in crime control in partnership with public agencies, 'emphasizing that crime is a shared challenge' (p. 48). Individuals are especially encouraged to engage the services of community-based, non-profit and non-governmental organizations. But voluntary and commercial security arrangements are valued largely because they augment, not replace, state resources (cf. Hudson 2001 on the UK). For example, design changes to private sector products, such as motor vehicles, residential buildings, and shopping and leisure complexes, are promoted because they facilitate law enforcement and thereby reduce the opportunities for crime (DoSS 1996b, 68; see ISS 1997 for a review of environmental design initiatives in South Africa).

More generally, individuals are urged to contribute directly to state institutions of criminal justice. South Africans are to invest confidence, hitherto lacking, in the formal system of criminal justice, providing the necessary information – by reporting crime and testifying in court – without which the state is 'helpless' to act (DoSS 1996b, 48). This is unsurprising given the historical background of profound public distrust of state justice and the current context wherein both political authorities and citizens demand (doubtless for different reasons) that the criminal justice structures be both effective and legitimate. But the public is not merely to assist state officials in the performance of their duties. Indeed, '[e]ffective crime prevention requires that communities are actively concerned and involved in *all* aspects of crime prevention' (*ibid.*) [emphasis added]. This includes community input into the setting of local policing priorities, the structuring of local crime prevention strategies and the construction of local crime profiles necessary to problem-solving. It also includes, under the *Victim Empowerment and Support* programme (Pillar 1), a greater role for victims in the criminal justice process through offender-victim mediation schemes, as well as complaints audits and evaluations of customer satisfaction with police service. The provision of public policing has become increasingly more market-like (consider the name change from South African Police to South African Police *Service*). A new contractual image of policing emerges, which see individuals and communities as 'customers' and 'users' of police services (cf. Stenson 1995; Garland 1996; O'Malley and Palmer 1996). A draft discussion document issued (circa 1996) by the reconstructed Ministry of Safety and Security promoted a vision of the 'Police Service' as 'accessible' and 'accountable' to citizens, and as 'user-friendly, effective and reliable'. This was later echoed in the Ministry's White Paper (DoSS 1998), demonstrating that individual and community choice, activism and participation are key features of liberal democratic policing.

Victims as emotive Alongside this model of the responsible, rational individual is another that positions the actual and potential victims as disenchanted, isolated, frightened and angry. This second model operates in terms of the division erected between reason and feeling (cf. Foucault 1977). It isolates the emotions and passions, presenting these as obstacles to the development of a human rights culture and a crime-resistant society. The emotions and passions appear as a source of intolerance, disorder and even crime.

> [T]he absence of victim-aid services has added to the sense of powerlessness of victims and has contributed to public perceptions that perpetrators lie at the heart of crime prevention strategies in South Africa. Not only does this often generate the quest for informal retributive justice which is criminal in nature but it also breathes life into popular resistance to human rights issues ...
>
> (DoSS 1996b, 21)

On this view, citizens feel betrayed, if not ignored, by the criminal justice system which they regard, not entirely incorrectly, as prioritising the needs of offenders. For example, where the state assumes 'ownership' of the solutions to crime, where victims become mere observes of court proceedings which appear foreign to them and where lax bail conditions exist, then victims may try to reclaim a sense of power within the informal justice arena or through campaigning for capital punishment, no bail and aggressive police tactics. Self-policing initiatives may seem rational and logical given current levels of crime and public perceptions of police as ineffective, inefficient and corrupt. But they were not seen positively within the new discourse on crime. Rather, the NCPS portrays informal justice mechanisms, in particular the politically aligned para-military structures, as inciting and exacerbating the almost primordial desires of individuals for revenge and retribution.

But if victims sometimes act criminally against offenders; they also sometimes perpetrate crimes more generally against others – family members, neighbours, employees, strangers – within their local environment.

> Victims of past or current criminal activity if untreated, frequently become perpetrators of either retributive violence or of violence displaced within the social or domestic arena.
> (DoSS 1996b, 20)

The line between victim and criminal becomes blurred. Perhaps the prominence accorded victims in this new discourse on crime is best understood as a preventative measure in and of itself. This is less an interest in enrolling the responsible individual in crime prevention activities than in preventing the victim from becoming an offender. Reliance is placed on the criminal justice system to provide victim-aid services (under Pillar 1), such as counselling, and a referral directorate to deal with the effects of crime. These services 'treat' and 'heal' victims of crime who feel a sense of rage, insecurity and helplessness. Additionally, the justice system is to attend to and accommodate victim demands regarding the fate of offenders thereby improving public perceptions of the accessibility and effectiveness of the formal system. Immediately, however, a problem presents itself: as emotive individuals, victims are unlikely to be placated by government strategies which promise not severe punishments or lengthy prison terms, but due process, effective and efficient service delivery, restorative justice, rehabilitation and the like. The challenge facing government, then, is to respond to the expressed concerns of victims and potential victims, but without retreating from its commitment to building a human rights culture. Whereas in other jurisdictions, such as the US, the raw emotional energy of victims is harnessed to crime control developments thus providing a public role for, and value to, cruelty and vengeance (Simon 2001), in South Africa the emotions are to be contained and brought under control if a rational response to crime is to prevail.

Conclusion

Analysts contend that at both a conceptual and practical level the NCPS has waned in influence. They charge that the crime prevention approach articulated in the NCPS was rapidly overtaken by a focus on increased law enforcement and enhanced crime control (see Dixon 2006; Rauch 2001; Samara 2003; Shaw 2002; Simpson and Rauch 1999; van Zyl Smit and van der Spuy 2004). For example, Shaw (2002, 126) offers the following assessment of the NCPS:

> … prevention interventions have (after a relatively short period) been seen as too long term and perhaps too uncertain to confront the country's crime crisis, and there is a renewed focus now on law enforcement interventions.

On this view, while the NCPS remains today a 'good strategy on paper' (Shaw 2002), it no longer provides the framework for understanding or managing South Africa's crime problem.

Such accounts are misleading. The NCPS was as much about building public and market confidence in the capacity of state institutions to govern as about reducing crime, and both were tied to a model of strong sovereign controls. A credible, competent and publicly accountable police force, in particular, emerged as a key index of successful democratization. More generally, the establishment of a legitimate, efficient and effective criminal justice system was seen as crucial to ensuring that public and private interests maintained faith in government structures. In the 'new' South Africa, a well-functioning criminal justice system comes to symbolise the strength of the state. Legal controls thus function as a key mechanism to generate and demonstrate authority (Stenson 2005). A strong police force and criminal justice system signal that the state is an efficient and predictable guarantor of basic levels of safety and security, minimum conditions for existence.

A well-functioning criminal justice system is also crucial to the reduction of crime. On the one hand, sovereign controls provide a 'vital foundation' (DoSS 1996b) for successful crime prevention. As international experience shows, the effectiveness of crime prevention is limited if not sufficiently backed up by the threat of rapid and repressive law enforcement and criminal justice response. On the other hand, crime control deters potential and actual offenders, both by raising the legal costs of engaging in crime and by making the experience of imprisonment and other sanctions so distasteful that reoffending will not occur – general and specific deterrence respectively.

The law enforcement focus of more recent criminal justice policies does not therefore significantly depart from the NCPS. Rather, it represents an extension of the concern, expressed in the NCPS, with the symbolic and instrumental functions of punitive controls.

Reliance on coercive technologies to control crime and maintain public order is not the sole prerogative of the state and its criminal justice agencies and the next chapter considers the punitive measures now at the forefront of private security activities.

Chapter 3

Crime Control and the Private Security Industry

This is not a club. It is a business and we're in it for the money.
National Chair, South African National Security Employers' Association (SANSEA).(*Security Focus* November 1997, 4)

Introduction

A private security trade association magazine, *Security Focus*, describes its readership as comprised of 'the security professional and security equipment installer to top officials in mining organisations, financial institutions and government bodies … i.e. somebody who does not have to be convinced that *crime is a problem* but is interested instead, in knowing how to plan, design, implement and evaluate solutions to persistent security problems' [emphasis added]. Similarly, the marketing of security products and services emphasizes the problem of crime. For instance, a promotional piece on the growing field of gate automation for commercial and residential applications stated that 'given the escalating crime rate in South Africa, people are increasingly looking to their perimeters as the front line of defence against intruders' (*Security Today*, Oct./Nov. 1997, 36). Another advertisement claimed that covert cameras provide companies that are facing profit losses due to theft with 'an excellent way of actually detecting crime by … "discrete monitoring"' (*Security Focus*, September 1997, 23). Consider as a further example two high-profile private security projects in Durban, South Africa: a lucrative guarding contract at a shopping complex that was awarded to Khulani-Springbok Patrols (Pty) Ltd included the brief to 'stamp out crime' (*Security Focus*, October 1997, 8); and, a proposed BID (Business Improvement District) that included the employment of private security on the public beachfront in an effort to reduce crime (Nedcor December 1995). As these examples suggest, the private security industry is a key performer in crime control whether in relation to the policing of 'mass private property', the private sector or indeed, the public domain. Crime is imagined not merely as the 'natural' environment within which commercial security providers operate and flourish, but as the principle *object* of private security regulatory strategies and techniques: crime is targeted as a marketable resource, which held a great deal of potential for expansion.

Private security has consistently presented itself as the partner of the South African Police Service (SAPS), rather than their competitors in crime control: 'The security industry is in fact a pillar of law and order which complements the Department of Safety and Security', proclaim key industry members (<www.securityalliance.co.za> accessed 01 June 2007). Government and the SAPS have advanced a similar view of the relationship between the two policing sectors (DoSS 1996b; SAPS 1996; also Baker 2002; Berg 2004). On occasion, this has translated into coordinated action against crime, for example a joint private security–police project to clean up the public beachfront (Nedcor December 1995; see also Chapter 4). More usually, though, private security operates relatively independently of the SAPS – the former concentrated mainly in city centres and suburbs, the latter operating principally in the townships (Shaw 2002) – both armed with considerable coercive powers (discussed further below).

There are few studies of the crime control activities of private security. More than a decade ago, Johnston (1992) remarked that the 'loss' and 'crime' distinction traditionally drawn by scholars – which linked the logics of crime control to public police activities and loss prevention to private security – left a distinctive feature of contemporary policing largely unexplored; that is, the extent to which these objectives had become complementary purposes in the context of an increasingly neoliberal political economy. Indeed, the complementarity of these objectives is often spelled out quite explicitly by private security agencies in their own public representations; these businesses adopt identifiers such as 'AntiCrime Force Training Academy and Guard Division'. Yet, the view of private security as interested primarily, if not exclusively, in loss prevention has persisted in the literature. For example, Garland (2000) exposed the myths of sovereign crime control while maintaining that private security arrangements promote the client's interest, above the public's interest, through an emphasis on preventing and reducing loss at private sites rather than prosecuting and punishing offenders. Similarly, although Ericson and Haggerty (1997) fundamentally reassessed police work and organization, they nonetheless retained the standard view of private security as 'quintessentially oriented toward compliance enforcement and loss prevention' (p. 50), rather than criminal investigation and criminal law enforcement.

Of the relatively few accounts of the industry's crime control role, most tend toward a negative image of power – power as ultimately and fundamentally oppressive. Rigakos's (2002) innovative Toronto-based study of Intelligarde International, for example, yields valuable empirical data on the company's law enforcement functions. Also of importance is the attention paid to the firm's reliance on coercive strategies to maintain social order, lending support to South's (1997) suggestions that coercive measures are now at the forefront of industry activities. Rigakos's analysis, however, is limited by an underlying equation of power with submission and domination and with perpetual and total surveillance (possibly a result of his attempt to fuse a Marxist economic logic with a Foucauldian disciplinary logic). His main research concerns centred on the excesses of power, on resistance to control and on the economic interests driving 'the parapolice surveillance systems'. However, by framing power in terms of subjection and prohibitions, he largely ignored the productive and positive aspects of power. As Foucault observed in a 1977 interview: 'The interdiction, the refusal, the prohibition, far from being essential forms of power, are only its limits, power in its frustrated or extreme forms. The relations of power are above all, productive' (Foucault 1988, 118).

This chapter examines the security industry's operation of preventative and punitive crime-management strategies, which are measures that impact directly on individual bodies. Rather than simply being seen as repressive or negative, such techniques are regarded in this chapter as productive, as they seek to promote and shape individual agency in particular ways. I ask how these tools imagine, at the same time as they seek to act on, the subjects of government.

In exploring the coercive and punitive techniques used by private security to manage crime, I am directly engaging with the assumption, contained in much of the governmentality literature, of a general move, in liberal societies, towards 'action-at-a-distance' (Miller and Rose 1990); that is, subtle techniques of persuasion and inducements for linking up the projects of political authorities and the subjective aspirations of individuals. On this view, governing authorities are spatially distant from the governed and rely primarily on compliance-based techniques that act indirectly on population categories to which individuals are linked, rather than directly targeting the individuals themselves. Regarding criminal justice, Feeley and Simon (1994) argued that the aim of the new risk-management strategies is not to adjudicate culpability, diagnose or treat particular individuals, but to identify, classify and administer problematic sectors of the population (see also Ericson and Haggerty 1997).

Various aspects of these arguments have been critiqued. Weir (1996), in her study of the 'government of pregnancy', showed that suggestions of the disappearance of individual bodies as the proper target of governance were premature. O'Malley (1994; 1996b) demonstrated a linkage between the advanced liberal model of individual responsibility and punitive penalties: individuals were to actively engage in rational choice-making in all aspects of life and were to be held personally responsible for the consequences of such decisions. Simon (2001) himself described a 'punitive mentality' in the US, which served an expressive rather than an instrumental function. Others acknowledge the persistence of coercive tactics – as a hang-on effect of sovereign strategies that no longer bear out the realities of 'high crime societies' (Garland 2000); as a disciplinary tool for shaping the moral agency of incarcerated populations and operating alongside actuarial analyses of security risk factors (Hannah-Moffat 1999); or as a 'negative practice of control' centred on the excluded, the non-consumer, the anti-citizen – those seemingly beyond the preferred responsibilization strategies (Rose 1999, especially Chapter 7).

This chapter argues that the continued use of coercion is not just limited to the excluded, the anti-citizens, those on the margins. It explores the *routine* use of coercion in contemporary practices to regulate conduct. In addressing these concerns I rely primarily, though not exclusively, on material drawn from private security advertisements and company publications. These self-representations are important indicators of the practice of private security – its subjects, the objectives it sets for itself, the knowledge and techniques drawn on to achieve these practical objectives and the authorities that authorize it. This is supplemented by material from interviews conducted, in the mid-1990s in Cape Town, with senior private-security management. While private security obviously varies across nations, the increasingly transnational character (Johnston 2000) of the industry and the similarity of industry development in South Africa, Europe and North America indicate that the observations in this chapter are not geographically limited, but have a wider relevance.

The remainder of the chapter is divided into four broad areas. First, I offer a profile of South Africa's private security industry, comparing some aspects to developments elsewhere, particularly in Canada, Britain and America. This descriptive account indicates substantial industry expansion since the 1980s and in the section that follows I explore the specific problem to which private security emerged as a solution. I consider how this problem was assembled and under what conditions, demonstrating that the content of the problem has shifted considerably over time. Thirdly, I examine the preventative and punitive measures by which private security seeks to govern the conduct of the criminal offender. Here, I deal with the particular configuration of state/non-state use of coercion in practices of crime control and the implications for the nature of the South African state. Fourthly, I focus on the disciplinary and surveillance techniques through which the private security guard has come to be understood and regulated as a productive member of a labour force. Taken together, the latter two areas specify multiple objectifications of those to be governed.

Profiling Private Security

Definitional inconsistencies and unreliable record-keeping practices are familiar enough concerns in much private-security research in the English-speaking world (see Johnston 2000; Jones and Newburn 1995). This has prompted at least one writer to comment that '[t]he only consistent and reliable statement that is continually made … is that it is hard to obtain consistent and reliable information' (South 1988, 23). South Africa proves no exception (see Grant 1989; Shaw 2002). Official data is only available from 1990 onwards when the industry's statutory regulatory body became operational; the Security Officers Act (SOA) was passed in October 1987, but only promulgated in April 1989. These statistics are at best incomplete. Private-security calculations exclude in-house guards, private investigators, parastatals (for example, ESKOM security), security divisions within large companies (for example, ABSA Security) and local authority security[1] since the legal requirement to register with the statutory regulatory body only applied to contract security firms and employees. The legislation distinguished between contract and in-house security on the basis of the relationship between provider and user: contract security refers to the provision of security services on a market basis while in-house security is defined as 'a service rendered by an employee on behalf of his [sic] employer' (section 1(b)). Moreover, the legislation had no force or effect in the former self-governing homelands and the TBVC states (Transkei, Bophuthatswana, Venda and Ciskei). Official calculations for the better part of the 1990s thus exclude private security operating in these areas. The existence of any other centralized database for these regions is doubtful as only

1 Local authority structures, such as the Durban Municipal Security Department, 'ha[d] amongst its duties the protection of municipal property, including electricity sub-stations, bus depots, civic buildings and personnel' (NIM 1996, 12).

the former Bophuthatswana had its own private security legislation (NIM 1996). Shaw's work appears to suggest that the official data for much of the 1990s failed to capture private-security activity in three of nine provinces – Northern Cape, Mpumalanga and North West (Shaw 2001). Thus the statistics offered below should be treated less as representations of an objective reality than as broad indicators of market trends.

The available data indicates that large-scale growth began about 1975, during the period of heightened political opposition to the apartheid regime. One early estimate put sales in contract security products and services in South Africa at R141 million for 1978, R350 million in 1983 and R600 million in 1986 – an average annual growth of 18 per cent (Grant 1989). As in other countries (Johnston 1992; 2000), private-security growth steadied after this initial period of rapid expansion, though dramatic increases were recorded in the closing decade of the twentieth century with the decline of apartheid (in relation to Canada, see CCJS 2004). In 1990, the approximate size of the South African contract security market exceeded R1 billion (Nedcor/ISS *Crime Index* 1997, A9). In 1995, turnover increased to just under R2 billion, with around 3,000 registered companies and 190,000 registered personnel (Shaw 1995). By 1997, sales had soared to approximately R9 billion (*Security Focus* 1997), with 4,499 authorized firms and 362,297 officially recognized security officers[2] (*The Financial Mail* 1997, 51–52). By comparison, members of the South African Police Service numbered 141,000 and commercial security sales amounted to roughly nine times that of the SAPS budget (DoSS 1996a). Private-security employment continues to exceed that of the public police. By 2002, the number of registered security officers had increased by 33 per cent (Gould and Lamb 2004), while the number of police had fallen to 121,000, in large part because of a hiring moratorium (Minnaar and Mistry 2004). Private security outnumbered the police by ratios estimated to be as high as 7:1 (Berg 2004; Irish 1999; Kempa and Shearing 2002). According to the most recent numbers released by the industry's statutory regulatory body, as of March 2006 there were 296,901 active security officers, a further 689,845 inactive officers and a total of 4,763 security companies (PSIRA 2006).

As these figures indicate, private security is indeed a sizeable and profitable business, with several firms now listed on the Johannesburg Stock Exchange.

Staffed security services – static and patrolling guards, alarm monitoring, cash-in-transit and armed reaction – remained the largest and most visible market sector with an estimated annual turnover of R3.6 billion and approximately 114,000 employees. Electronic systems (card access, CCTV, turnkey systems, satellite tracking) retain slightly smaller market shares (*The Financial Mail* 1997, 51–52; *Security Focus* October 1997). Private security elsewhere also displayed a similar distribution of services which suggests a more complex interaction between the two leading market components than that implied in early predictions of the replacement of labour-intensive operations by electronic surveillance technology (see South 1988). In most jurisdictions today, including South Africa, North America, New

2 The total number of registered security officers included 116,825 actively employed individuals, 175,000 inactive though previously employed and 70,472 never employed (*The Financial Mail* 1997, 52).

Zealand and parts of Europe, it is private security that provides the initial response to alarm call-outs; in South Africa, as well as the US, this includes the dispatch of armed reaction units (Johnston 2000). According to the Chair of the South African Electronic Security Distributors Association, South African monitoring companies, with one exception, also install alarms and most offer armed rapid response services typically consisting of two security officers per vehicle (*Security Today*, Oct/Nov. 1997). Verification of alarm systems usually occurs through normal telephonic communication, with clients expecting a four-minute maximum response time for a 'normal alarm condition'.

Pointing to the increased market importance of monitoring and armed reaction, one estimate put the medium-term annual growth rate of this area at 25 per cent (*The Financial Mail* 1997, 51). *The Financial Mail* reported on the extraordinary income potential of this sector:

> Creating a monitoring station is expensive, but unlike guarding the overheads are constant and all income is profit, once the break-even point has passed. The average charge is R100 a month. 'It costs no more to monitor one terminal (client) than it does to monitor 1000,' says [the chair of the industry's regulatory body].
>
> 'It costs R10,000 a month to keep an armed response unit on the road. Clients pay R75 a month, which means a unit has to cover an area with 135 clients to break even. Every additional client is profit. Many units cover areas with 300 clients.'
>
> *The Financial Mail* (1997, 51)

Toward the close of the twentieth century, the number of registered monitoring and armed response firms stood at 673 (Irish 1999). Significantly, the greatest expansion to date has occurred in the domestic alarms and domestic patrols sectors (*The Financial Mail* 1997; Grant 1989). This has included township residents (Shaw 2002), though these policing strategies remain remarkably racialized: users are overwhelmingly white while 'only 2% of blacks have a private security or armed response system' (Valji, Harris and Simpson 2004). It is not that blacks lack confidence in private security measures, but rather that they are priced out of the commercial security market (Baker 2002; Dixon 2004; Robertshaw *et al* 2001). The implications that flow from this lack of purchasing power are discussed in detail in the following chapters. The main point here is that private security not only plays a role reminiscent of the state's conventional law and order function, but increasingly provides such services to the category of individuals – the predominately white middle-classes – traditionally regarded as the primary consumers of public policing.

In short, existing research points to the diversification and extension of contract security services for commercial, industrial, retail and government use, including the regular maintenance of public order. It also suggests an expansion of private security activities to the (domestic) household segment, including the surrounding residential streets whether publicly or privately owned. Private security has become increasingly involved in the provision of routine security.

From 'Club' to 'Business'

The private security industry initially operated much like a 'club'. Membership was exclusive and largely restricted at the administrative levels to those with police, intelligence and military backgrounds. Interestingly, the early firms were owned and managed predominately by former members of various colonial forces opposed to the political liberalization of Rhodesia, Kenya and Zambia (Grant 1989; Shaw 2002). These individuals found a receptive home in the South African private security industry, which like its state counterparts was militaristic and racist in nature. The dominance of these English speakers gradually gave way as Afrikaners with combat experience began to enter the industry.

The emergent old boy network facilitated close ties between the apartheid regime and the private security industry. One of the most nefarious and covert links between the government and private security involved the establishment, by state security forces in the first half of the 1980s, of private security firms as fronts[3] for the illegal trade in weapons, ivory and diamonds (NIM 1996) – all activities in support of the maintenance of the embargoed and crumbling pariah state. More generally, throughout the 1980s the state actively encouraged private security growth and development with the view to deploying private security as a complementary force to supplement the public police, increasing the repressive capacity of the apartheid regime (interviews with security company CEO and with security company manager, January 1998). Reflecting on the historical conditions of the time, a key industry figure stated:

> ... the wider social climate was in a state of extreme turbulence. General instability followed the 1976 protests, and the early 1980s saw a state of near anarchy in the townships which was part of the strategy of ungovernability used in particular by the ANC. Instability and war within and on the borders of the frontline states put severe pressure on the State's resources to provide security and maintain acceptable levels of order.
>
> For these reasons the state believed that there was a need for a closer relationship with private security in an attempt to contain not only the threats of violence and terrorism, but the rising crime levels associated both with the unrest and high unemployment and poverty.
>
> (Ibbotson 1994)

Of course, the state's mandate and private security interests were not necessarily similar, but they came to coalesce around the issue of white property and privilege. The state's primary concern centred on maintaining sovereign control over territory and increasingly this extended to securing white property as commercial and industrial sites in particular came to be seen as suitable targets in the anti-apartheid struggle (Prior 1989). In this context, the protection of white propertied interests came to be identified with the fight against Communism and the 'black threat'. Several statutes compelled citizens to perform policing roles in support of the maintenance of apartheid. For example, 'After influx control was "abolished" [1986]

---

3 Many of these survived into the twenty-first century as legitimate businesses and retained aspects of their paramilitary and covert institutional character (see NIM 1996).

the Prevention of Illegal Squatting Act was amended [1988] to compel landowners to evict squatters rather than have the police be seen to be performing unpopular forced removals' (Schärf 1989, 210). Evictions were at the landowners' expense and private security were often employed to perform the forced removals. For private security, the obligation placed on white South Africans to assist in defending the state by 'look[ing] after themselves and safeguard[ing] their own assets' provided the opportunity to turn a profit (*Security Focus* 1988 in Grant 1989, 111). However, although certainly seeking to exploit the profit potential in policing, private security firms did not portray themselves in market-based terms; in large part this was because the prevailing discourse linked security to state sovereignty. Rather, they consciously and strategically represented themselves as 'complementary and hopefully, playing our role in countering crime' (*ibid.*).

In an effort to cultivate closer ties with the state, the industry – more specifically, senior security personnel – advocated for legislative controls. Self-regulation through volunteer bodies, such as the South African Security Association, founded in 1965, had failed to inspire government confidence as it did not incorporate large numbers of small companies or the more problematic 'fly-by-nights'. Statutory regulation offered a greater measure of discipline and professionalism, as well as increased legitimacy, to private security as a key state ally. Legislative action also appealed to government, though for different reasons. It promised knowledge, an indispensable element of the state's interventionist strategy of rule, and it affirmed the state's claimed monopoly over the power to define the legitimate use of force.

The National Key Points Act (102 of 1980) provided the state with direct access to and control over private security. Designed to meet the apartheid state's national security interests (Grant 1989), it empowered the Minister of Defence to declare any area or place, for example a fuel depot or electricity substation, to be of strategic importance to state sovereignty or security and therefore in need of special safeguarding measures.[4] Once a site was designated a national key point, the Minister could compel the owner to provide such security measures or himself assume any or all of the duties of the owner in this respect, including any contracts with private security firms. The Act further authorized the Minister to prescribe the employment, training and powers of key-point guards. Key Points contracts were actively sought after, not only because they were very lucrative, but also because they placed a positive value on, and encouraged the further development of, the paramilitary skills and networks of middle and senior management personnel; also, the attainment of Key Point contracts propelled the security firms into elite status.

While the Key Points Act enabled the mobilization of non-state security providers under public auspices, the Security Officers Act (SOA) (92 of 1987) provided for more informal links into the state security apparatus and enrolled the Minister of Law and Order and the SAP in the regulation of the industry. The principle objective of the

4 This should be read alongside the Sabotage Act 1962, which authorized the death penalty for anyone endangering law and order, public safety, health and the free movement of traffic; jeopardizing the supply of fuel, food, water, light and power; hindering medical and municipal services; trespassing on any land or building; or destroying private or public property.

SOA was the creation of an industry-led regulatory board to 'exercise control over the occupation of security officers, and to maintain, promote and protect the status of that occupation' – the industry focus of the legislation befitting of a club. Interviews with the CEO of a prominent security firm and with a former Security Officers Board (SOB) member revealed a widely held industry view: the focus on promoting and protecting the industry signalled the state's intention to produce a corps of security officers capable of assisting in the containment of violence, terrorism and crime. Indeed, the SOA granted the Minister of Law and Order and the South African Police (SAP) significant authority in the control of private security, thus providing at least the potential for the identification of industry objectives with state security interests (cf. Grant 1989). The initial constitution of the SOB, the main mechanism for exercising control over the industry, is an example. Section 4 (parts of which were later amended and/or repealed) stipulated the composition of the SOB: six security officers; a SAP commissioned officer; an officer with functions as defined by the Internal Security Act (74 of 1982); and any other two persons considered by the Minister as 'fit and proper ... to serve on the Board'. Board appointments and removals were at the discretion of the Minister, though requirements existed as to the selection of security officers as SOB members. Security officers were to be chosen by the Minister from a list compiled by the Commissioner of Police who exercised complete discretion in this regard. The list consisted of names, submitted by security officers and organizations or associations, who the Commissioner considered 'competent and willing, and ... fit and proper' to serve on the SOB. Where no names or an insufficient number were submitted, the list was complied at the Commissioner's absolute discretion. This selection procedure did not apply to the filling of SOB vacancies, which was entirely 'at the Minister's pleasure'. While not ostensibly part of the repressive state security legislative framework (Grant 1989), the SOA nonetheless provided the possibility of transforming private security into 'para police' in orientation, if not in function: the extensive police influence in respect of the industry's regulatory body held out the possibility of stacking the board with members sympathetic to the apartheid regime's national security policy. Interviewees suggested that the pivotal role of the Minister of Law and Order, especially in regulating security officer training, gave the state considerable scope to shape the nature and direction of private security activities. Interviews with senior industry personnel, along with the extant literature (NIM 1996; Schärf 1989; Shaw 2002), indicates that the state made 'ordinary', localized use of private security in the removal of squatters and to protect white schools and commercial interests, capitalizing on the public order and counter-insurgency training of private security personnel.

In some contrast to all of this, there was a concern by key elements in the industry, beginning in the early 1990s, to sever, or at least significantly curtail, links with the state and to recast private security as 'a business ... in it for the money', as the largest private security employers association crudely put it (see the quote at the beginning of this chapter). No doubt there was a large element of self-preservation in such manoeuvres. Given its early institutional links with the apartheid regime, the industry certainly sought to legitimize itself in the eyes of the incoming African National Congress (ANC) government by drawing on the ideals of neutrality and efficiency inherent in market discourses and thus securing its place in the 'new' order. But the reframing of the industry – from a 'club' to a 'business' – must be located within a wider shift toward a neoliberal politics, which promoted the market as an organizing principle for all spheres of life, including policing (whether undertaken by state or non-state security agencies). At the discursive level, it thus became possible to speak of policing as a profitable *enterprise*, shaped by market forces.

Within the context of a neoliberal economy, safety and security came to be posed less in terms of state sovereignty and national security, and more in relation to the notion of active, responsibilized citizenship. The management of crime and associated risks through private security measures is reconceptualized as an individual and collective responsibility owed to oneself and one's family, rather than as a patriotic duty. Private security expanded considerably, both in size and scope, in a context where crime was no longer predominately an affront to the state, but was to an increasing extent *everyone's concern* – literally so, as crime spilt out of the townships into the mainly white city centres and suburban enclaves. Private security offered consumers the fantasy of total security and control, providing users with 'peace of mind' (as suggested by a guarding-company ad) in the home, at work, in the leisure centres etc., whereas the SAPS could only promise – and often failed to deliver – to bring crime down to acceptable levels. Punitive and repressive measures – for example, armed patrol and reaction – were advanced as the mechanism for achieving this fantasy of total security; in other words, militaristic solutions to what was essentially a social problem – crime (on the punitive culture of private security see: Singh and Kempa 2007).

In promoting itself as a business independent of the state, the industry gave a new focus to the consumer market in legislative controls. Industry-led initiatives advocated changes to the composition of the SOB, in particular the elimination of police presence on the Board and the inclusion of consumer representation. Proposals also suggested that rank-and-file employees, and not only middle to senior management and owners, should have a place on the Board. Taken together, these measures indicate that the industry no longer positioned itself as a 'closed club' of employers and senior police personnel, but rather as increasingly open and responsive to a (potentially) wider range of interests expressed by users and ground level employees. Arguments that the focus of legislative control should be altered from one of industry protection to public protection, in line with the regulation of other occupations (Ibbotson in *Security Today* Oct/Nov. 1997, 4), were also part of the discursive shift from 'club' to 'business'. This reflects the emergent view of private security as a legitimate business, and one located in a broader set of relations, rather than operating in the shadows of the state. Private security played an increasingly important role in the public domain – it not only guarded 'mass private property' but increasingly operated to secure more fully public spaces, such as 'ordinary' residential streets and beachfronts.

Governing the Criminal

South African private security training manuals of the 1980s, as recalled by one prominent member of the local industry during an interview, were riddled with references to the 'enemy'. This focus on the 'enemy' was inscribed into law with the introduction of the National Key Points Act in 1980. The legislation compelled major security firms to safeguard strategic installations and places against 'terrorist activities, sabotage, espionage or subversion' and placed these firms under the direct control of the Minister of Defence. The involvement in defence functions enhanced the paramilitary character of private security (Grant 1989; Shaw 2002).

Concern with the 'enemy' was not, however, confined to those companies providing key-point services, but was industry-wide. An advertisement in a local trade association magazine is illustrative:

> Who controls your labour force? You can have the best management and production system in the world and still be plagued with labour unrest. This unrest could take the form of illegal strike, subversion, intimidation, sabotage or management character assassination perpetrated by Communist [sic] backed legal or illegal organisations.
>
> (*Security Focus* 1989 in Grant 1989, 94)

Underpinned by an Afrikaner nationalist criminology, a distinctively South African brand of positivism (van Zyl Smit 1989), the 'enemy' was explicitly racialized: it had a black face. Portrayed as morally corrupt and racially inferior, this individual was, on this view, prone by nature to violate the laws of civilization. As the target of private security interventions, the 'enemy' – the terrorist, the saboteur, the communist (the red scare), *Die Swart Gevaar* (the black danger) – was to be vanquished.

Although contemporary training manuals retain references to the liberation movements of the past as 'the enemy' (Powell 1999), it is the 'criminal' that appears as a prime object of private security practices. Seen in rational choice terms, this opportunistic individual responds to situations and circumstances that offer the possibility of committing crimes with relative ease and for rewards greater than the perceived costs. One can thus dispense with the need for special theories of offender motivation or causal analyses of criminality. The criminal appears neither as abnormal (or subnormal) nor as especially different from the average individual. Therefore, the rational choice model has a democraticizing effect: everyone – black or white, ANC or National Party supporter – is a potential offender. Criminality is not symptomatic of moral or racial degeneracy. Rather, the decision to offend depends on the quite rational exercise of a cost–benefit calculus (see Crawford 1998 for a critical review of rational choice theory in criminology). Thus, little, if any, value is to be had by probing the mind or mapping the neural pathways of offenders (Cohen 1985). Instead, the *preventative and punitive* strategies of private security concentrate on modifying and influencing the behaviours and movements of individuals, impacting on the body itself (O'Malley 1994, 1996b).

Behaviour, as Cohen (1985) observes, *is* what matters. The regulation of the actions of the body comes to depend on the transformation not of desires or motivations, but of the physical and social settings within which individuals conduct themselves (Feeley and Simon 1994; Reichman 1986). Manipulations of the environment or the effects of crime aim to raise the costs of criminal activity relative to the anticipated gains. Faced with an excess of costs, there arises, in the criminal, 'a little more interest in avoiding the penalty than in risking the crime' (Foucault 1977, 94). The regulation and control of the actions of rational choice criminals thus occurs precisely through their capacity for reasoned calculation in decision-making. Where private security once sought to control the 'enemy' by eliminating their capacity for action, it now seeks to govern the 'criminal' by altering the balance of the cost–benefit equation that underpins rational conduct (on governmental practices, Rose 1999; on policing and government, Stenson 1993; O'Malley 1992).

This logic is well illustrated in the case of the previously discussed staffed security services, the leading commercial market sector. Static and mobile patrolling, for example, secure property and personal security through deterrence, multiplying the disadvantages – detection, access etc. – of engaging in unauthorized activities. Consider also perimeter security devices (for example, walls, fencing, wire), the fourth largest market segment with an estimated turnover of R410 million (*Security Focus* 1997). These aim to prevent crime and other risks by increasing the physical difficulty of effecting unauthorized intrusions. That individuals seek to maximize their pleasure and minimize their pain does not appear as especially troubling. Indeed, private security accepts this as the truth about people and seeks to use it to prevent problem behaviour and to maintain security.

While it can be argued, following Foucault (1977, 94), that the effectiveness of guarding, perimeter devices and other measures results from the 'idea of pain, displeasure [and] inconvenience' alone, I would further suggest that crime control techniques make generous use of the 'actual sensation of pain'; in this respect, they quite literally seize hold of the criminal's body. Take the mundane example of perimeter walls; in South Africa's urban centres and peripheries, it is not uncommon for the walls enclosing residences and small businesses to be capped off with shards of coloured glass. The bottom half of haphazardly broken bottles are arranged to create an uneven surface designed to puncture the flesh of individuals intent on scaling the wall. Another perimeter security device – 'Rotary-Razor-Spike' – consists of a horizontal metal skewer encircled by a series of long, rotating spikes flanked by serrated edges (*Security Focus* 1997). Mounted on walls, gates or fences, this device does not simply add height to existing barriers; rather, as individuals try for a sure grip or footing in order to propel themselves over the top, the mechanism rotates causing them to lose balance. The individuals fall forward, impaling themselves on the 'razor-spikes' or they fall backwards, instinctively grabbing onto the nearest object for support – the razor-sharp projections, in this case. Similarly, in a 1998 W5 programme ('In Security') on the North American industry, electric fencing was portrayed as a physical penalty, directly affecting the body. In one especially memorable clip, a retailer highlighted the versatile nature of electric fencing: 'we can decide if we want to cook you, fry you or bake you.' All of these measures seek to regulate the rates of specific offences by increasing the difficulty of effecting unauthorized access and at the same time, they aim to impress upon each individual, in the most corporeal of senses, responsibility for the consequences of their actions.

Punitiveness can also be detected in staffed security services. In South Africa, guards are routinely armed; in addition, as previously noted, the combination of guarding and electronic monitoring has led to the marked growth of armed reaction units[5] (NIM 1996, Shaw 1995). Rapid firepower constitutes an integral element in the guarding of homes and commercial premises and in cash transportation.

---

5 Johnston (2000) points to the increasingly transnational character of South Africa's security industry with the UK-based company Chubb, for example, now providing armed response services in South Africa.

> The old .38 special Rossi ... has been replaced by the canvas-holstered 9 mm Browning; where the single-shot Greener held pride of place, the 12-guage pump action Remington is used. Semi- and automatic weapons are now standard in the industry's arsenal in its bid to combat the growing incidence of murder and robbery in SA's low-intensity war.
> (*The Financial Mail* 1997, 51)

Such interventions target the body, but not as an expression of a desire for 'cruelty' (Simon 2001). The ultimate aim is not the humiliation, torture or destruction of the criminal. Far from being an end in itself, physical pain is a resource for impressing upon offenders the individual responsibility for the consequences of their freely chosen actions (O'Malley 1994). Electric fencing may offer the option of cooking, frying or baking the body, but the precise character of the penalty is clearly communicated to individuals: signs not only indicate that a particular fence is electrified, but also specify the exact voltage. Placards affixed on perimeter walls announce the presence of armed response units and the use of coloured glass visibly highlights the hazards involved in unauthorized intrusion of property. The criminal as a rational choice actor is to be provided with information on the costs of criminal offending to be weighed up against perceived benefits. And as rationally choosing individuals, criminals are also to be held responsible for the choices they make. The argument, within the situational crime prevention literature, that 'the focus of concern is shifted to situations rather than individuals or groups' (Crawford 1998, 72) is misleading: the individual has not disappeared, but rather is the target of punitive interventions linked to contemporary models of individual responsibility and choice. The fact that penalties for offending are exacted on the body of the criminal should come as no surprise, for where else, on the rational choice view, should these be directed? Surely not to the mind or soul. Thus, private security practices and techniques both presuppose and produce the criminal as rational and responsibilized.

The Authority of Authority

The commonly held view (for example, Ericson and Haggerty 1997; Shearing and Stenning 1983, 1984) that private security possesses an almost singular concern with prevention, accompanied by a marked disinterest in detection, apprehension and punishment, needs revising. As should by now be evident, private security undertakes both preventive and reactive functions; the latter including the application of punitive penalties in response to the occurrence of crime. This raises the question of the legitimization of private security's coercive authority. As South (1997) points out in his discussion of the privatization of the legitimate use of force in the UK, it is not the state's claim to exclusive control of the means of coercion that is at issue here. 'The monopoly claimed by the state', Ryan and Ward (1989) observe, ' ... is over the power to *define* the legitimate use of force ... This power does not necessarily depend on the State *owning* the means of force or employing the individuals who use it' (in South 1997, 109). This helps make sense of the debates regarding the law enforcement powers of private security personnel.

Like their Western counterparts, private security personnel in South Africa do not operate with special – that is, peace officer – powers. Instead they exercise powers accorded to 'private persons' – this category being subdivided into 'any person', on the one hand, and owners, lawful occupiers or managers of property and their agents, on the other (on Canada, see Shearing and Stenning 1982). Unlike in most other jurisdictions, however, the legal authority given to 'ordinary private citizens' in South Africa is far-reaching.[6] Considerable scope exists, under the Criminal Procedure Act (51 of 1977), for guards, armed reaction teams and other categories of security officers to act with significant coercive might – from forced entry to search and seizure, arrest, physical force and even lethal force.

Thus, as 'private persons', security personnel are empowered to arrest, without a warrant, anyone seen to be engaged in an affray and anyone 'reasonably' believed to have committed *any* offence and who is fleeing a pursuing individual who 'reasonably' appears to be authorized to effect an arrest for that particular offence. The term 'reasonable' is open to wide interpretation. Private security may also, without a warrant, arrest and pursue any person who commits, attempts to commit or is reasonably suspected of committing any Schedule 1 offence. Schedule 1 offences are wide-ranging, falling (more or less) into three broad categories: property offences – arson, malicious injury to property, breaking or entering, theft, knowingly receiving stolen property, fraud and forgery; crimes against the person – murder, culpable homicide, rape, indecent assault, sodomy, robbery, kidnapping, childstealing (the official term), assault with grievous bodily harm; and offences against the state – treason, sedition, public violence, offences related to coinage. Further still, as agents of the owner, occupier or manager of property, private security may arrest without a warrant any person found committing *any* offence on or in respect of that property.

In order to effect an arrest in any of the above circumstances, security personnel are authorized to break open, enter and search any premises on which the person to be arrested is known or reasonably suspected to be. Furthermore, they are empowered to use reasonable force, and lethal force in relation to Schedule 1 offences, where an arrest can not be effected by other means and where resistance occurs, or where the suspect flees.

Certain categories of guards operate with even greater legal powers. The National Key Points Act (102 of 1980) enables the state to declare, under certain circumstances, any privately or publicly owned place or area a National Key Point and thereby regulate any private security company involved in protecting the said key point. Such regulation includes the extension of the powers of guards regarding search and seizure, arrest and use of force. Key point guards 'are authorized to demand identification and an explanation of the presence of all persons found at a key point … and are specifically empowered to destroy articles perceived to present a danger to persons or property' (Grant 1989, 108). Further, firearms were a requirement for all key point guards.

There has been little, if any, expression of public or political concern with the extensive powers enjoyed by private security. Thus, while key point guards are now

---

6 How this came about is an important issue, though beyond the scope of this book. The discussion would require consideration of the racialized politics of citizenship and the relations of obligation that tied the citizen to the state, including the duty owed by citizens to defend the state against threats to its sovereignty.

commonly unarmed (NIM 1996), such disarming did not occur in response to, nor did it stimulate, demands to curb private security access to force. Instead, as a report on the industry suggests, 'with the new dispensation [the] regulations have become more lax' (NIM 1996, 4) – a mere relaxation of rules rather than a policy shift.

Such debate as exists, centres not on restricting or reducing the far-reaching powers of private security, but on the possibility of conferring peace officer status on industry personnel. Industry proposals to extend, to its senior personnel, peace officer status or 'at least the power of arrest without warrant, the power to demand a name and address and the powers of search/seizure after arrest', have been rejected by state officials (Eveleth 1997). It appears that the state may be reacting not so much to the content of such proposals, but to the way in which arguments have been framed. Typical of the industry's line of argument is the following excerpt from a position paper of the SOB:

> Where the state's financial, human and other resources are insufficient to provide a comprehensive police service on its own, it may be seen as [the state's] constitutional duty to assist private security in any other reasonable manner possible to extend the protection or rights of the members of society.
>
> (Eveleth 1997)

The view that the state is legally obligated to grant additional powers to private security strikes at the very heart of the matter: it threatens to undermine the state's claim to a monopoly over the power to decide, on a case-by-case basis, when and to whom the right to use force will be extended.

The state does not appear to be especially concerned with securing exclusive ownership of the means of coercion. Indeed, if private security activities do not routinely include the public police it is not, as Shearing and Stenning (1983) and others claim, because the industry devalues policing strategies involving the application of force. Rather, it is because the state has extended legitimacy to the use of force by private security (cf. South 1997). The security industry has recourse to an expansive and innovative repertoire of coercive sanctions, including physical measures, that it can bring to bear on individual bodies without the need for the mediating presence of the state. Even in the exercise of law enforcement powers it is significant that, although the Criminal Procedure Act (51 of 1977) requires private security to hand over any articles seized to a police official, no such stipulation exists with respect to bodies seized (arrested etc.).

Consequently the role of the state has been redefined. In policing, as in other areas, the state takes on the role of manager and facilitator (Lacey 1994; Rose 1999). It is no longer required to meet all the security demands of the population (taken either individually or collectively). Rather, the state is tasked with setting up a framework in which these enormous, and at times conflicting, demands can be met *appropriately* by a range of providers, including private security. This meshes well with the emergent view of crime as 'everyone's business'. Individuals are to be active participants in security, not by turning in the first instance to the state, but by voluntarily entering into contractual arrangements with private security for the management of crime (O'Malley 1992). The management of crime, as I have suggested, involves both preventing offences and responding to those that have occurred in order to hold criminals responsible for the consequences of their actions. Offenders who, for various reasons, cannot be adequately dealt with through private security arrangements become the responsibility of the state, targets of its vengeance-seeking penal strategies (Hudson 2001; Simon 2001).

Several commentators argue that the control technologies deployed by policing authorities are also applied to the watchers themselves. Thus, in relation to Intelligarde, Rigakos maintained that its 'perpetual system of examination and its hyperpanoptic imagination visualizes and digatizes the environment to be policed, the employees that police it, and those falling within its gaze'(Rigakos 2002, 119). In a different context, Ericson and Haggerty observed that 'police managers adopt .... risk profiling techniques ... that are parallel in logic and format to the risk profiling techniques their officers apply to members of other populations as part of their routine surveillance work' (Ericson and Haggerty 1997, 36). Such arguments imply that control strategies reflect and construct a singular image of subject populations: both the watched and the watchers are understood in a parallel fashion. In contrast, the section below outlines a different set of control strategies for managing security guards, who are the watchers. These disciplinary technologies specify a moral subject of habits rather than a rational, responsible and autonomous individual as discussed above.

'Better People, Better Trained, Better Managed'[7]: Disciplining the Guard

Beginning in the early 1990s, a new discourse started to take shape in which improvements to the employment conditions, development and training of security guards emerged as a central concern of industry. Proposals and programmes to institute equal opportunity employment, establish benefits schemes, rationalize managerial authority and the like, treated security guards as individuals, each with their own particular and specific characteristics, rather than as an undifferentiated mass. For example, following its 1993 study on racial imbalances[8] within the industry's management structures, the Security Association of South Africa (SASA) sought to initiate

> a process of building, training and growing people [such that they may] progress as quickly as it is practically possible to their *individual levels of competency*.
>
> (*Security Focus* October 1997, 40) [emphasis added]

In this and similar projects for regulating the workforce, industrial productivity and individual development became complementary objectives:

> The end result [of leadership training] will be that previously disadvantaged persons will rise above their colleagues, both black and white, and take on positions in which they

7 This is the motto of a successful South Africa private security company.

8 Racial imbalances continue: the vast majority of security guards are black compared to approximately four per cent of security employers, managers and special response units (Irish 1999).

> will be able to make a meaningful and professional contribution to the profitability of the company and thus, they themselves will be meaningfully empowered.
>
> (*ibid.*, 41)

These projects articulated a new relationship between guards and employers. This was no longer a relationship of domination established in the form of the individual will of the employer: 'the days of telling an employee to just hand in his uniform, without notice, are long gone' (*Security Today* Oct/Nov. 1997, 22–3). Indeed, guards come to be recognized in all their positivity – not as objects to be ignored or completely dominated, but as subjects with capacities and attitudes that can be used to govern them.

The figure of the security guard assumed a new visibility in the security enterprise. The guard occupied a primary place in advertisements, as an 'Ambassador' of the company and the client: 'We offer the best ... security personnel, believing their image and bearing must reflect well on both our company and ours' (Monitoring company ad in *Security Today*, Oct/Nov. 1997). Security personnel also appeared in the mission statements of private security firms: '... we are committed to improving the quality of life of all employees through equal opportunity employment and continuous development ...' (Grey Security Services). The guard, it seems, was a product of the security process. That is, the industry sought to manufacture competent and skilled security guards. At the same time, one must fabricate compliant subjects, for as one CEO stated: 'guards tend not be diligent when performing their security duties' (interview, 3 December 1997).

In certain key respects, then, security employers and the industry's statutory regulatory body act to shape, shift, modify and transform the conduct of private security personnel. This section examines the devices used to produce individual subjects who are simultaneously compliant and useful. I outline a policy of constant coercions on the body that extend throughout the process of selecting, training and managing security guards.

Selection and Registration

Guarding firms account for over half of all registered companies and the vast majority of individuals actively working in the industry are employed in the guarding sector (PSIRA 2006; also Berg 2004; *The Financial Mail* 1997; NIM 1996). Racial imbalances have persisted: security employers, managers and special response units are overwhelmingly white while most security guards are black (Irish 1999). The guarding sector also experienced massive staff turnover, with one industry insider putting the figure at 200 per cent per year (Ibottson 1994). This situation can be linked to such factors as low pay, poor working conditions, the routine nature of the job and the almost limitless recruitment pool. In this regard, South Africa's private security industry is not unlike that of Britain (South 1988; Johnston 1992; 2000), Canada (Shearing *et al* 1980) or the US (Cunningham and Taylor 1985; Cunningham *et al* 1991).

The following questions thus assume particular importance. What was the recruitment pool from which guarding firms can draw? How did the industry imagine the ideal or suitable recruitment candidate to be? What were the eligibility requirements for employment as a guard? What procedures existed for registration as a security officer?

The SOA (92 of 1987) provided for the mandatory registration of all contract security guards by the SOB. Eligibility extended to anyone 18 years or older and no minimum education requirements existed. Documentation permitting the description and analysis of individual features accompanied all applications for registration. The SOA required the submission of copies of identity records and a clear and complete set of fingerprints taken by the police: these were cross-checked to ensure a match. However, reports indicate that security company management sometimes took fingerprints themselves with the approval of the resource-strapped police. 'This le[ft] the system open to abuse because it allow[ed] a guard or the company he or she [worked] for to submit a false set of fingerprints, to be registered with the Board even if he or she ha[d] a criminal record. There [were] no other mechanisms in place to ensure that the fingerprints and the identity documents submitted match[ed]' (NIM 1996, 5).

Criminal histories were examined for convictions of 'serious' offences (that is, those listed in the Schedule to the Act). Criminal convictions for these offences constituted grounds for disqualification, though this was by no means automatic as the SOB had the discretionary authority to nevertheless effect registration. At issue was not the mere existence of a criminal record, but the type and nature of the crime committed and thus the moral character of the individual. The aim was to identify and exclude those individuals whose conduct revealed dispositions at odds with the economic interests of private security: deceit and greed (convictions for theft, fraud, forgery, robbery, knowingly receiving stolen goods, housebreaking with intent to commit an offence, illicit dealing in or possession of precious metals or stones); indiscretion (violations of the Protection of Information Act); anger and rage (murder, homicide, kidnapping, arson); and sexual depravity (rape, indecent assault, sodomy, bestiality). We have, then, not a binary division between criminals and non-criminals, but multiple separations – the petty offender and the career criminal, the individual convicted of serious crimes who lacks sound judgment and those who exhibit dangerous qualities. It is the absence of self-restraint or weak self-control that posed a problem for profit.

Guarding firms also showed concern with the moral habits of prospective employees. Psycho-social techniques – panel interviewing, aptitude tests and psychometric testing – operated alongside the profiling of an applicant's employment and criminal history. Psychometric testing in particular formed an integral part of the recruitment process of most large to mid-size companies. One of the largest cash-in-transit operators, Fidelity Guards, only employed those who passed a psychometric test (*The Financial Mail* 1997, 52). These psychological techniques, as Rose (1999) remarked, coded defects of moral character as defects of personality. Aptitude testing, another recruitment tool, measured an individual's potential to learn new skills. That is to say, it produced knowledge of habits of work. Further, psychometric testing and aptitude testing made it possible to both isolate each applicant in their own particularity and to compare individuals, that is, to differentiate among them according to the norm.

In general, the guard was addressed as a subject of moral habits and competencies whose productivity could be maximized through disciplinary coercion, continuous surveillance and training.

Training

The SOA granted the SOB the discretionary power to 'take such steps as it may deem expedient or necessary in connection with the training of security officers, the giving of advice in connection with such training, the determination of the standards of such training, and the promotion of the maintenance of those standards' (s. 3 (c)). Industry-wide training standards were formulated by the SOB, which also offered training for all levels of security officers. However, as the former chair of the largest guarding employers association remarked, the industry viewed the SOB-run programmes as 'too comprehensive, leading to the poaching of trained guards by other companies … [and] to [a potential] increase [in] the costs of security, again allowing larger companies to be undercut by smaller operators' (in Shaw 1995, 81). Accordingly, some medium to large firms opted to establish their own separate training units, offering employees basic training as stipulated by the SOB, as well as more specialized training in order to meet particular client needs. Commercial training facilities later cropped up to 'sell' trained guards to security companies without training units. Cilliers (1997) maintained that in early 1993, 17 SOB-accredited training centres existed countrywide; by July 1995 the figure rose to 160; and by April 1997 it stood at 370. According to a more recent study, there were 533 officially recognized training centres in 2003 (Gould and Lamb 2004).

The glossy marketing brochure of one contract security firm outlined the basic curriculum taught at its training facility. The course stressed loss prevention skills (access and loss control, fire prevention and alarm systems, equipment identification), as well as crime control and order maintenance skills (legal powers, self-defence, first aid, emergency procedures, safety, report writing, record keeping, communications, public relations, junior leadership). As private security operators and the SOB recognized, such training schemes provided the opportunity to enhance and maintain a professional image of the security guard at both organizational and industry levels. Training helped to constitute the guard as a competent security practitioner who was knowledgeable about strategies and techniques for controlling crime, maintaining order and preventing loss. It also enabled the guard to convey and demonstrate such competency to clients and the public more generally, through report writing, record-keeping, personal demeanour and so on. In other words, it was through and by means of programmes of training that guarding emerged as a semi-skilled profession: training 'acts as a form of gate-keeping for entrance to the industry … [and] it enables guards to choose a career within the industry' (Shaw 1995, 81).

Thus, the question confronting the private security industry concerned how to make each recruit useful and the training of guards profitable. How can one organize the time of training to assure its control and usefulness?

Training was divided into five successive stages. Each segment lasted one week and concluded with an exam. Progression through the five training levels involved tasks of increasing complexity marking the gradual acquisition of knowledge and good habits. One of the problems with the SOB training programmes for entry level guards is that the programmes were too comprehensive; the training did not correspond to the use to be made of these individuals. In contrast, commercial training facilities and individual companies offered new recruits basic training in the practical aspects of guarding. Training programmes provided instruction on the mechanics of record-keeping, report-writing, equipment identification, alarm-monitoring and self-defence; on the appropriate procedures to follow in the event of floods or accidents; on the legal authority to protect property, profits and persons, and to respond to crime and disorder.[9] But more than this – and most crucially – these programmes sought to inculcate habits of obedience so that workers would adhere automatically and without question to the myriad requirements and routines that surrounded and characterized the security-guard occupation. While patrolling or performing other security functions, guards were not to exercise independent judgment. Rather, they were to follow standard practices and procedures – for reporting on the use of one's time 'on the job', for dealing with inquires from the public, and for responding to crime, fires and emergency situations. As one industry executive put it, while 'innovative solutions [to security problems] tend to come from the security management level', compliance is a character trait of most entry-level personnel (interview, January 1998).

Training was intended to produce docile and utilizable bodies; that is, bodies that are skilled and at the same time obedient. Guards who followed regulations and procedures not so much because they were compelled to do so, but because they were willing to do so, finding that approach in their own best interest. As South (1988, 37) noted of the requirement to write reports: 'Although inevitably regarded as an arduous task, staff *can* none the less see report writing as a professional commitment and, further, one which gives them a respectability and professional sub-cultural affinity to the broader law enforcement enterprise.'

The system for ranking guards also emphasized conformity and obedience. Ranks classified and distributed individuals according to the way in which they moved through the training stages and therefore according to the use that could be made of them. Guards who successfully completed a week of basic training earned an 'E' grade; and most guards remained at this level. Each higher grade required an additional week of training, with the highest level, grade 'A', signalling a total of five weeks of training. The SOB anticipated that such systematized ranking would ensure uniformity in training standards, would demonstrate the competence of every guard,

9 In light of the previous discussion about the routine arming of static and mobile guards, it is interesting to note the absence of basic firearm training for new recruits. The police issued firearm licenses to individual firms based on SOB information on the number of registered employees and inspections of company premises. The legislation allowed the company to temporarily license its firearms to any competent employee who had been trained. However, no provision existed for verifying the quality of firearm training. The Network of Independent Monitors (NIM) documented the inadequacy of such training. One guard interviewed claimed to have been instructed on the use of a firearm, by another guard, in less than five minutes (NIM 1996, 6). The report also suggests that companies denied a licence often hire guards who have their own personal licensed weapons.

and would enable distinctions to be drawn between individual guards on the basis of the amount of training that each one had undertaken. This system offered an instance of a disciplinary technique for situating the individual within the multitude, for enhancing the obedience of individuals and for increasing their aptitude. In practice, however, standardized examinations across different training centres did not exist and these facilities tended to operate with in-house, rather than external, instructors. This means that attempts to compare and differentiate between individual guards on the basis of a standard recognizable qualification proved unsuccessful. This also suggests that guards coming through a company's training programme might be taught skills that were not necessarily, or easily, transferable within the industry, thus discouraging individuals from seeing guarding as a long-term career.

In sum, training instructed guards, but also supervised the conduct and habits of each and every guard, as well as and hierarchized skills and aptitudes. However, as with any governmental strategy the regime of private security training was marked by failures.

Supervision and Management

Private security firms operated techniques for controlling and transforming the routines of security guards. Guarding firms faced the problem of how to supervise guards working at client sites without requiring the physical presence of managers. This problem was met by the development of electronic surveillance systems that monitored and disciplined the conduct of guards by dividing up time, space and activity.

Most security companies, in response to a collective agreement on wages reached in 1996, rostered their guards on a '5 on, 2 off' basis – five shifts of 12 hours each per week, followed by two days of rest (*Security Today*, Oct/Nov 1997). Electronic surveillance systems sought to ensure that the 60 hours of time paid was not being wasted. A number of interruptions to shift-work existed – tiredness, laziness, boredom and disinterest. Loss of time and individual idleness were distinct possibilities: 'Stop your guard from having a peaceful night's sleep', announced an ad for Mag-Touch, an electronic monitoring device. But it was not only a question of eliminating inconveniences, disturbances or distractions to work. It was also a question 'of extracting, from time, ever more available moments and, from each moment, even more useful forces'; in other words, of deriving the maximum advantages (Foucault 1977, 154).

An industry magazine featured an ad for 'a new generation guard control system' (*Security Focus* November 1997). Performer Guard Patrol Systems promoted electronic surveillance technology as a management tool that ensured that 'guards are on duty and are, in fact, doing their patrols' and at the same time, optimized the efficiency and economy of patrols. The main control box, located on-site, instructed the guard when and where to begin a patrol and set out how long the patrol should take. The unit could be programmed for a maximum of 48 patrols daily, 7 days a week and 'each patrol [could] have different parameters'. Performer thus divided up the patrol shift according to a strict timetable of continuous exercises. Guards were subjected to a series of external signals and relays that imposed tasks that were both repetitive and different:

> When a patrol must start, Performer alerts the guards and randomly selects a point [to] begin. The guard will remove the hand-held unit from the control box, and walk to the first point … he completes the patrol by going to the rest of the points in the order that the box has told him to … the guard will replace the hand held unit in the control box … [which] will then download the information … If any points have been missed, the point will be displayed to the guard, and he must go to that point to complete the patrol … the control box will [then] radio the control room and a 'patrol complete' message will be logged.

The onset of the device triggered the required behaviour, which was an immediate and automatic reaction to the command signals. If the guard missed a patrol, or failed to complete it within the designated time, or where an emergency situation existed, then 'the control room [was] immediately notified by radio, and action [could] be taken'. Such action no doubt included either dispatching 'back-up' or activating management strategies to deal with dilatory and inefficient employees.

The Performer system imposed temporal norms that aimed to induce habits of obedience, but also to augment the productive forces of the body, to increase the skills of each guard, to coordinate these skills, and to accelerate movements in order to achieve the optimal number and speed of patrols. Performer thus came to depend on, as it gave rise to, knowledge of how long the average guard needed to complete a given patrol route, and of the standard time it took to go between check points. Performer was programmed with these normative settings, which individual guards were required to match, and if unsuccessful, were judged against. And chance interruptions to this schedule were rendered predictable and calculable, and hence manageable: 'human error' resulted in the control box redisplaying the missed check point to the guard; crime, fires, floods etc. resulted in immediate radio notification to the control room.

In sum, such forms of electronic surveillance coerced by imposing external directives for action requiring the unquestioning compliance of the guard. Security guards were not to engage in creative or independent decision-making as to how best to secure the site. Rather, their movements and activities were controlled both spatially and temporally: the Performer control box enabled security management to establish the precise location of individual guards at specified time intervals. By means of surveillance technology, patrolling guards were distributed in both space and time. Electronic monitoring systems also operated as procedures for knowledge, rendering the performance of each guard visible and permitting comparisons between guards on the same patrol shift. More generally, surveillance systems increased the efficiency and economy of guarding activity by matching the route and duration of patrols. They generated information that enabled the security firm to demonstrate, to the contracting agency, the productivity and efficiency of its security services (the claim of 48 patrols daily); and they ensured the safety of the guards themselves.

Electronic supervision of guards certainly coerced, but without the need for physical violence. Performer Guard Control Systems may have had a gun sight as its logo, but it did not rely on force to constrain guards to comply with patrol routines. Rather, it exercised a constant pressure to conform, and it elaborated signals and rules that the guard must allow to operate automatically and uninterrupted within herself or himself. Performer was, I suggest, a diagram for power that acted by ordering bodies in time and space.

Conclusion

This chapter has provided detailed information on developments and trends in South Africa's private security industry. The operation and expansion of this very lucrative trade was situated within a particular problem–space: that of the obligation placed on citizens to assume responsibility for their own self-protection, which in part involved the voluntary engagement of the security services offered by multiple and competing providers other than the state (O'Malley 1992, 1996b). I have shown that private security marketization and employment were structured predominately around the issue of crime. The routine provision of armed patrols and armed rapid response and the invocation of powers of arrest, of the application of force, of search and seizure suggest that private security increasingly adopted features popularly seen as characteristic of the public police: that is to say, a focus (though not exclusively) on crime, reactive controls and legal powers.

These observations give us pause to reconsider the comment, often heard in international circles, that contemporary reforms of the public police made them more like private security in orientation and function (that is, a concern with prevention, problem-solving techniques, mediation and conciliation; a reliance on knowledge and resources other than the law; the decentralization of authority; and an elevation of the status of the victim). Thus, for example, Shearing, widely recognized for his enormous contributions to the sociology of policing, contended that community policing, especially of the problem-solving sort, has meant that the public police are adopting a preventative future-oriented risk management orientation similar to that pursued by private security (Shearing 1997; also Bayley and Shearing 1996; Brogden and Shearing 1993; Shaw and Shearing 1998; Shearing 1994). Similarly, in their analysis of public policing within risk society, Ericson and Haggerty (1997) maintained that the police, in promoting risk management strategies over coercive controls and punishment, operated much like a private security organization. Problem-solving and preventative strategies may have been pioneered by private security, but as this chapter demonstrates, one should be wary of assuming that these remain at the forefront of private security activities. Indeed, South (1997) commented on an emergent shift, occurring in most Western countries, from private *security* to private *police*, a sentiment echoed by Rigakos (2002) in his analysis of Intelligarde, the 'new parapolice' in Canada; this is the incorporation of a crime control function alongside loss prevention and the increasing recourse to coercive techniques of policing. If the public police are becoming more 'private security like' it is in relation to features which no longer characterize today's private security industry.

However, I am also suggesting that contemporary developments in South African private security strategies and practices did not necessarily display a high degree of coherency. As the industry expanded within the context of changing forms of governance, private security practices came to embody rather different and contradictory assumptions of the individual. For instance, I have pointed out that a rational choice model and ideals of individual responsibility, enterprise and innovation informed the current image of the criminal and potential criminal, while regimented conformity, normative judgment and correction were linked to perceptions of the private security guard. Private security's punitive interventions targeted the corporal body with the view to either correcting moral and behavioural conduct or holding the individual accountable for the outcome(s) of actions taken; in either case, the objective was to ensure that behaviour occurred within designated parameters. It is imperative to note that both the security guard and the (actual or potential) offender were clearly raced and classed. The vast majority of guards came from the black underclass. So too the criminal, given private security's concentration in largely white areas and private security's integral role in sealing off these communities from 'outsiders', especially the surrounding townships (Shaw 2002; see also Chapter 4). The enterprise form valued and promoted by neoliberals and the global market economies is unrewarded if enacted by the criminal, but also by the security guard in the context of his or her normal work routines. Both the rational choice offender and the security guard are seen to be 'free', active subjects; but in the case of the former, freedom is to be responsibilized while in the latter it is to be disciplined.

I have analyzed some of the coercive techniques through which private security came to know and regulate individuals in terms of these divergent specifications of freedom: coercion is not counterposed to freedom. In seeking to prevent and respond to crime and other risks, private security made routine use of punitive measures that impacted directly on individual bodies. Perhaps we are seeing an attempt to redefine the authority to coerce and to punish as within the competence of non-state authorities: private security not only prevents crime, but punishes as well. Chapter 5 explores how crime control and punishment were contested and divided up between political and social authorities.

While the discussion above addresses private-sector involvement in policing, the following chapter considers the impact of private-sector interests and influence at the level of the public police institution.

Chapter 4

Crime Control and Corporate Enterprises

> If we don't manage crime we'll be out of business.
>
> CEO, Business Against Crime Western Cape.
> (*Cape Argus* 20 April 1998)

> Crime prevention and control is mainly the responsibility of government. Indeed, many believe the most important function of the state is the safety and security of its citizens … But the crime problem also needs the attention of government at every level, as well as of business, labour and all other sectors of society.
>
> (Nedcor December 1995, 3)

Introduction

In the mid-1990s, two high-profile corporate-sponsored business campaigns against crime emerged in South Africa – The Nedcor Project on Crime, Violence and Investment, and Business Against Crime (BAC). Through such campaigns, the private sector became consciously and collectively involved in restructuring state crime control practices and policies. This was achieved primarily by offering assistance to government for the transformation of the SAPS (South African Police Service) into a 'better trained and equipped police force' (Nedcor August 1995, 4). Business supported an enhanced police capacity for rapid response through its donation of 100 BMWs toward a special anti-hijacking highway patrol unit that had as one of its focal concerns sophisticated crime syndicates that targeted high-end or luxury vehicles. Industry provided government with technical expertise, which facilitated access to the latest technological advances, such as CCTV and cellphone networks, that were used for surveillance and crime detection within key commercial districts, but also served the purpose of upgrading police services in underprivileged communities. The private sector promoted discourses of numeracy and the extension of market disciplines to criminal justice agencies: the introduction of performance indicators and business plans at (police) station level, which established a degree of consonance between the broad programmatic objectives of accountability, transparency and efficiency, and more concrete strategies for the allocation of scarce operational resources; the development of a 'reliable' crime information system to chart the specific characteristics of crime as an object to be governed – its spatial coordinates, trends, costs. At the same time, these business-sponsored anti-crime initiatives revealed that industry also assumed some degree of responsibility for the routine management of its own security risks and needs especially in relation to economic crime.

The BAC and Nedcor anti-crime campaigns constitute an important yet largely overlooked development in the post-apartheid governance of crime: the significant extension of commercial influence over the nature and direction of public policing. Historically, business organizations invested substantially in contract or in-house security products and services: guards, alarm systems, etc. Today, the use of essentially private solutions to corporate 'problems' is increasingly complemented by the provision of financial, technological and other support to criminal justice agencies with the express view of augmenting the reactive capabilities of the state in a particular direction that is predominately conductive to the interests of the powerful. While South Africans of all races find reassurance in a reactive police force (Shaw 2002), corporate interests are not necessarily co-extensive with the security needs of the black underclass whose marginalization and powerlessness are further entrenched as a result of greater corporate involvement in shaping the state's crime control agenda. This leads to the conclusion that state and non-state security policy and practice reflect the priorities of a very limited 'public interest' (Shearing 2006), to the point that 'security' increasingly stands as a 'club good' monopolized by the few (Crawford 2006).

This chapter examines how the corporate sector came to see its crime control responsibilities as including not only the enactment of independent routines for self-protection, but also, and more unusually, the funding of public policing to enable government to perform its crime-fighting duties. It also considers the social and political implications of such corporate sponsorship.

BAC and Nedcor, in contrast to the private security companies previously discussed, understood policing to be the basis for profit, rather than profitable in and of itself. Policing was seen to provide the necessary foundation for the operation of a free market. The relation between policing, security and 'foundational orders' was articulated by Clifford Shearing when he wrote of the 'significance of peace as a "foundation order" on which other orders – for instance, the order of financial markets – depend and policing as an activity that seeks to maintain this foundation' (Shearing 1992, 400). As the Nedcor quote at the outset of this chapter illustrates, corporate enterprise unambiguously identified the state as the primary guarantor of public safety and security. Business anti-crime campaigns therefore set out to assist the state in fulfilling its leadership role in practices of crime control, thereby securing the foundational basis for rational and efficient market relations.

While governmentality studies document private sector reliance on privatized security services, they tend to ignore, as Hudson (2001) remarks, the extent to which individual and community activism is usually accompanied by demands for more, and more punitive, state action, not less. In the sphere of crime and prevention, Hudson notes, 'privatization is an adjunct, not an alternative to, state provision' (*ibid.*, 156). While business and individual citizens alike were understood to have an active role in independently calculating and managing their own crime risks, Nedcor and BAC took the view that responsibility for safety and security rested mainly with government. It was the absence of sovereign authority in the crime control arena that posed a problem and corporate South Africa urged government not only to coordinate the emergent network of state and non-state security providers, but also, and perhaps most crucially, to demonstrate competence in reactive law enforcement. While the corporate sector supported a reactive crime fighting strategy, there was no suggestion that the law should be always and everywhere equally enforced. Instead, the 'usual suspects' – the black underclass, in particular young, black men – continued to bear the brunt of the law.

The centrality of coercive techniques and strategies in business anti-crime initiatives was vividly captured in BAC's original corporate logo: barbed wire in the shape of a gunsight. Private sector promotion of coercive controls, as the basis for governing social and market relations, remains largely unaddressed in the governmentality and risk literatures. While these bodies of literature do not entirely discount punitive logics and practices, they nevertheless point to the displacement of law enforcement by compliance-based policing (Ericson and Haggerty 1997) and the prioritization of subtle, indirect strategies of governing more generally (Feeley and Simon 1994; Rose 1999). The BAC and Nedcor case suggests, however, that we look carefully at the intersection of direct and indirect mechanisms of liberal rule in crime control, and the conditions under which one comes to prominence over the other.

BAC and Nedcor present empirically interesting and theoretically relevant sites for analysis. Unfortunately, they have hitherto received very little attention from criminologists or sociologists; accounts of corporate South Africa's anti-crime campaigns are mainly limited to the business management and economics literatures. Nor has the corporate sponsorship of police and criminal justice reform generated much public debate. In part this is due to the practical need, in light of high recorded crime rates, for a police institution with an explicit crime control, rather than political, function, as well as widespread popular support for harsher criminal justice responses (Shaw 2002). Yet, the growing role of the corporate sector in the governance of crime and criminal justice warrants closer scrutiny.

The remainder of this chapter focuses on four broad areas. The first section describes the 'partnerships' that developed between business and government in the context of managing the 'crime problem' and outlines how industry perceived its role in relation to that of government. The second section questions the apparent 'naturalness' of such alliances and suggests that the interests of both 'partners' were not necessarily identical. These associations arose in part because both sides came to see crime as a threat to the country's shared socio-economic future. The perceived necessity to promote a properly functioning, legitimate and publicly-accountable legal system gained added saliency for the corporate sector in South Africa due to the felt sense of political vulnerability during the post-apartheid period. Attempts to persuade government of the utility of partnerships with the corporate sector had added urgency because of this. The third section examines the targets of corporate projects aimed at bolstering public policing and highlights the reconfiguration along socio-economic and racial lines of social space in the exercise of surveillance and crime control. I conclude by commenting on the apparent paradox that freedom (of market responses, of individual choice) requires for its guarantee, the existence of a strong sovereign authority armed with considerable coercive powers operating in conjunction with collectively-organized corporate power operating with considerable powers of its own.

The chapter draws on BAC and Nedcor publications. This is supplemented by material from interviews conducted, in the mid-1990s in South Africa, with representatives from BAC and the National Business Initiative (NBI), which initially managed the project.

Security Investments

Corporate concerns in the latter part of the 1980s centred mainly on 'political violence, labour relations, government policy and financial issues' (Nedcor December 1995, 10). Urged by the (then) Minister of Law and Order to 'look after themselves and safeguard their own assets' (Grant 1989, 111), business organizations invested substantially in a variety of self-protective measures such as in-house security and private security products and services. Some of these interventions had a public face, such as the use of in-house security personnel to police mining towns (Brogden and Shearing 1993). But this did not amount to an overall plan by commerce to influence the nature or direction of public policing more generally.

By the mid-1990s, corporate concerns had shifted to crime, investor relations and government strategies on security and macroeconomic development. This period witnessed the establishment, in 1995, of both the Nedcor Project and BAC. The aim of these two independent, corporate-sponsored anti-crime initiatives was to inform and transform state crime control policies and practices. These campaigns evinced what O'Malley and Palmer (1996) call 'voluntary collectivism', where the 'business community' is configured in terms of relational ties voluntarily established between individual firms in the context of managing the 'crime problem'. Both projects operated within a framework of a 'partnership' model, wherein government was deemed the primary provider of safety and security. Envisioned as short-term crisis management interventions, the Nedcor Project and BAC sought to 'empower' government to play a more successful leadership role in the 'fight against crime' (Fourie and Mhangwana 1996).

The Nedcor Project

The Nedcor Project on Crime, Violence and Investment was established in April 1995 as a 'public service'. The publication of the *Final Report* in April 1996 and the *Executive Summary of the Main Report* in June 1996 effectively marked the conclusion of the Project. However, a subsequent joint venture between Nedcor Ltd, the Institute for Security Studies (ISS) and BAC resulted in ongoing updates of the Project's results, published as the *Nedcor/ISS Crime Index*. Moreover, a comprehensive database of crime statistics originally compiled by the Project was later housed at, and made accessible through, the BAC national office.

Nedcor Ltd, the holding company of Permanent Bank, Peoples Bank, Nedbank, Syfrets Ltd, Cape of Good Hope Bank, UAL Merchant Bank Ltd, NedEnterprises and NedTravel, sponsored the R3m Project. This Project aimed to inform business on possible contributions to the 'fight against crime', where crime prevention and control rested 'ultimately' and 'exclusively' with government: 'business has a variety of vital roles to play in assisting government in its responsibility to safeguard the security of all South Africans' (Nedcor April 1996, 8). These 'vital roles' were expressed in terms of a 'partnership', with business interests centring mainly on the sphere in which crime and violence impact on investment.

1. Presentation on causes, prevention and control of crime
2. Permanent assets for the country in crime combating
3. Communications Program
4. Reports produced in co-operation with other organizations
5. Co-operative work with government
6. Survey: impact of crime on foreign investment
7. National Crime Survey
8. Publication: 'Stop Crime'
9. Study: local authorities
10. Project Report

Figure 4.1 Nedcor's 10-Step Stop Crime Programme
Adapted from Nedcor, December 1995

Combining research and consultation with over 100 international and domestic organizations, the Project identified both the parameters of the 'crime problem' and the possible solutions (*ibid.*, 2–3). This included an overview of the 'actual' situation for 1995–96; the identification of the 'fundamental causes' of current crime; an assessment of the impact of crime on foreign investment and the development of strategies to provide investors with a 'better understanding' of the crime situation to ensure their ongoing commitment to South African markets; the specification of business initiatives to reduce the impact of crime on society, as well as on the business sector; and, the identification of large-scale business interventions to address crime at the national level. According to a Project briefing paper, 'Nedcor believes that the information gathered will serve as a databank which will provide the foundation for broadly based initiatives to reduce levels of crime and their impact on our economy.'

A ten-step programme, 'Stop Crime', designed to implement the above objectives appeared toward the end of 1995 (see Figure 4.1). The programme was in essence an enumeration and communications strategy. The Project configured its partnership role in terms of the accumulation and dissemination of knowledge deemed necessary for both the governance of crime and the evaluation of the success of such crime control efforts. The computerized results of data obtained through survey devices were used to produce statistical information on crime – incidence rate, trends, effects and the like. Nedcor's survey of 500 domestic businesses across service sectors and racial groups – the first of its kind – quantified the cost of crime by using such measures as profitability margins, public confidence (in state anti-crime measures) and a 'six-point scale of perceived risk' of personal and corporate victimization. Another original study of 70 companies in the UK, USA, France, Belgium, Brazil, Peru and Columbia computed the relative importance, for foreign investment decisions, of 22 factors including crime, violence and corruption. The expressed aim was to situate South Africa's investment favourability globally in comparative terms relating to its political, economic, social and (crucially) security climate. A third step in the 'Stop Crime' programme – a computerized inventory of 'permanent assets' in the 'fight against crime' – amassed an impressive database: a 'name bank' of crime prevention experts with 500 entries and a list of over 700 available national and international 'resource materials' (literature, policy documents, case studies etc.).

Rose (1991) has made the general relationship between statistics and democracy clear (see also Comaroff and Comaroff 2006; Haggerty 2001). Statistical knowledge and measurement are key mechanisms through which reality can be 'objectively' and 'reliably' captured and plotted. Numercized knowledge of the domain(s) to be managed enables the exercise of socio-political authority. Action, especially effective action, can only be undertaken where knowledge of the problem exists. At the same time, statistical practices are crucial to the constitution of calculating, self-directed subjects who not only govern themselves in approved ways, but who also scrutinize state activities. The perceived value of numerical information about crime, just when the new liberal democracy was faced with 'the problem of crime', is made plain in Nedcor documents:

> [S]tatistics are vital. In a modern society all policy-makers and implementation relies on statistics. This is also true of policies on crime prevention as well as the identification, detection and conviction of criminals.
>
> (Nedcor April 1996, 6)

But it is not only government that was to have routine access to this knowledge. The public too was to be informed and the 'Stop Crime' strategy aimed to communicate knowledge about crime to industry and communities, as well as to local authorities and central state departments. Provisions for the routine answering of enquiries from community groups and local authorities on the causes, prevention and control of crime were set in place. Workshops were conducted with local authorities. Collaborative projects were undertaken with other corporate bodies – for example, the Business Initiative Against Crime and Corruption conference (BIACC), organized together with Business South Africa (BSA) and the Council of South African Banks (COSAB) discussed below[1] – and with government – for example, the working group on a national crime prevention strategy. One thousand 'interested people' received the Project's monthly newsletters. The publication of the 'Stop Crime' strategy as a newspaper insert in the *Sunday Times* and the *Sowetan* and its distribution through Nedbank branches aimed to reach approximately 900,000 readers. In this way, the Project promoted and participated in, shaped and structured a quantitative public discourse on security.

Representations of crime, interventionist measures and assessments of such measures must all, it seems, be conducted in the language of numbers. The mapping of crime's particular dimensions – its causes, cycles, victims, perpetrators, frequency,

---

1 COSAB is a collective business body. BSA is a mandated business organization focusing on macro-economic growth.

costs etc. – provides the basis for the state's performance of its 'crime prevention and control function' (that is, the detection and apprehension of criminals through the police, the adjudication of cases through the justice department, and the execution of sentences through correctional services). Further, it is on the basis of numericized information depicting crime's statistical dynamics that commerce sought to hold government to account and itself undertook various activities against crime. The latter involved industry participation in public policing, effected principally, though not exclusively, through assistance rendered to the South African Police Service (SAPS). (The implications arising from this private calculation of numbers, which was seen to provide the conditions for state action, are discussed below.)

Business Against Crime

BAC emerged out of the BIACC conference, held at Johannesburg's World Trade Centre in August 1995. BSA and COSAB, with the assistance of the Nedcor Project, organized the conference in response to an appeal by the state president for cooperation between public and private sectors in dealing with crime, corruption and violence.

> During 1995 he [President Mandela] appealed to the business community at a gathering of … Business South Africa … he said, I need you, we need your help, we need your functional and technical expertise and your capability and wherever possible your resources to assist us in the fight against crime.
>
> BAC Western Cape Director (interview 4 December 1997)

Opened by President Mandela (as he was then), this high-profile event included participants from the corporate and banking sectors, along with six cabinet ministers, and senior police and defence officials. Varying accounts put the number of conference delegates between 400 and 500, with 84 discussion groups. Conference objectives included clarifying the crime control roles and responsibilities of business and of government and developing a process of coordination.

The official conference summary[2] presented to President Mandela, government ministers and the media at the end of September 1995 unambiguously identified the state as the principle guarantor of public safety and security. However, the corporate sector sought a significant role for itself, not least in managing its own crime risks, and the document recommended that business 'form a working group on corruption to work towards self-regulation' (BSA circular No. 113/95). More than this though, the conference summary highlighted that business was uniquely placed to assist government in performing its security functions because of the special expertise and

2 For reasons that remain unclear, both the Nedcor Project and BSA produced separate conference reports. BSA distributed its version to government and the media; the final document reflected some input from the Nedcor Project. In effect the circulation of this report pre-empted the work of the Action Committee, an elected body of 20 conference delegates expressly created to 'make recommendations to BSA for endorsement in order to present these to President Mandela' (BAC circa 1996). The committee met for the first time one month *after* the release of the BSA conference summary.

resources that the corporate sector had to offer. This expanded role for commerce was linked to an emergent view of crime, especially violent crime, as the single greatest threat to post-apartheid national reconstruction programmes. South Africa was presented as being in the midst of a crime wave of crisis proportions that endangered not only the operation and survival of individual enterprises, but the country's economic growth, development and overall well-being. Corporate involvement in public policing was explicitly framed in terms of instrumental financial motivations: 'The direct and indirect costs of crime to the business community are likely to ensure that a well targeted anti-crime initiative by the business community will be a productive investment and is likely to yield a productive cost/benefit ratio' (BAC circa 1996).

Corporate South Africa's contribution to overall levels of security was to be nothing less than assisting government in setting a national framework and strategic plan for an integrated multi-sectoral attack on crime. The BIACC document proposed a working group of government representatives and other stakeholders (citizens, churches and commerce) to develop a national strategic approach to address crime and that would serve to coordinate efforts among different state departments and between these government agencies and individuals, communities and organizations. Industry was also to empower criminal justice agencies, as a well-functioning reactive system in particular was seen to provide the main line of defence against crime and the criminals. Thus, the conference summary envisioned a campaign that would include specific business-endorsed projects such as 'Community Police Force Forums', 'reward schemes for identifying criminals' and 'crimewatch phone, TV and radio services', all designed to promote public support of, and confidence in, the police.

The report also offered some free legal advice, suggesting the introduction of a series of interim legislative changes to achieve practical (lower crime levels) and symbolic ('to demonstrate [political] will' and 'to show that crime doesn't pay') gains in respect of certain offences, most of which involved violence. Crimes such as murder, rape, use of a weapon in the commission of a crime, possession of illegal firearms, vehicle hijacking, dealing in stolen goods, drug trafficking, extortion, witness intimidation and bribery of government officials were listed and characterized as 'detrimental to the national morale'. The interventions proposed to respond to these crimes were highly repressive and included: the search of person and property without a warrant; denial of bail to further the aims of preventive detention; maximum mandatory sentencing; the denial of parole; and the elimination of young offender status.

To facilitate the implementation of the report's recommendations and the coordination of private/public partnerships, the conference-elected Action Committee was transformed, towards the end of September 1995, into BAC under the auspices of BSA and managed by the NBI.[3] BAC provided a private-sector platform that was imbued with the institutional capacity to assist government in the reduction of overall levels of crime. A collaborative venture, BAC pooled the substantial

3 NBI is a collective business body focusing on socio-economic development. In 1996, BAC became independent of both NBI and BSA.

resources (financial, technical, human and other) of individual firms. Funded entirely by company contributions (R25 million in 2005 alone), the BAC umbrella covered diverse market sectors – from financial and banking services to travel, tourism and recreation.

How did business come to perceive the need to have a *collective* body dedicated to fighting crime? How did it come to pass that individual organizations having initiated independent projects in support of government's efforts against crime subsequently endorsed BAC? Nedcor Ltd had established the R3m Project on Crime, Violence and Investment shortly before donating over R500,000 to BAC and becoming one of its board members. Why was a collective anti-crime body so appealing to individual companies? Commenting on the creation of BAC, an NBI interviewee suggested that the growth and volume of crime accounted for this collaborative approach taken by industry: 'corporate business felt that crime was a main issue that required a single standing body'. The issue of crime was self-evidently the greatest threat to national economic growth and success and it was this threat that united individual companies in a fight against the (new) common enemy; crime had replaced political violence, communism and the liberation movements. Each individual firm would still provide for its own self-protection, but they were also to act cooperatively, as members of the 'business community' and as responsible corporate citizens, to help safeguard South Africa's future. There emerged then some sense of a moral mission understood as a desire to 'do good works' that benefit society. Organizations voluntarily participated in BAC because individuated and isolated action could be expected to have little impact on the general threat posed by crime to society. Indeed, *ad hoc* and sensationalist interventions by individual companies could conceivably act to amplify the problem by raising general levels of fear, while offering little in the way of concrete and sustainable solutions. Any such bad news could reasonably be expected to further contribute to the loss of skilled employees (through emigration) and foreign and domestic disinvestment (Fourie and Mhangwana 1995). The perceived benefits of collective participation in anti-crime campaigns included not only a rise in general levels of security, investment and productivity, but also more high-visibility marketing opportunities (BAC circa 1996) than would normally be available to individual firms, and opportunities for displaying, to senior state officials, good corporate citizenship. I should note here also that government wanted business to make collective representations on the formulation of a national policy and strategy on crime – the absence of which, the BIACC conference concluded, was a major contributing factor to the current 'crime crisis'.

Organizational Structure

BAC sponsors included a wide range of mid- to large-size organizations, described by one BAC interviewee as 'the champions of industry'. Organizational sponsors represented a variety of market sectors:

- advertising (for example, TBWA Hunt Lascaris)
- the chemical industry (for example, Plascon)
- financial and banking (for example, Liberty Life, Nedcor Ltd)

- food and beverage (for example, Nando's)
- industrial and infrastructural development (for example, the Barlows Group)
- information technology (for example, IBM)
- media (for example, Independent Newspapers, SABC Radio and TV, M-Net)
- mining (for example, Anglo American)
- motor vehicle manufacturing (for example, BMW)
- professional services (for example, Andersen Consulting, Deloitte & Touche)
- public utilities (ESKOM)
- travel, tourism and recreation (for example, South African Breweries).

The BAC Board of Directors consisted mainly, although not exclusively, of its financial sponsors. Meetings were chaired by a chairperson, but day-to-day activities came under the purview of a managing director. A number of working groups were struck and concentrated organizational efforts around key focal areas. These areas included: the promotion of BAC and the mobilization of citizen involvement in crime prevention and control measures; white-collar crime; legislative and judicial review and criminal justice transformation; the formulation and implementation of strategic policies on crime, especially a national crime prevention strategy; the collation, processing, distribution and management of crime data and information; and, capacity-building and resourcing of the SAPS (that is, management training, satellite communication links and vehicle donations).

BAC structures were also organized at provincial levels, in KwaZulu-Natal, the Eastern Cape and the Western Cape, and more recently in the Northern Cape, North West Province and Mpumalanga. The emergence of these branches took into account the fact that many of government's national crime policies were to be implemented at provincial levels and it also reflected the existence of specific regionally-based business interests and needs. The discussion in this chapter, however, only pertains to national BAC programmes.

Strange Alliances

Goffman (1959; 1961) argues that the everyday, routine activities of individuals and institutions depend on and give rise to shared assumptions of meaning. Unsurprisingly, therefore, industry publications convey a certain obviousness about corporate ventures in public policing. In several documents relating to possible contributions to the 'fight against crime', common-sense understandings about rising crime and the need to respond appropriately are invoked. On this view, crime only emerged as a significant social problem in the closing decade of the twentieth century.

> Until the early 1990s, crime was a relatively minor issue for business. Political violence, labour relations, government policy and financial issues were the dominant concerns of business decision-makers.
>
> (Nedcor December 1995, 10)

While during this period individual citizens certainly had to protect themselves, corporate South Africa 'largely ignored the crime situation, or hoped that it would be taken care of by the police' (*ibid.*, 14). All this changed. 'Today, studies show that crime is the key factor negatively affecting business confidence in the future' (*ibid.*, 10). Industry could ill-afford to ignore the threats posed by crime, nor could it expect government to address them by itself. Certainly, 'the primary responsibility to ensure a crime-free environment rests with the state, and in particular the Ministry of Safety and Security' (Fourie and Mhangwana 1996, 8). But truly successful intervention required a multi-agency approach and the establishment of partnerships between government, industry and other parties affected by crime: 'effective and sustainable crime prevention is only possible through coherent and integrated strategies supported by all sectors of society' (BAC circa 1996; see also Chapter 2). Business was thus to assist government, providing expertise as well as financial, technical and other resources to both develop a national strategic plan to coordinate this multi-agency approach and enhance police performance especially.

Undoubtedly, at the beginning of the transition period, many police personnel lacked basic detective and investigative skills. This skills set was largely discarded during the apartheid years in favour of techniques of torture and *en masse* detention and relocation. Transition in the SAPS implied deep organizational and cultural reform (Brogden and Shearing 1993; Cawthra 1992). However, exclusive concern with attempts to reorient the SAPS toward crime control contributes little or nothing to our understanding of how corporate South Africa came to see the solution to problems posed by crime as bound up with transformations of the police. After all, the police are neither the only, nor even the primary, agents of policing in modern society (Ericson and Haggerty 1997; Grant 1989; Johnston 1992; Shaw 2002; Shearing and Stenning 1982; South 1988). It is not surprising, therefore, to find in the Nedcor Project *Final Report* and *Briefing Paper* to the BIACC that commerce may confront crime in several ways with varying degrees of police contact and involvement (see also the discussion in Chapter 3). For example, business may retreat into its privatized spaces, employing in-house or contract security and/or providing victim support services to its employees when warranted. Donations may be made, whether financial or material, to local cooperative projects operating within urban and industrial areas, for example, police-endorsed Business Watch schemes; or industry may lend support to the crime prevention initiatives of mandated business organizations like BSA. Alternatively, industry may fund a business body such as BAC. None of these options is mutually exclusive; a point that was made by Johnston (1992) as regards the range of possibilities open to individuals for participation in policing in the UK. For example, ABSA Bank, the South African banking group, was a participant in BIACC, a contributor to BAC and an employer of a huge contingent of in-house private security.

Moreover, it is not at all obvious that government, in developing and implementing its crime control policies, should necessarily come to see this activity as somehow bound up with the economic interests of private enterprise; or that issues of policing, the administration of justice and imprisonment should occupy an important place within state programmes for macro-economic growth and social development (Dixon 2006). Nor can one assume that in joining forces to combat crime, business and government were acting in terms of identical interests.

In interrogating the self-evident nature or 'naturalness' of private/public partnerships in crime control, I am not seeking to uncover hidden motives or conspiratorial intent. My aim is not to debunk industry claims that it was motivated by concerns about high crime levels. Instead, my interest lies with the conditions and factors that enabled the formation of such alliances between business and government, and with how these partnerships came to be seen as somewhat 'natural'. Here, language plays a key technical role, translating the different and diverse values and objectives of capital and government so that each came to see its own interests and needs as in some way commensurate with those of the other. As Miller and Rose (1990, 10) argued, following the approach developed by Callon and Latour (1981):

> ... alliances [are] formed not only because one agent is dependent upon another for funds, legitimacy or some other resource which can be used for persuasion or compulsion, but also because one actor comes to convince another that their problems or goals are intrinsically linked, that their interests are consonant, that each can solve their difficulties or achieve their ends by joining forces or working along the same lines.

In the 'flexible' and 'mobile' alliance established between commerce and government, crime levels came to provide a measure of South Africa's socio-economic progress. But different interpretations existed as to the precise nature of this relation. For government, the question of safety and security was a question of social justice and equality, of the integration of economic growth and social development, and of the democratization of state structures (see ANC 1994). For commerce, basic levels of safety and security provided the foundation for the operation of a free (that is, deregulated) market, for market investment and expansion, and for improved economic performance ('growth of real output per person'), 'leaving no group untouched by the benefits of growth' (South African Foundation 1996). There was common agreement, though, that crime was a social issue: crime had become 'everyone's problem'. Further, both business and government agreed that their respective interests and objectives could be met by an efficient, effective, professional and legitimate legal system organized around a reactive, crime-fighting model. In sum, these developments can be understood less in terms of the supposed blurring or disintegration of private and public sector boundaries and more by reference to the strategies of persuasion and negotiation by means of which various state agencies (police, justice, finance) and commerce came to form anti-crime partnerships without relinquishing their formal independence and autonomy (cf. Miller and Rose 1990).

Below, I argue that government was able to count on industry support in the 'fight against crime' in part because big business perceived the need to legitimate itself in the eyes of the political authorities by appealing to a particular image of responsible corporate citizenship. In the section below I offer a more detailed discussion of the shared understanding, evident in the private/public anti-crime partnerships, of a link between safety and security and the country's socio-economic future.

Crime, the State and the Economy

The 'crime problem' brought into focus a series of macro-economic concerns for corporate South Africa: concerns about the emigration of skilled individuals, attracting the tourist dollar and perhaps most crucially, securing new client bases and retaining existing new ones. In relation to investment decisions, a Nedcor survey of nearly 500 South African businesses – 'white and black owned', across service sectors and of all sizes – found general agreement that rising crime levels inhibited 'fixed investment in new operations, or the expansion of existing operations', with small black-owned enterprises facing the most serious threat. Over 55 per cent of interviewees spontaneously identified crime as one obstacle to business expansion and almost 40 per cent regarded it as *the* most serious factor (Nedcor December 1995, 10). High rates of crime, especially violent offences, together with public perceptions of increased risks to personal safety were therefore understood to undermine the confidence of business owners, executives and investors in the very socio-political environment in which they operated. Crime control was already predominately a state responsibility. This was so because government had an enabling role to play vis-à-vis the economy, since by ensuring a basic level of security the state provides the necessary condition for the successful functioning of a free market (cf. Gordon 1991; Rose 1999, especially Chapter 4). Thus, early Nedcor and BAC proposals called on government to immediately develop a national strategic policy to manage crime (thereby demonstrating state leadership in fighting crime) and to integrate this strategy within the country's *Reconstruction and Development Programme* (thereby signalling state recognition of the crucial link between safety and security and socio-economic restructuring). Business assisted government both in formulating the NCPS – as a participant of the Interdepartmental Task Group – and in implementing it – through BAC, which directed its early efforts toward supporting the NCPS Secretariat. (See Chapter 2 for a detailed discussion of the NCPS.)

In addition to a national plan, commerce identified a well-resourced criminal justice system and public police force as key institutional mechanisms by which government would maintain basic levels of public safety and security. The funding and staffing of the justice department and the police became an index of what was termed the 'political will [of government] to seriously tackle the crime problem' (Nedcor April 1996, 18). According to Nedcor and BAC, the lack of adequate resourcing undermined the professionalism of criminal justice departments, aggravating an already existing crime situation that accompanied the rapid transition to democratic rule.

> In respect of the SAPS, extremely low salaries, violent working conditions, understaffing, community scepticism and other factors have led to many resignations and, in turn, to low rates of detection and apprehension of criminals. Once again, criminals perceive that with a remote chance of being arrested (combined with low chances of coming to trial and even lower chance of being convicted) they can safely increase the scale of their activities.
>
> (Nedcor April 1996, 5)

But because mere criticism of the existing situation could reasonably be expected to produce negative outcomes – disinvestment, emigration of skilled individuals – corporate South Africa offered constructive assistance, committing funds, technical and other resources, and expertise toward improving the efficiency and efficacy of state law enforcement agencies.

Transforming the SAPS

BAC introduced a number of SAPS-related 'special projects'.[4] To a large degree, these reflected support for what some researchers call a 'professional crime-fighting' model of policing (see Moore, Trojanowicz and Kelling 1988). This can be characterized by reference to its reliance on motorized patrols, visible police presence, surveillance and other technologies, and centralized authority structures in the control of crime. The aim of the BAC 'special projects' was to assist the police to demonstrate competence in reactive law enforcement and commitment to responsive public service (see Bayley 1995 on improving technical capacity for policing in other transitional democracies).

Several of these BAC projects focused on rendering the SAPS more responsive to the specific security concerns of corporate South Africa and its investors. For example, proposals for the use of CCTV in metropolitan city centres and for the provision of offices and residential quarters to the SAPS in central business districts in Johannesburg, addressed industry's perceptions of inner city decay and rising crime. Both proposals held out the possibility of deterring potential offenders through increased surveillance and of detecting crimes in progress through enhanced police presence.

Consider also the donation of 100 BMWs fitted out as police cruisers, which were the core of a special anti-hijacking highway patrol unit in the Gauteng province. Various accounts had emerged that testified to the high degree of violence that usually accompanied car hijackings. These also identified upper-class business executives and investors as likely victims of sophisticated syndicates that specifically targeted 'luxury vehicles' (Wright 1995; also Nedcor August 1995, April 1996). Porous borders to the north were said to make it easy to transport stolen vehicles to nearby territories where they were altered and resold or stripped for parts; and the absence of inter-regional agreement on combating this type of crime ensured low rates of recovery and arrest (AA South Africa 1995; BAC circa 1996). But not only was Gauteng the 'gateway' for the illegal car export trade given its proximity to surrounding countries, it was also South Africa's industrial heartland. Hijacking in Gauteng posed particular problems because any '[i]ncrease in personal risk and concerns over safety inevitably leads to a decline in confidence in the operating environment of business' (Nedcor December 1995, 10). What the proposal for a highway patrol unit indicates, as did the other two BAC initiatives, was that corporate South Africa actively mobilized to create a reassuringly visible and mobile police presence.

Perhaps surprisingly given the recent history of apartheid policing, the view of the police as 'essential for any solution to the current crime crises' seems to have been held by most of the adult population, including those living in South Africa's townships (Nedcor February 1996, 4; also, Shaw 2002). This shared view of the role of the police was taken to suggest that perceptions of ill-equipped and unprofessional police also inhibited more local forms of investment. Thus a number

4 All BAC initiatives with the police were later consolidated under the Support Partnership with Police Stations Project (SPPS) (Nedcor/ISS Crime Index 1997, G3).

of other BAC 'special projects' focused on transforming state policing within 'previously disadvantaged' communities, ostensibly in order to tap into the potential for market growth and development that existed at the lower end of the socio-economic spectrum. These initiatives aimed to address the historical imbalance in the distribution of policing resources (Brogden and Shearing 1993) by the supply of new technology, for example cellphones to facilitate police communications in underprivileged areas. Other projects focused on training police management in the more efficient use of existing resources; for example, Project Lifeline, which sought to enhance the 'operational performance' of 100 of the most 'needy' police stations through the transfer of management skills (BAC circa 1996).

Management discourses framed the search for the best use of existing resources at station level (Crawford 1994; Garland 1996; McLaughlin and Murji 1997; Rose 1999). The search entailed the creation of a 'fact base' to document the current situation and to map out areas for improvement. A not untypical example of this, which was revealed through field observation, concerned one police station just outside Cape Town which had a fleet of four police cars of which, at any one time, three were out of commission awaiting repairs. Solutions to such resource concerns were not necessarily the prerogative of station management. Indeed, both police personnel (workers) and community members (consumers of police services) were encouraged to participate in processes for shaping resource use and deployment. However, the authority to evaluate and approve proffered solutions rested with the SAPS Provincial Steering Committee, and so, in the final instance, control over operational matters remained with centralized authority structures within the police.

Each idea proposed to the provincial committees required an 'implementation plan' that incorporated performance indicators to 'monitor progress and impact', and those 'essential needs' that could not be met without additional funding from either the public or private sectors were to be the subject of a 'business plan'. Acquiring extra resources became 'conditional upon evidence of economy, efficiency and effectiveness' (Loader 1994, 521). Together, these measures indicate that police decision-making operated according to a set of managerial practices that provided for the routine and repeated numericized and monetarized evaluation and revision of the decision taken. Project Lifeline and the cellphone initiative illustrate the belief that the growth potential of micro-, small- and medium-range businesses in less privileged communities depended, at least in part, on the local police possessing the technical capacity and managerial skills to maintain the law and order foundation that underpins the operation of the free market. Such projects do not, however, exhibit much in the way of democratic control of the policy agenda *per se* by these communities.

In different ways, all of the BAC 'special projects' conveyed a particular image of police professionalism. This placed particular emphasis on external cues, such as access to state-of-the art equipment. Successful professional policing, it seemed, depended heavily on the exploitation, for crime control purposes, of the latest technological innovations.[5] The image of police professionalism also incorporated

5 A focus on enhanced technical capacity also featured significantly in donor-assisted projects in post-apartheid South Africa (van der Spuy 2000) and other transitional democracies (Bayley 1995). However, the international donor community, unlike corporate South Africa,

notions of accountability: police management are accountable professionals who invite input from police personnel and community members to aid the resolution of station resource problems. The station commander 'of the future must emerge as a responsible professional who is self-regulating in his/her personal conduct, who accepts accountability as a personal challenge' (M. Palmer 1995 in O'Malley and Palmer 1996, 146). Accountability was still channelled upwards, to centralized police authority structures; but increasingly it was also channelled outwards, toward private-sector sponsors/consumers of the provision of police services, such as BAC. In either case, accountability came to centre on the quality, economy and effectiveness of service delivery (Crawford 1994; Lacey 1994; Loader 1994; McLaughlin and Murji 1997).

Fighting the 'Crime Problem' with Numbers[6]

Both the Nedcor Project and BAC agreed that investor concerns could be assuaged not only by a show of force on the part of the state, but also needed other more indirect measures, such as the provision of 'accurate' crime data. The implicit view was partly that investors draw conclusions about the security of their investments on the basis of statistical measures such as the crime rate. Thus, the availability of appropriate, up-to-date statistics could go a long way toward altering the 'perceptions of existing and potential investors toward the negative phenomena of crime and violence' (Nedcor August 1995, 5).

This points to the importance of numericized information in the management of the crime problem. Statistics were, in the words of the Nedcor Project, 'vital' to the development, implementation and evaluation of state anti-crime policies (Nedcor April 1996). Statistical information is crucial to the exercise of socio-political authority (Rose 1991; 1996b) because action, especially effective action, can only be undertaken where knowledge of the problem exists: 'professionals, planners and politicians can be mobilised to greater effectiveness if they know the size of the challenge facing them as they strive to provide services of all kinds, including safety and security' (Nedcor April 1996, 6-7). In its delivery of security services, government was subjected to assessments conducted in numerical terms: crime rates, number of arrests, conviction rates, security budgets, police remuneration packages, personnel recruitment and so forth.

Numbers also hold special significance for the governance of crime because of the relation established between practices of quantification and practices of liberal democratic citizenship (Comaroff and Comaroff 2006; Haggerty 2001). I highlight

---

was not the driving force behind criminal justice reforms (see also, van der Spuy *et al* 1998; van Zyl Smit and van der Spuy 2004).

Recently, strategic partnerships have developed between foreign donors and BAC South Africa. For example, in 2002 USAID, BAC and the South African Department of Justice cooperated in launching the Criminal Justice Strengthening Programme, which aimed to increase the capacity of the state to 'respond swiftly and forcefully' to crime (<www.sn.apc.org/usaidsa/speech49.html>, accessed 01 June 2007).

6 In this section I draw on Rose's (1991, 1999) account of the relation between numbers and democracy.

here two forms that this relationship may take. First, there is a link between police record-keeping and the 'crime reporter' role. The determination of the size of the 'actual crime situation' (Fourie and Mhangwana 1995) requires that citizens be willing to report criminal activity and 'suspicious' people to police authorities. Business employers and employees, as well as the public more generally, are all understood to have an active part to play in the management of crime by providing the police with information that enables them to calculate the extent of the problem and devise appropriate solutions: 'As long as the public is not prepared to report criminal activities, within and outside the company, it will not be possible to stamp out crime' (*ibid.*, 11). This is notwithstanding that the lack of fit between statistical measures and 'reality' may not so much reflect the failure of citizens to assume the responsibility for reporting crime, but rather the failure of the police to gain public confidence and trust. Secondly, individuals and associations are not only resources for, and objects of, statistical calculation, but are themselves required to become the kind of calculating citizens that liberal democracy expects (Rose 1991; 1999). On the one hand, crime statistics proliferate throughout Nedcor and BAC publications illustrating that public scrutiny of state activity – a key feature of liberalism (Gordon 1991) – occurs within the technical and seemingly objective, framework offered by numbers. Discussions about the quite complex experiences of criminality and victimization and about state policies and practices become debates about the 'crime rate' (see Comaroff and Comaroff 2006; Hudson 2001; Shaw 1997, 2002). On the other hand, individuals are guided in their everyday conduct by facts and figures, not by subjective perceptions or anecdotal information on crime. The same applies to business organizations: the computer and electronics industry, for example, began to make decisions on how to manage the substantial risk of theft of its 'goods in transit', in terms of information cooperatively produced by industry members and stored in a common database (BAC circa 1996). The successful management of crime requires the active participation of a knowledgeable public (O'Malley and Palmer 1996).

Yet numbers do not just provide the basis for action; rather statistical calculation itself is a way of acting on experience. Through police recording procedures, victim and household surveys, Geographical Information Systems and other techniques of inscription, 'crime' emerged as an object that is knowable and manageable: as a routine, predictable and systematic phenomena (Garland 1997) with identifiable spatial and temporal coordinates. Statistics do not simply represent or capture a pre-existing reality – they actually help constitute it (Comaroff and Comaroff 2006; Haggerty 2001). The constitutive role of numbers is well illustrated in Nedcor's call for 'accurate' and 'reliable' crime data to allow for international comparisons in order to both 'judge the severity' of South Africa's crime situation and determine what the *normal crime levels should be* (Nedcor December 1995, 1). Standardized calculations of the incidence of crime per 100,000 population enabled comparisons to be drawn between South Africa's crime rate and that of other countries. In this way, Nedcor could establish that while South Africa's overall crime rate compared favourably with that of the developed West, its murder and assault rates far exceeded international averages; in this way too, Nedcor could project an ideal norm for levels of violent crime in South Africa.

'Centres of Calculation' In his book, *Science in Action*, Bruno Latour advanced the idea of 'centres of calculation' (1987), an idea subsequently developed by Miller and Rose (1990) in the context of their analysis of liberal governance. This idea gains specific purchase in terms of evolving strategies of governance in post-apartheid South Africa: 'Over the past 2 years the provision of statistics on crime and violence in South Africa has become a growth industry' (Nedcor April 1996, 6). Both the Nedcor Project and BAC participated in this development by reworking and synthesizing 'official' material and collecting new data. Police-recorded crime rates were recalibrated using revised population estimates in order to compare crime trends across the entire South African territory (including the former homelands and self-governing states). In so doing, Nedcor sought to 'add value' (Starr and Corson 1987) to official statistics.

New efforts were mounted to produce statistical measures of the views and experiences of business operators and investors. An example of this was the Nedcor survey of the impact of crime on domestic business and on foreign investment decisions. A further example is the previously discussed BAC proposal for the collection and aggregation of data on the theft of computer and electronic goods in transit. Other studies, such as Nedcor's National Crime Survey in 1995, provided new statistical information on the number of South African households affected by property offences or crimes against the person; on the costs of crime at the level of the individual and of society (medical costs, extra insurance); on public opinion on crime and on possible solutions to crime. In effect, Nedcor and BAC operated as 'centres of calculation', producing statistics that seemed to reveal some degree of compatibility between the different concerns, objectives and interests of private enterprise, political authorities and the citizenry.

This 'private' collection of numbers certainly had commercial value, but was not a commercial venture as such. That is to say, Nedcor and BAC were not in the business of 'selling repackaged public data and privately collected statistics, statistical models, and analytical skills' (Starr and Corson 1987, 415). Instead, Nedcor and BAC freely offered the statistical information that they gathered to government and other interested users; this free circulation of crime statistics stood in some contrast to the apartheid period (Comaroff and Comaroff 2006). Indeed, dissemination and communication of this information was a key strategic objective within these corporate anti-crime campaigns. For example, Nedcor, BAC and the Institute for Security Studies cooperated in the publication of the Nedcor/ISS Crime Index for circulation to 2,000 organizations and individuals in the public and private sectors. The aim was to 'provide a ready reference resource for crime prevention practitioners, policy makers and organisations involved in crime prevention initiatives'. The Index was to 'provide ongoing information about the crime situation in South Africa based on research and information from different organisations', offering 'an overview each month of an area of crime, the current available statistics from the South African Police Services and [an] update [of] these statistics as they are made available' (Nedcor/ISS Crime Index 1997, i).

Consider another example: an NCPS programme involving BAC, labour, consumer bodies and various government departments (for example, Justice, Finance) that proposed to integrate information from private and public sources on the 'incidence', 'trends' and 'developments' in relation to corruption and commercial crime. Government needed this statistical data generally so that it could make and justify decisions as to the setting of priorities, the allocation of limited resources, the training of police and internal auditors, and legislative changes. Industry likewise needed such information as the basis for self-regulatory mechanisms: codes of conduct, assessment of organizational policies on financial decision-making, evaluation of the actions of employees and so forth (DoSS 1996b, 72–3). To sum up, Nedcor and BAC participated in and helped produce a 'public habitat of numbers' (Rose 1991, 1999) that became crucial to the liberal democratic governance of crime in South Africa. Within this public habitat, business operators, investors and employees, along with government officials and the citizenry more generally, could calculate the risks posed by crime to the achievement of their specific objectives and decide what to do about it. In so doing, they established some common ground – the domain of mutual (in)security.

Responsible Corporate Citizenship

A Nedcor Project survey in 1995 found that foreign companies were deterred not so much by 'ordinary' crime – even though these rates were high – as by perceptions of political and social instability in South Africa. In fact, crime, violence and corruption, along with interest rates, investor protection, power costs and availability of raw materials, were understood as less of a negative influence on foreign investment decisions than were concerns about the potential for market growth. Such growth was understood to be determined by political and social stability in South Africa and the country's macro-economic policies. While it was certainly possible to regard high levels of crime and violence in South Africa as indicative of political instability, none of the companies surveyed perceived such a connection. The Nedcor survey determined that what tended to worry foreign investors was not the amount, but the type, of crime and violence. It was thought that disinvestment was likely to occur if violence, no matter how occasional or sparse, had a political edge to it (Nedcor April 1996, 4).

Corporate involvement in the management of the 'crime problem' thus had multiple motives in addition to the desire to secure a client base. Undoubtedly corporate actors understood their motivations in terms of a desire to 'do good works' and show themselves as helping disadvantaged communities and society as a whole. This was perhaps most evident at the regional, rather than national, level of BAC. Promotional material by BAC KwaZulu-Natal, for example, appealed directly to the moral sensibilities of corporate actors. On the front cover appeared an enlarged image of a dove bearing the following message: 'In order for evil to abound all that is required is that good people do nothing.' Businesses were instructed that 'your involvement is the key to peace and order', an instructions that was accompanied by the image of a disembodied hand with the index finger pointing to the reader. BAC KwaZulu-Natal 'challenge[d]' corporate enterprises to exercise leadership and 'champion crime prevention in [their] area' in the tradition of those great morally-charged medieval knights on horseback who, without fear, looked down their lances at the approaching enemy (this was the accompanying image on the promotional material). Corporate actors were thus partly animated by conscience.

However, corporate participation in anti-crime measures was especially occasioned by the political vulnerability of industry. Corporate practices during apartheid and the immense powers accrued by corporate bodies in the pre-democratic era later gave rise to a sense of political vulnerability. Many of the companies involved with BAC and the Nedcor Project provided indirect and direct support to the apartheid regime. An example is Eskom, the national electricity supplier and BAC Board member. In a submission to the Truth and Reconciliation Commission (TRC), Eskom acknowledged that 'it did not always behave like a model corporate citizen' and apologized to 'all black South Africans in general, and black Eskom employees in particular' for its actions which, until the late 1980s, 'entertained' and 'perpetuated' apartheid policies (Eskom 1997).

The TRC also received an amnesty application implicating Nedbank, part of the Nedcor group, in a security police operation to divert funds from the National Union of Mineworkers (*The Mail* & *Guardian* online, 26 January 1999). Not only Nedbank, but banking institutions more generally, appear to have played an instrumental role in the apprehension of anti-apartheid activists using banking transactions, particularly withdrawals from ATMs (automated teller machines), as a way to track the movements of 'enemies of the state'.[7] Further, the ANC discussion document, *The State and Social Transformation*, identified capital as a whole, rather than individual firms or particular market sectors, as an 'important and central factor in the totality of forces responsible for the anti-human misery baptised as Apartheid' (ANC 1996, 5.1). Thus industry, in the post-apartheid period, needed to demonstrate unequivocal commitment to the new democratic order.

Such commitment needed to be more than passing the institutional equivalent of a loyalty oath. It was not that industry might simply present an ideological challenge to the new state; rather, the immense powers and benefits accrued by corporate South Africa under the apartheid system were at stake. Consider the example of the mining industry and its veritable 'army' of in-house security amassed to police entire towns and equipped with the same array of weapons as the police, including 'quirts, dogs, teargas, horses, water canons, shotguns, Casspirs (the armoured vehicles used by the police in the townships) and helicopters' (Schärf 1989, 212). Consider again the public utility, Eskom, commonly referred to as a 'parastatal': it had operated relatively independently of the apartheid government as it had powers normally associated with a state. The loss or blunting of the coercive capacity to order social relations was a distinct possibility in the face of a new post-apartheid government anxious to flex its regulatory muscle. For example, the Security Officers Act (92 of 1987) created the option of subjecting in-house security to the same controls as the contract sector, and ministerial supervision of parastatals intensified in keeping with the new government's cautious attitude on privatization (*The Mail* & *Guardian* online, 29 June 1994; see also ANC 1994, 57). Further, the national *Reconstruction and Development Programme* set forth state interventionist strategies to substantially transform the mining, minerals, pulp and paper, tourism and financial industries –

7 Charles Small, personal communication, 1998.

precisely those sectors from which the Nedcor Project and BAC drew their support. Measures such as wage determinations, 'black economic empowerment', monetary policies (for example, interest rates), trade policies (for example, tariff reductions on imports), nationalisation and anti-trust legislation aimed to address the monopolies, insularity, lack of accountability and relative autonomy previously enjoyed by industry under the apartheid system (ANC 1994, especially Chapter 4). In the hopes of forestalling and even preventing the restructuring of its powers and operation, business sought to provide public reassurances that it did not challenge the authority of the state, especially in relation to security issues.

Industry therefore engaged in a series of high visibility anti-crime initiatives designed to represent itself as a 'responsible corporate citizen' (BAC circa 1996; but see also, Johnston 1992 on responsible citizenship and corporate sponsorship of police in the UK). These measures were aimed not so much to eliminate or even reduce crime, but instead they had a high symbolic value, seeking to reassure, persuade and convince government of the good intentions of commerce: 'The objective of Business Against Crime is to empower state agents and to strengthen existing initiatives' (Fourie and Mhangwana 1996, 7). Business sought to show itself as providing supportive capacity to government. This can be illustrated by considering three high-profile industry projects in the field of public policing: BAC itself; BAC proposals on white-collar crime and corruption; and Cellwatch, a partnership programme in the Gauteng province involving business, the SAPS and the 'public'.

Marketing Sponsorship

Why would private enterprise fund BAC? What is the expected 'return' on such investments? The following answer suggests itself: it is a calculated attempt by organizations to publicly demonstrate that they are good corporate citizens; that they are willing to 'put their money where their mouth is' and contribute financially to the strengthening of governmental capacity to fight crime. In effect, sponsorship is a marketing exercise, something made abundantly clear in the Agreement entered into by BAC and its sponsors. The first paragraph of the document is especially revealing: 'BAC was established in August 1995 by the business sector in order to *materially support* the governmental authorities' anti-crime programs and to *show* public commitment by business to that support' [emphasis added]. Nowhere does the Agreement outline the manner in which sponsors may participate – if at all – in expenditure decisions. Funders appear concerned less to do good than to be seen to be doing good: 'The value to the Sponsor in linking themselves to the aims of BAC is of normal marketing exposure ... These associations are highly desirable at this time and positive association for the Sponsor to his [sic] target consumer is high [sic] probable.'

This Agreement, with the exception of the first paragraph, provided specific content to this notion of exposure motivation. Three sponsorship tiers existed, each with specific 'rewards'. 'Founding sponsors' donated R500,000 or more per annum. Their association with BAC would then be publicly communicated in a number of ways. The sponsor's name and logo would be featured 'regularly' in BAC print media campaigns. Sponsors could expect their brand presence to be 'deliberately and systematically raised on public platforms' including 'speeches and interviews, or TV and radio talk shows and in general PR activities'. Corporate logos subsequently appeared on BAC corporate stationary and were included in quarterly newsletters for, and briefing sessions and meetings with, the corporate sector only. Founding sponsors were also given permission to use the BAC logo and 'other devices' in their own marketing programmes, at the point of sale or in promotional campaigns, and were permitted unspecified use of any BAC research. Interestingly, BAC also facilitated direct access to relevant ministries and departments for its sponsors, again illustrating that business sought avenues by which to reassure, persuade and convince government of its good intentions.

'Major Sponsors' who contributed between R100,000 and R500,000 per year obtained similar benefits. The exception was that PR exercises, such as speeches, interviews and TV and radio talk shows, did not so feature the brand presence of the more limited sponsors. Major Sponsors were given permission to use, without restriction, any BAC research and could incorporate the BAC logo in their own advertising campaigns. The use of the BAC logo in promotional activities, however, was subject to specific approval.

Finally, donations of under R100,000 per annum earned the 'Sponsor' the right to use BAC data and information; to display the BAC logo on its corporate stationary; and to use, subject to approval, the BAC association in promotional campaigns. The Sponsor's name and logo would also be included in BAC print media campaigns, corporate briefing sessions and in newsletters circulated to the corporate sector.

In sum, individual organizations were enticed by the marketing prospects associated with sponsorship of BAC. Investments in state anti-crime measures were to be publicized by contributors themselves. Such publication merged with routine promotional practices – at the point of sale, in promotional programmes and on corporate stationary. Moreover, displays of corporate citizenship were undertaken by BAC itself. Indeed, one of BAC's strategic priorities was its communications programme: the name and logo of BAC sponsors were featured on BAC letterhead, in quarterly newsletters, in speeches, interviews and TV and radio shows. Thus, advertisement strategies pursued under the BAC banner opened up a large public domain in which industry seamlessly linked advertising products to potential consumers, with a demonstration of support for the criminal justice system and government more generally.

Corruption and White-Collar Crime

As a demonstration of good corporate citizenship, commerce sought to address corruption and white-collar crime. Both BAC and the Nedcor Project had insisted early on that 'business should help to put its own house in order' (Nedcor December 1995, 16). This call gained added urgency as commercial crime was identified in the NCPS and the 1996 Annual Police Plan as a high priority issue. Industry members were urged to assume responsibility, individually, and collectively as the 'business community', for managing their own security risks. This involved transforming the unethical business culture that took root during the sanctions era as well as developing in-house measures so that companies could manage the risk of commercial crime internally, without criminal justice involvement (BAC circa 1996). At the same time, however, industry sought to demonstrate its confidence in the ability of state agencies to deal effectively with crime. Tension thus existed between the desire to display corporate responsibility by publicly acknowledging corruption and commercial crime as significant threats to the nation's future, and the particular interventions business relied on when resolving specific incidents of white-collar crime.

This section will consider four projects developed by BAC to address white-collar crime and corruption (BAC circa 1996). These projects evinced a strong preference for informal mechanisms, at both industry-wide and company levels, to control and prevent commercial crime. At industry level, an ethical business culture was to be promoted by 'exerting peer pressure' in the form of a one-page Charter of Ethics. Voluntary endorsement of the Charter would be indicated on company letterhead thereby representing 'a public commitment to an ethical way of doing business'. At company level, guidelines for the 'prevention, detection and response of commercial crime' were developed by BAC's Commercial Crime Working Group. The guidelines aimed to 'assist companies in assessing their risk profile, indicate how to allocate responsibility among employees, steps to consider when the crime is committed and the involvement of law enforcement agencies' (BAC circa 1996). The involvement of law enforcement officials was limited by industry perceptions of both the very nature of commercial crime ('non-violent' and 'non-confrontational') and the criminal justice system's incapacity to process cases efficiently ('the enormous backlog of reported cases and the long periods of investigations and court appearances') (BAC circa 1996). And despite a pilot project for corporate donations of computers, scanners and software to ensure continuity between the investigative and prosecutorial stages and to improve case management, increased reliance on the criminal justice system was effectively discouraged. First, the industry view of commercial crime as inherently 'non-violent' and 'non-confrontational' meant that such acts were defined as not being in the criminal justice arena, and the formal system was seen as primarily oriented towards violent offences. Secondly, a framework for a coordinated public–private approach to the prevention and control of commercial crime was under consideration only – the subject of a pre-scoping exercise – and it never materialized in practice.

Such a partnership framework for the prevention and control of commercial crime would consider at least two roles for private enterprise: that of the eyewitness who reports the incident to the state authorities; and that of the expert witness who assists criminal justice officials in understanding the complex accounting practices, computerized networks and other means by which the offence was committed. For reasons pertaining to the institution of privacy (Reiss 1987) and the particular features of commercial crime,[8] independent police discovery of such offences is

8 Commercial crime is usually committed in the context of the offender's routine employment duties. The offence can endure over a long period of time – months even years; and often the visibility of the offence depends on its cumulative effects; pinching a few pennies from individual bank accounts is not noticeable until one happens upon several instances of this type of fraud.

unlikely. Thus, the eyewitness becomes key to the process whereby an event enters the formal legal system as a case of fraud or corruption, etc. But this is precisely the role that industry was reluctant to assume. BAC did not seek to encourage business employees and managers to report incidents of corruption to the police. Rather, it advocated the implementation of self-regulatory measures. Doubtless, industry's strategy on corruption reflected and solidified the different objectives of the state and private enterprise. The state's concern was with the legal guilt or innocence of the accused while business emphasized the prevention of similar future acts and at times sought to enrol transgressors in order to achieve this goal (cf. Shearing and Stenning 1982, 1983; Johnston 1992). But there is another issue: regular, instead of occasional, involvement of the criminal justice system might signal that corruption is widespread, even endemic, and this would strike at the very heart of the corporate citizenship project.

Roving 'Eyes': The Cellwatch Programme

The Nedcor Project (December 1995, 11) identified Cellwatch as a successful example of a business-supported programme aimed at preventing and controlling crime. Cellwatch was a cooperative venture involving the SAPS, Radio 702, Vodacom and cellphone users that aimed to reduce the incidence of car thefts and hijackings in the province of Gauteng and improve recovery rates by creating the 'perception of an increased number of "eyes" watching any attempted vehicle crime'. The scheme worked, first, by the SAPS providing descriptions and registration numbers of stolen cars to the radio station (subject to a SAPS assessment of 'chance of recovery' – only those deemed to have a 'high chance of recovery' could expect airtime). Radio 702 would then broadcast the details of the stolen car (and, in the event, news of its recovery) and urge listeners to call a Cellwatch hotline to report sightings. Vodacom managed the hotline and worked to channel selected calls through to the SAPS. A web of seemingly constant surveillance could thus be created: the criminal would be deterred by the perception of an increased risk of detection – every cellphone user, whether in a car or on the street, becomes a potential 'watcher'. What remained unclear was how swift the police response could be, given the mediating role of Radio 702 and Vodacom.

A number of comments on the Cellwatch programme are in order. First, whatever the motivation for police and Radio 702 involvement – and one can not assume the interests of all actors in this alliance to be identical – Cellwatch was primarily of symbolic value to Vodacom. What was appealing about Cellwatch, as the Nedcor Project noted, is that it showed commerce as willing to make financial and technological investments in public anti-crime measures, and to do so without delay. Certainly the programme had real effects as it was estimated that half of the stolen cars filtered into the scheme were recovered. But were car crimes the primary concern of Vodacom, the programme deliverables would surely inspire little confidence: the number of cars recovered was but a proportion of all *officially recorded* car crimes. Further, measures of changes in the rate of car crime (the deterrent effect) were noticeably absent in subsequent advertising of programme success.

Secondly, as Davis (1990, especially Chapter 4) observed of 'post-liberal' Los Angeles, electronic technologies are well suited to an exclusionary politics in which surveillance functions to secure the social boundaries of race and class. Note that Radio 702 identified its listener base as primarily 'upper income adults between the ages of 25 and 49'. Note, too, the fairly restricted ownership of cellphones, which was largely confined to middle- and upper-income individuals. Lastly, note that only upmarket cars tended to be included in the programme. It is easy to imagine the 'eyes' focusing on those whose skin colour seems at odds with the make of the car – that is, on the marginalized 'Other', particularly black males. Surveillance practically sorts people into categories (the young black male in the BMW into the car thief category) in order to administer them. However, all individuals, not only marginalized populations, are snared in the web of surveillance (Ericson and Haggerty 2000). Surveillance also impinges on the freedoms of the very persons employing such security measures. Take the example of the cartoon image accompanying the Nedcor Project's documentation of the Cellwatch programme. Three cars are in a row, each occupied by two people (six pairs of eyes), all of whom are talking on cellphones. Behind this row of cars is a fourth car with a driver also talking on a cellphone. The space between all of the cars has been erased and it seems that the car frames have buckled inwards, trapping the occupants. The car has become a confinement cell, driver and passenger imprisoned and subjected to the unrelenting, penetrating gaze not of one identifiable person, but of many unknown individuals – the occupant of the car behind, adjacent or in front may be watching; so, too, may be the person on the cellphone who is crossing the street or sitting in the outdoor patio of the cafe.

'Ordinary Crime' and the Securitization of Social Space

What were the objects of corporate anti-crime projects? What specific kinds of targets were envisioned and enacted in industry-endorsed crime control strategies? In this section I argue that BAC and Nedcor programmes attended largely to 'ordinary crime', especially that which impacted on industry investments and profit margins – public nuisance (aggressive panhandling, drunkenness), vandalism, shoplifting, theft, possession of stolen property. Ordinary crime emerged as a category distinguishable from 'corruption'. The name of BAC's predecessor – Business Initiative Against Crime and Corruption – clearly conveys such distinctions. The Nedcor Project also differentiated between ordinary crime and commercial crime: 'high levels of crime make day-to-day business almost impossible ... there are also significant levels of crime within the business sector, in the form of fraud and corruption' (Nedcor December 1995, 11). Business had certainly developed several specific and practical projects to address corruption and white-collar offences. As already noted, these tended to treat the category of commercial crime as outside of the public arena and, in the main, as the responsibility of private enterprise. However, far greater concern was paid to what can be termed as public order issues. In other words, business interest centred squarely on the foundational basis for the free play of the production and consumer markets, a foundation for which government was deemed the principle guarantor.

While public order encompassed issues relating to personal safety, corporate-sponsored anti-crime projects also separated out ordinary crime from 'violence'. Take, for example, the title of the Nedcor initiative: the 'Nedcor Project on Crime, Violence and Investment'. Industry research indicated that violence, especially violence directed against the person, impinged on the daily operation of businesses (see Fisher 1991, on the US). In one study, approximately 50 per cent of the nearly 500 firms surveyed saw 'themselves and their businesses to be "very much" or "constantly" at risk of crime'. The study also found that most interviewees (66 per cent) were not at all convinced by government's anti-crime initiatives and that 40 per cent were willing to contribute to *any* scheme, whether by government and/or industry, to reduce crime levels (Nedcor December 1995, 10). Yet, most practical proposals put forward in the corporate anti-crime campaigns focused not on violent personal offences (murder, rape), but on ordinary crime (theft, shoplifting, public nuisance).

How is it possible to account for this? A number of different, though related, explanations exist. One, BAC and Nedcor members secured their own personnel against risks to personal safety – whether in the office, to and from the office or even, as in the case of executives and others, at home – by employing in-house or contract security. Unlike smaller businesses, these private arrangements did not substantially reduce profits (*ibid.*). Two, as the same study confirms, individual firms were willing to invest and otherwise support industry interventions as long as these were 'visible in [their] impact and aimed at reducing the crime risks ... specific to business and its employees' (*ibid.*). Similarly, private enterprise, as previously shown, appeared less interested in reducing general crime levels (for example, violent, personal offences), than in participating in highly visible anti-crime campaigns designed to project an image of responsible corporate citizenship. In sum, targeting ordinary crime, such as shoplifting, vandalism and panhandling, addressed the quite specific investment and profit concerns of business operators. It also promised to produce immediate and visible effects, in particular a re-energized and vibrant trading environment. Finally, those projects directed against ordinary crime offered the best chance of 'success' in that the primary objects of such schemes were the actions of the poor and marginalized, the very sectors least able to mobilize effective resistance. This last point is especially significant: it suggests that the focus on ordinary crime was bound up with attempts to recolonize urban spaces by effecting (and securing existing) boundaries between different populations divided along socio-economic, racial and other lines (cf. Davis 1990, especially Chapter 4; Hermer and Mosher 2002; Huey *et al* 2005; Samora 2003). Across a variety of sites, 'circuits of inclusion and exclusion' (Rose 1999) were secured through the imposition of repressive legal controls, as well as through the introduction of more subtle and indirect techniques. I explore this point through an in-depth examination of two corporate-sponsored projects on public policing, details of which were taken from Nedcor's 'Stop Crime' publication (December 1995).

The Christmas Spirit

In Pretoria, the local SAPS and 'business community', represented by the Pretoria Chamber of Commerce, cooperated in launching Operation Christmas in the city centre's business district (CBD). Operation Christmas began on 25 November

1994 and ended on Christmas Eve. It was initiated in response to twin problems facing businesses in the CBD area. On the one hand, a concern with what was called 'seasonal crime', though the more accurate reference would be seasonal increases in crime. This included shoplifting, bribery, fraud and robbery, which were offences impacting directly on daily trading. On the other hand, a declining number of shoppers due to fears of congregating drunks and drug addicts and perceived risk of robbery, car theft and break-ins. Operation Christmas thus aimed to 'provide a safe trading environment for Pretoria's businesses' by 'apprehend[ing] criminals of all kinds operating in the Pretoria CBD' (Nedcor December 1995). Towards this end, the SAPS assigned 40 extra officers to foot patrol duty in the CBD area. Visible police presence was seen to have both preventive and reactive features (Moore and Trojanowicz 1988; Wilson and Kelling 1982). Foot patrols would deter potential criminals. They would also serve a crime detection purpose: patrol officers may chance upon crimes in progress and were well placed to receive and follow up tips from shop-owners about criminal activity and 'suspicious' people in the CBD area. Moreover, increased police visibility by itself was assumed to reassure business operators and shoppers alike that 'something was being done'.

The success of Operation Christmas was measured by the volume of trade, with businesses 'reporting their busiest Christmas season for seven years' (Nedcor December 1995). Success indicators also included the number of arrests made during the operational period and recorded crime levels declined by 40 per cent. Details of the most 'significant arrests' were provided by Nedcor: these accounted for over half (125) of the total (225) arrests made during this period. A small number of these 'significant arrests' were for violent offences. A far greater number, by contrast, were for crimes that can be characterized as property-related – possession of stolen property, shoplifting, fraud, possession of car-breaking equipment. Arrests within this latter group can be readily recognized as 'significant' in that theft, fraud and the like threaten business interests, making it difficult for operators to profitably run their enterprises.

However, public drunkenness also accounted for a large number of the 'significant arrests' and this suggests that Operation Christmas was also 'significant' for less palatable reasons. This business–police venture had as much to do about crime as it did about defining and enforcing particularistic conceptions of public order. After all, it was predominately the poor and the marginalized – street kids, the unemployed, street hawkers – who were most likely to be nabbed by the long arm of the law; not necessarily because they committed more crimes or did so without much skill, but because they were unable to mobilize effective opposition to such periodic police sweeps (see Samara 2003 for a discussion of the policing of vulnerable sectors, especially street kids, in Cape Town; on Canada see Hermer and Mosher 2002; on the UK, see Loader 1994). An 'aggressive order maintenance' (Wilson and Kelling 1982) approach to policing, what Huey *et al* (2005) term 'image-oriented policing', was put in place. This was a kind of social cleansing of public streets and commercial corridors where drunks and other disreputable and unruly people were rounded up and moved on and, if they 'protested', locked up. That arrests for public drunkenness, possession of stolen property etc. were deemed 'significant' had less to do with the nature of the offences than with the implications arising from the application of the criminal law: arrest removed (even if temporarily) 'problem populations' from the CBD area, thus contributing to a 'safe trading environment'. Here, safety relates to social perceptions of threat in that these problem populations comprised the black underclass, a grouping that was the product, as well as the target, of the policies of the former regime. The policing of the CBD area thus overlaid the spatial segregation of the apartheid city: Operation Christmas constituted certain categories of individuals as legitimate consumers and promised to insulate them from undesirable others seen to occupy an illegitimate place in commercial centres.

Remaking the City Centre

Business also acted collectively, with rather limited direct involvement on the part of the state, to manage specific crime risks within their immediate environment. For example, faced with inner-city decay, rising crime and corporate retreat to the suburbs, private enterprises in central Johannesburg and Durban cooperated in establishing Business Improvement District (BID) schemes. Composed of property owners and their tenants, and receiving the support of the municipalities and local SAPS, these inner city 'private governments' (the official term) 'provide[d] services to [their] members where local authorities are unable to do so' (Nedcor December 1995). These services included the structural upgrading of city centres, addressing issues such as 'the environment (street lighting), signage, security screens [and] streetscape design (investing in a pedestrian-friendly city environment)' (*ibid.*). Certainly the physical remodelling of the city centre can have quite benign implications; for example, the refurbishment of derelict buildings or increased social interchange due to the transformation of streets from motorized to pedestrianized access routes. But as Davis (1990) reminds us in his description of 'post-liberal' LA, architectural design may merge with racist discourses, inscribing into the structural fabric of the city itself social divisions of space and facilitating the policing of such boundaries. Disturbingly, Davis's account of privatized pedestrian corridors in the new downtown LA business centres – as a sanctuary for middle- and upper-class whites, as a fortified space hostile to the poor and sealed off from the nearby barrios and ghettos to which marginalized populations are consigned – mirrors not only South Africa's past, but also its present. Contemporary Johannesburg and Durban, for example, continue to bear the hallmarks of spatial segregation with access to their city centres limited by inadequate and dangerous transportation systems linking the surrounding townships to the downtown areas. Conceiving of township inhabitants primarily as workers, rather than as legitimate consumers of the retail, recreational or other products on offer downtown, buses and taxis[9] ferry individuals into and out of the city centres starting several hours before dawn until the early evening. At some distance from the townships or 'locations', trains operate from dawn to late evening. The BIDs agenda did not include improvements to public transport or crime control on trains and buses, at stations and taxi ranks or on those taxi routes

9 Known locally as 'kombis', minivans accommodating (normally) up to 14 passengers provide an inexpensive mode of transport within city centres and between these and outlying areas. These minivans operate on a 'hail-and-ride' basis.

which were the objects of violent clashes between different operators each vying for control; such omissions make clear that it was not township dwellers that were to be enticed into the city centres.

Moreover, the newly-improved business districts remained isolating of the poor and marginalized because to a large extent such spaces were policed privately (see Chapter 3 for a discussion of private security). The Durban BID, for instance, proposed a voluntary financial contribution by businesses toward the employment of private security to police 'blocks' such as the beachfront and the CBD.[10] Private security was primarily responsive to commercial interests, which were not necessarily co-extensive with liberal democratic principles such as human rights and equality (Brogden and Shearing 1993; Nina and Russell 1997).

What were the targets of such policing measures? A cartoon illustration (Nedcor December 1995) promoting BIDs characterized the scheme as a giant broom cleaning, in both a literal and figurative sense, city streets: dirt, scattered newspapers, empty cans and bottles and discarded banana skins are swept up along with (three) gun-toting robbers. While the robbers featured predominately in the cartoon drawing, the accompanying text made no mention of armed robbery. Instead, the text highlighted the issue of begging, and advocated that the public be 'encouraged to purchase meal vouchers to hand out to beggars, which [could] be redeemed at city center feeding schemes'. Industry support for a voucher system and feeding scheme was a calculated display of good corporate citizenship. It aimed to show business as willing to share responsibility (with government) for poverty within its immediate environment. Of course, it also addressed the quite specific industry concerns that the homeless, street kids, alcoholics and drug addicts were driving legitimate firms and shoppers from the city centres. The introduction of meal vouchers aimed to ensure that panhandlers did not receive money or cigarettes that could be used to obtain 'inappropriate' consumables such as alcohol, glue or drugs. One could only benefit from public generosity if one behaved responsibly. On this view, a meal voucher was worthless to the vagrant begging for money for the next drink. And the network of feeding schemes distributed 'undesirables' within time-space matrices: the homeless, alcoholic panhandler was to be lured away from vital trading or tourist areas for certain periods of time during the day and evening by the promise of food. Presumably, those who refused to participate in these schemes, and those who remained recalcitrant, were moved on or faced arrest for any one of a host of public nuisance offences such as public drunkenness or loitering. Thus, we

10 No mention was made of how the private patrols would relate to the SAPS. This is a key question in the US BIDs programmes which served as models for the South African schemes. In Philadelphia (Seamon 1995) and St Louis (Mokwa and Stoehner 1995), for instance, public and private forces functioned in tandem within a 'public safety network'; close operational links between the two were developed with private security serving in a supportive capacity, attending to crime prevention, public service requests (from residents and tourists) and traffic concerns, thus leaving police officials free to engage in crime control and rapid emergency response. As in South Africa, the primary targets of such public-private partnerships were panhandlers and petty criminals; unlike in South Africa, private security were unarmed, had severely limited authority to arrest and use force, and were actively discouraged from playing a crime control role.

have here two control strategies at work. One aimed to responsiblize the actions of the marginalized and the disreputable. For those who seemed impervious to such exhortations, a variety of more repressive measures were available to manage the risks that they posed (cf. Rose 1999; Stenson 1995, 2005).

But BIDs also drew attention to another aspect of the problem of begging: those people who gave money to panhandlers. The contribution of these well-meaning, but misguided, individuals to the problem can be summed up thus: begging would not exist, or at least not exist to the extent it currently did, except for the large pool of people willing to provide handouts. The average citizen thus received instruction on responsible charity giving (meal vouchers, not money). The well-meaning individual was to play a moralizing role, ensuring that irresponsible behaviour such as alcoholism and drug addiction remained unrewarded, at least on the streets.

Conclusion

Corporate sponsorship of the public police became evident in many countries towards the end of the twentieth century (see Dupont *et al* 2003 for Australia; Ericson and Haggerty 1997 for Canada; Johnston 1992 for Britain). But the South African situation appears to display certain unique features: the involvement of business took a more collective form; the initiatives targeted police operational practices; and the transformation of these practices was linked much more to the imperatives of crime control than to crime prevention. The additive impacts of state and non-state security policy and practice were largely in the service of the interests of the well-to-do segments of the population. Corporate interests, as demonstrated, were not necessarily co-extensive with the security needs of the black underclass whose marginalization and powerlessness were further entrenched as a result of business initiatives against crime. This leads to the conclusion that 'security regimes' reflect the priorities of a very limited 'public interest' (Shearing 2006), to the point that 'security' increasingly stands as a 'club good' monopolized by the few (Crawford 2006).

The partnerships between corporate South Africa and government should not be seen simply as responses to rampant crime. Rather, such developments are perhaps better understood by reference to a context wherein the roles and functions of governing authorities were being significantly remodulated and revised (O'Malley 1992; O'Malley and Palmer 1996; Stenson 1993; also Rose 1999). For the government as for industry, state action no longer comprised the 'delivery of goods [and social services] to a passive citizenry' (ANC 1994, 6). Instead, an enabling role came to the fore, one which aimed to foster the exercise of free choice, responsibility, independence and efficiency in all spheres of life. As regards the economic sphere, the state provided the necessary condition for the establishment of rational and efficient market relations by maintaining basic levels of public tranquillity and security. It is thus through the discursive construction of the state as the primary guarantor of public safety that commercial anti-crime investments became tied to transformations of the SAPS.

The apparent need for a strong sovereign authority – to control crime and thereby enable the operation of a free market – is perhaps best understood not as a vestige of an *ancien régime* for governing (Garland 1996), nor as a core principle of liberal rule (Stenson 1999, 2005), but in terms of its articulation with specific political programmes and the achievement of particular ends set out in local political agendas (O'Malley 1992). It is in part because crime posed a threat at the macro-economic level – that is to inward foreign investment – that business in South Africa organized collectively to assist government in playing its leadership role in practices of crime control. I have discussed the various kinds of technical expertise offered by business to enable the police to respond directly and forcefully to crime and the threat of crime. This involved the innovative use of existing technology, such as cellphone networks, for crime control purposes (for example, surveillance), uses that were not part of the original product design. Further, the application of legal powers was focused on the poor and the marginalized and on controlling the threats posed by risky populations within urban spaces. Industry also promoted reliance on statistical resources in the 'fight against crime'. Through various statistical devices, such as crime indices and performance audits, political authorities were able to 'conduct the conduct' of members of the public and police from a distance. Subsequently, citizens were expected to moderate their behaviour in light of information on 'actual' crime levels while police performance was measured by matching resources to outputs.

However, all this might be beside the point since business partnerships with government were also entered into amidst the palpable sense of political vulnerability among the corporate sector. Whatever else, corporate South Africa was anxious to guard and preserve its own power, including its power to marshal coercive forces in the maintenance of its own interests. Crime control was a tactical manoeuvre calculated to help forestall attempts to curb corporate influence, monopoly power and access to the organized means of violence. The BAC and Nedcor campaigns, therefore, projected an image of 'good corporate citizens' and high profile anti-crime initiatives were intended to reassure, persuade and convince government that business was not a challenge to state authority. Here, then, we see the mobilization of discourses of responsibilized citizenship for decidedly illiberal ends.

Chapter 5

Crime Control and Community Authorities

> The people's courts play a nation-building role … [they have] a long term role even when we have a new government and even if this government is a people's government. They are not a temporary phenomena related to the struggle against apartheid. They will continue to play a role because people feel more comfortable in the people's court than in the formal court.
>
> Shela Mgubane, community activist
> Community Courts Conference (Port Elizabeth 1993)
> (in Nina 1995a, 45)

Introduction

On 4 March 1997, a mother whose son had committed assault with a bat appeared before the relevant authorities. She recounted how she had apologized to the victim for her son's actions. Although the victim had initially rejected this apology because of the brutality of the assault, she later accepted it. This account by the offender's mother was given to the authorities in the absence of both the victim and the offender (who had since run away from home). The victim was summoned to verify the events as relayed by the mother.

This case, revealed through fieldwork, is interesting for – amongst other reasons – the following reason: it was not the public police or the formal state courts, but the street committee that exercised authority in this matter. These community structures, located within the poorest sections of urban black townships and informal settlements, were formed by township inhabitants to address various concerns, including crime and insecurity, within their immediate locale (Schärf 1989; Seekings 2001). Where the affluent, predominately white, urban population had ready recourse to the police as well as the private security industry, poor, black, township residents – the most likely victims of crime, especially violence (Shaw 2002) – had little option but to enlist the services of voluntary, community-based structures such as street committees if their security needs were to be assured. The concentration and proliferation of street committees in poor black communities indexes a persistent and marked condition of inequality in the distribution of and access to policing resources.

The form and content of street committees have changed over time, as has the response of political authorities. Oral testimony indicates that prior to the mid-70s, street committees,[1] especially those operating in townships in and around Cape Town, attended to disputes between neighbours and to issues of urban township living: price hikes in rents, bread and milk; routes and costs of buses and trains; poor signage, street lighting and housing conditions; funeral expenses. The apartheid regime established informal links with the committees because it needed information for its regulatory interests, such as influx control and housing allocation. This relationship appeared mutually beneficial: street committees were aware of all newcomers to the townships and whether they held valid work and residential permits, while government officials were in a position to address the administrative-related concerns of rent increases, bus routes and so on.

The mid-70s to mid-80s saw a politicization and polarization of street committees. Previously, the committees worked with, yet remained independent of, state structures. This changed as the state sought to co-opt committee chairs and other senior members into local government schemes, and offered them positions as community councillors. This was part of a much wider shift in national policy following the 1976 Soweto uprisings, in which rule was still to be accomplished through command but was now to be administered by blacks themselves. Some street committee members, realizing that this limited empowerment of the individual was at the price of collective freedom (that is, for all Africans), either resigned from the committees or restricted the committees' role to managing disputes as opposed to operating as a civic association. Others made a strategic decision to align themselves with the apartheid regime and became community councillors; the committees that they headed assisted local authorities in implementing apartheid policies, but less so as a means of securing attention to poor housing conditions etc. and more as an end in itself.

Popular opposition to the local governing bodies and their associates – denounced as 'state puppets' – grew throughout the early 1980s. During the next few years new community structures sprang up which, together with those committees free of community council influence, were broadly aligned to the anti-apartheid struggle (Ditlhage nd). Oral evidence suggests that both old and new street committees were sites for the practise of a local and national politics of freedom. Established as institutions of 'people's power' (Seekings 2001), the committees operated parallel to state systems, signalling both a defiance of state authority, especially in the realm of policing and justice, and the capacity for self-rule. Street committees coordinated and policed local consumer and rent boycotts in opposition to township councils and by extension the central state who set up the councils as a substitute for the extension of national political rights to blacks (Seekings 1992b). At the same time, street committees were sites for pre-figuring justice (Schärf and Ngcokoto 1990): they articulated and enforced a non-racist vision of justice, society and morality grounded in notions of popular democracy (see also Crais 1998; Nina 1995a). Thus, street committees not only contested state power, but also provided alternative

1 In tracing out the history of interaction between street committees and the apartheid regime, I draw substantially from Schärf's work (1989, 1991; see also Burman and Schärf 1990). The discussion is also informed by interviews I conducted and which are detailed in the 'Methods' section of this chapter.

structures for ordering individual and collective existence. As these community-based structures became increasingly politicized, state repression intensified: participants were detained, arrested and tried for treason, sedition or subversion (Pavlich 1992). By 1988, these measures succeeded in crushing most of the estimated 400 people's courts in operation throughout the country.

Doubtless, I have oversimplified matters; but my concern lies less in providing a detailed historical account than in stressing the changing character of the street committees and of apartheid policies in regard to these township structures. Seen against this backdrop, a significant shift in the dynamics of township ordering was witnessed in the early 1990s. Under the umbrella of politically unaffiliated civic associations (the civics), street committees re-emerged with a strong anti-crime focus (Nina 1995a; Seekings 1992a and b). In the unfolding period of the negotiated transition to democracy, the civics and state authorities entered into discussions over reforms to urban policy, including the division of crime control roles and responsibilities at the township level and the establishment of a cooperative approach to managing crime.

With the aim of consolidating their gains and strengthening their bargaining power, the civics initiated projects to regulate the street committees. In particular, training programmes run by non-governmental organizations (NGOs) (Nina 1995a) came to provide the answer to concerns expressed by civic leaders and others about the lack of accountability to the 'community' and the 'excesses' of the people's courts of the late 1980s including summary and severe punishments. The training involved a form of civics education that included discussion about the importance of rights, process and procedure, precisely the types of tradition widely recognized as lacking in developing nations and that restricted the prospects of political transformation. Thus, under the banner of crime control, efforts were mounted to cultivate democratic sensibilities, that is, a set of core ethical values that would shape the ways in which individuals understood and ordered their own lives and those of others. This amounted to a form of 'democratization through crime'. Crucially, street committees were encouraged and taught to 'act within the law rather than outside it', as a member of the Western Cape Anti-Crime Forum explained (interview 5 December 1997). The training programmes maintained the relative autonomy of the street committees and their members while introducing procedures and processes to render their decisions visible and open to evaluation at the township-wide, regional and/or national levels of the civics.

Street committees had to be made knowable to civics, but also to state officials. Political authorities desired knowledge of the inherent nature and internal norms of the street committees, not so much to reinforce or extend the state's power and control over such structures as to ensure and augment local responsibility for crime control. As Seekings (1992a, 186–7) observed:

> the debate … has centred around the question of the potential role of the township courts in everyday crime prevention and settlement of disputes … the possible prefigurative role of the township courts has moved from a secondary concern to centre-stage … In what amounts to a partial and implicit repudiation of their earlier public analysis, state officials recognise that there are good local and non-party-political reasons for township residents to undertake illegal policing and judicial roles.

Rather than being viewed negatively, street committees came to acquire a more positive value linked to the self-fashioning of individual and collective existence.

In this chapter, following a discussion of methods, I document the contemporary operation of community-based anti-crime structures as simultaneously located on a technical and ethical register. Following leads from Stenson (2005, 1999) and colleagues, these localized projects and agendas for managing crime are best regarded as governmental in their own right, rather than as mere instances of abstract political strategies formulated elsewhere by state agents (Stenson and Factor 1994, 1996; Stenson and Watt 1999; also: O'Malley, Weir and Shearing 1997), because, as we have seen, township communities exercised local governing schemes long before the state made community responsibility for problem-solving a formal and generalized requirement.

The relevant literature tends to analyze strategies for communal and self-regulation in terms of their relation to the state. This is especially so because these accounts look for the origins of localized governing practices and finds them in the state. Street committees are often said to have come into existence because the state failed to adequately police the townships – either because it lacked the resources or because it had no interest (see Knox and Monaghan 2002; Nina 1995a; Schärf 1989). Of course, local governing bodies had to adjust themselves to state practices of rule; but they were not simply responsive or resistant to state policy. They were much more besides this. They had their own governmental agendas, and local actors sometimes enlisted state agencies in their local governing schemes and sometimes they themselves were enrolled in more formalized projects (O'Malley, Weir and Shearing 1997; Stenson 1998, 2005). While informal policing programmes certainly did not have the character of the veridical discourses examined by Foucault, it is possible to detect a certain rationality that is inscribed in these practices – a certain regularity in conceptions of the objects, subjects and tasks of government.

The next section investigates projects for the governmentalization of street committees. I analyze the NGO-sponsored training programmes for reshaping the self-ordering practices of the street committees. The training was crucial to the constitution of township residents as liberal democratic citizens and of street committee members as *anti-crime technicians*, para-experts who drew on non-scientific knowledge for regulating, understanding and modifying the conduct of others with whom they were 'in community'. While regarding ordinary citizens as competent calculators of the crime risks they face, NGO certification (Nina 1995a) and licensing (Roche 2002) programmes retained a rather technocratic view of security provision. Certificates and licenses rendered the street committees credible and legitimate in the eyes of state partners (for example, the police and municipal authorities), but mattered less to township residents whose reliance on these committees was more pragmatic than principled (Baker 2002).

In the final section, I look at the constraints on street committees and how these impacted on projects and strategies aimed at governing their operation. It is difficult to achieve and sustain active, responsibilized community involvement in problem-solving if their participation is voluntary and they lack crucial infrastructural resources – housing, electricity, running water – and often have to raise these themselves; that is, where the state fails to provide communities with basic conditions for existence.

This presents challenges to contemporary national and international developments to institute localized, community-based mechanisms in the crime control field – for example, community policing (Bayley and Shearing 1996), restorative justice (Braithwaite 1989; Roche 2002) – and in other fields such as health and education.

Research Methods

Practical rationalities of governance at the local level are evidenced not only in textual and documentary forms, but also in oral and cultural practices (Stenson 1998; Stenson and Factor 1994, 1996; Stenson and Watt 1999). Accordingly, this chapter draws on a range of methodologies.

Data collection occurred during 1995–97. This involved the use of semi-structured and open-ended interviews with: street committees; civic associations; anti-crime forums; NGOs working on community policing/safety issues in the Western Cape; former operatives of the African National Congress's (ANC) now defunct military wing; the South African Police Service (SAPS); policy advisors to the National Commissioner of Police, as well as to the national and provincial (Western Cape) Ministers of Safety and Security; and key researchers in the area of informal justice in South Africa. Documentation produced by the Community Peace Foundation, an NGO involved in the training of street committees, was also analyzed and were part of the discussions with respondents. In addition, the research included observations of the NY141/140/143 street committee (which I will refer to as NY141) in Guguletu, Western Cape. Guguletu had a well-developed civic structure, the South African National Civic Organization (SANCO), to which NY141 and most of the other street committees in the township were aligned, as well as a long history of self-policing (Holtzman 1994; Mncadi and Nina 1994; Nina 1995a; Ngcokoto 1997; Seekings 1992a and b).

Between February and April 1997, I attended seven of NY141's 'Tuesday meetings' held from 7–9 p.m. While these were public meetings, the meaning of the term 'public' is fairly restrictive; in this instance it referred to the mainly adult residents of a cluster of three streets – NY140, 141 and 143. Thus, access to the street committee had to be negotiated. A former secretary of the committee, who at the time of my research was also the publicity secretary of SANCO and an NGO fieldworker, facilitated my attendance at the weekly meetings. On my behalf, he approached the committee members and explained my interest in observing their proceedings. Consent was readily granted. He accompanied me on my first encounter with the committee, introducing me at the start of the meeting. He subsequently translated, for those members who spoke little or no English, the short presentation I was invited to make on my research interests.

This particular route to access the street committee appears a little unusual. Ngcokoto (1997), when researching Guguletu's NY153 street committee, was informed that permission to conduct interviews could only be granted by SANCO. Indeed, discussion with several researchers confirmed that direct negotiation with SANCO, rather than street committee members themselves, *was* the normal course of action for researchers. But this is not to suggest that the NY141 street committee made an exception in my particular case. Rather, this street committee was somewhat peculiar: it had routinely encountered academics since 1993,[2] which resulted in a degree of informality in relation to the granting of access, though access very much depended on 'sponsorship' by a committee member or other respectable resident of the locale. Thus, the attendees at one meeting included three foreigner researchers (including me). On another occasion, the Chair of the street committee extended an open invitation to anyone that I might have wanted to bring to future meetings.

The more or less continuous presence of outside observers also meant that the NY141 street committee was sensitive to language issues. All of the meetings were conducted in Xhosa[3] and many members had only a limited command of English. However, the committee anticipated the need for translators where visitors like myself, or parties to a dispute, spoke no or little Xhosa. This stands in contrast to Crehan and Shapiro's account of an NGO worker's encounter with a street committee: 'I had great difficulty understanding, because no one was prepared or even thought to translate, you know, this is their thing, this is clearly their meeting and I sort of stumbled along with the five words of Xhosa that I know …' (in Crehan and Shapiro nd, 13).

At the first meeting I attended, my sponsor acted as my interpreter. At the conclusion of that meeting, the committee resolved to ask a local resident to attend future Tuesday sessions as my translator (the resident, a single man over the age of 35 who lived with his mother, was considered a youth and thus did not regularly attend these meetings of adults). On the occasions that my translator was absent, the Chair of NY141 asked an elderly male committee member to perform this function; the same member later assisted as an interpreter in a case involving an Afrikaans-speaking complainant. My presence, far from being minimal, veered towards the intrusive as the Chair often deliberately interrupted the pace of the meetings to allow for a translation of the immediate proceedings.

The translations, which I noted in longhand, form the basis of the analysis that follows. A tape recorder was not used in an effort to minimize further disruption to the meetings. Undoubtedly, the details of particular disputes, some of which were resolved over the course of several meetings, were lost in the translation process. However, my interest lay less in rendering a faithful account of particular cases than in understanding how street committees produced truths about the subjects before them. Through what means, techniques and forms of knowledges did they operate, and with what effects?

---

2 In 1993–94, the committee underwent 'training' in human rights with an NGO affiliated with the University of the Western Cape. The content of this training is discussed in detail in this chapter. During the mid-1990s, students of the Institute of Criminology (University of Cape Town) visited the street committee as part of their fieldwork electives (Schärf – personal communication, 25 February 1999). In 1996, the same committee member who 'sponsored' me in my fieldwork research made a presentation on the nature, operation and role of the Guguletu residents' associations at the fifth annual National Conference on Police Accountability held in Chicago (Storer 1996).

3 One of South Africa's 11 official languages. Xhosa also denotes ethnicity (that is, of the Xhosa nation).

While NY141 appeared atypical in its interactions with, and courting of, researchers, its procedures and practices for managing conflict and restoring order resembled those of other SANCO-aligned street committees in Guguletu and elsewhere – for example, Alexandra (Gauteng), Port Elizabeth (Eastern Cape) and Pietermartizburg (KwaZulu-Natal) (see Nina 1995a). Indeed, in 1992 SANCO initiated, at national level, a self-regulatory project to standardize and regularize the structure and process of informal, community-based justice in the townships. In 1994, it adopted a uniform set of guidelines for the operation of street committees in Guguletu. I analyzed these and other NGO training documents.

Guguletu Street Committees: Structure and Process Since 1990

For a variety of reasons – the apartheid policy of racial segregation, anti-slum provisions and public health legislation (Parnell and Mabin 1995) – non-white populations were forcibly extracted from the inner city during the early twentieth century and exiled to areas well beyond the city centres. Vast numbers of people were consigned to small, often inhospitable tracts of land. The vernacular term for the townships – 'location' – bears witness to this removal imperative of the apartheid regime.[4]

One of the oldest black townships of Cape Town (Western Cape Province) is Guguletu. It was established in 1954 for migrant workers from the Eastern Cape employed in the Cape Town metropolitan area (Burman and Scharf 1990). It is divided into four quadrants – Sections 1 through 4 – and in the mid-1990s was home to approximately 350,000 inhabitants, most of whom were Xhosa-speaking. During the research period, two civic bodies coexisted in Guguletu: (a) the Western Cape Civic Association (WCCA), which had emerged in the 1980s as an umbrella body of various organizations (both black and coloured) opposed to the Community Councils and Urban Bantu Councils set up by the apartheid regime; and (b) SANCO, a coordination body formed in 1992, which encompassed myriad civic structures regardless of the political affiliation of those structures.

SANCO predominated: according to its publicity secretary in Guguletu who was also a former NY141 member, 95 per cent of the township was SANCO aligned (interview 28 May 1998). The organization was and remains a multi-tiered hierarchical structure. The highest level in the township, SANCO Guguletu-Local, comprised four branch (or zone) committees. Branch committees were composed of several area committees and these in turn were made up of a number of street committees, which were represented by the chairs and secretaries. Representatives at each level were democratically elected by their (adult) constituency. The civics liaised with local, provincial and national governments for the attainment of basic human needs for township residents, such as housing, sewerage, electricity and water. However, the primary function of the civics was not one of service delivery, but of 'monitoring

4 Although Burman and Schärf (1990) observed that in Cape Town separate black 'group areas' predated the apartheid policy by nearly 50 years: 'In 1901, legal measures forced almost all Africans to move into a specially created African town, Utivlugt (renamed Ndabeni in 1902)' (*ibid.*, 697). In 1927, Ndabeni residents were – again – forcibly relocated to a new township, Langa, and by 1935 Ndabeni no longer existed (*ibid.*, 698).

the behavior and action of the government at all levels' (Kobese 1996, 35). The civics no longer positioned themselves in competition with, or as surrogates for, state structures, but as representatives of township residents in negotiations with various political authorities for the provision of minimum conditions of existence (Seekings 1992b). Beyond this oversight role, the civics organized anti-crime drives at the local level, not in opposition to the state's ordering practices, but as an expression of the liberal democratic principle of responsible self-government.

The lowest tier in the civic associations, the street committees, sometimes called popular justice mechanisms (Nina 1995a) or people's courts (Schärf and Ngcokoto 1990), functioned as *community-based structures for the establishment and defence of communal security*. Generally, each committee exercised jurisdiction over residents of a particular street, normally 32 houses with, at times, upwards of 12 people per house. NY141 appears somewhat unusual as it encompassed three streets[5] in Guguletu Section 3. 'Community' here designates a zone of shared commitment to a rather limited geographic locale. Such commitment is voluntary, not imposed: 'community' consists of networks of relations entered into for mutual benefit, that is, for maximal protection against crime and other risks. Specific content also attached to the 'security' concept: the security role performed by street committees had both a social welfare and a social ordering component (Pavlich 1992; Schärf 1989, 1991). The social welfare component included the organization of and participation in various social events (for example, ceremonies surrounding births, marriages, initiations) and the operation of a kind of collective insurance policy where residents contributed a certain sum of money towards the funeral expenses incurred by any family in the street.[6] The disciplinary committee of the street committee undertook the social ordering function. Elected by the adults of the community, this sub-committee consisted of a chair, a secretary and an orderly of sorts, as well as the 15-member executive committee of the street committee. Only adults (both male and female) were allowed serve as street committee members, with age (24+), marital status (married, preferably with children) and home ownership signifying adulthood. The election of adults to the disciplinary committee occurred by way of nomination and seconding. Students and adults could volunteer for other types of community service. According to a street committee member, such volunteerism was considered a 'blessing', 'a commitment that is not challenged' (interview 28 May 1998).

The disciplinary committee dealt with various problems between neighbours. No distinction was made between civil and criminal cases; all problems heard by the disciplinary committee were seen as torts or civil harms (Schärf 1991; Williams 1996). This downgrading of crimes to problems suggested that the law was not the primary mechanism for ordering at the community level (discussed further below). Typical cases before the street committee included theft, robbery, property damage, alcohol-related incidents, physical assaults (stabbings, beatings, slappings),

5 One street committee member suggested that SANCO adopted the concept of an Area Committee from the NY141 structure (interview, 3 February 1997).

6 During the fieldwork period in NY141, each family contributed R5 after the death of any resident. In NY142, by contrast, R20 payments were deposited by residents into a bank account to be withdrawn in the event of a resident's death (Ngcokoto 1997, 11).

child welfare concerns and contractual issues (unfinished jobs, payment owing for completed work, debts). Intra-familial conflicts – for example, disputes over rightful occupation of a house or physical confrontations between relatives – were in the first instance handled within the extended family and only once this route was exhausted was recourse to the committee considered. The familial bond marked the limits of the street committee's authority and capacity to intervene. Family relationships appeared as the most important bond between individuals, but also the most fragile, its mechanisms of self-regulation easily disrupted. Care had to be taken to ensure that the autonomy of the family unit was not breached or compromised. Indeed, I did not, either during the course of the fieldwork or in the available literature for the post-1990 period, come across the involvement of the disciplinary committee in any case involving spouses (though reports indicate that marital disputes were addressed by street committees in the late 1980s; see: Burman and Schärf 1990).

Two other situations highlighted the question of the jurisdiction of street committees. The first was where a dispute occurred between parties who resided in different streets. In such an event, a meeting between the two relevant disciplinary committees was called so that the incident could be jointly resolved. Secondly, since the early-1990s, Guguletu street committees and those in Cape Town and elsewhere (for example, Alexandra, Gauteng) generally regarded child abuse, rape and murder as the responsibility of the state system of criminal justice (Kobese 1996; Mncadi and Nina 1994; Nina 1995a; Ngcokoto 1997; Schärf 1991). The reason why such cases were deemed beyond the purview of community structures remains unclear: perhaps competency in investigative skills was at issue or perhaps such cases evoked strong desires for the exclusion of the offender from the community through detention or imprisonment – sanctions understood as legitimately available to the state alone. But exceptions existed. Nina (1995a) notes the case of a single woman who reported a young man for attempted rape and physical assault: 'She decided to take the case to the police, because as a teacher in the community she has a reputation to maintain' (Nina 1995a, 66). Her father, an active committee member, along with the rest of the street committee, persuaded her to drop the charges and have the case heard at the community level. Nina offers no explanation for this departure from the general understanding of rape cases as the proper concern of state officials.

Yet, whatever the reasons and exceptions, it is certain that street committees usually directed particular complaints to the police authorities. Equally apparent, as several commentators remark, is that the police generally advised disputants to report specific matters – petty theft, debt repayments, physical assaults – to the street committee (Mncadi and Citabatwa 1996; Mncadi and Nina 1994; Ngcokoto 1997). Nina (1995a) argues that by 1993–94, an informal referral process existed between street committees in some Cape Town townships and the police, prosecutors and the Magistrates' Court. Clearly, the functional jurisdiction of street committees was one that was negotiated with state structures, rather than determined in isolation. It is tempting to attribute the development of this informal referral network to the strategic decision-making of particular individuals – the enlightened judge, the community-minded police commissioner or the highly respected committee member – in the context of rising crime rates and fear of crime, and visible limits and failures on the part of the police. However, the dividing up of crime control responsibilities between state officials and local authorities is better understood in terms of an emerging rationality of rule that constituted individuals as active and responsibilized citizens. Citizens, taken at the individual and collective level, were encouraged to assume an active role in resolving their own problems by seeking out approved ways of privately securing themselves against crime and other risks (see Stenson 1993, on the link between governmental rationalities and policing in the West). In the section on expertise, below, I discuss how street committee members were made responsible.

Spatial Arrangements and Crime Control Authority

Foucault's work highlights the importance of attending to the different ways in which space is constituted and organized in the exercise of power (see Foucault 1977). In his discussion on popular justice with the Maoists (Foucault 1980), he observed that the spatial arrangements of the court revealed much about the complex relations between individuals, knowledge and power. He described the people's court during the French Revolution as follows:

> judges behind a table, representing a third party standing between the people who were 'screaming for vengeance', and the accused who were either 'guilty' or 'innocent'; an investigation to establish the 'truth' or to obtain a 'confession'; deliberation in order to find out what was 'just' ...
>
> (Foucault 1980, 2)

For present purposes, Foucault's claims that is was impossible for the court (as a neutral intermediary between the masses and its enemies) to dispense popular justice are less interesting than his view that the relations between subjectivity, truth and politics were implicated in the very spatiality of the court. This suggests that the structural organization of the Guguletu disciplinary committees was crucial to the exercise of power.

During the fieldwork period, the disciplinary committee met in the garage of one of its members. As the garage was still being used for its original purpose, the meetings were often preceded by the laborious task of starting an old car and reversing it out. Unsurprisingly, the meeting place was dreary and inhospitable. The garage was poorly insulated, and during the winter months with no heating system and the south-easterly winds pounding the Cape Peninsula, little perceptible difference existed between the temperature inside and out. A naked bulb provided much needed light. Against the walls, long wooden benches were stacked one on top of the other. For the meeting, these were placed in rows, filling much of the space between the garage entrance and the back wall, with some benches lining the side walls. A small table and three chairs were set roughly a foot away from the rear wall. Here, with their backs to the wall and facing the entrance sat, in apparently no order, the Chair who facilitated the meeting, the Secretary who recorded the proceeding, and a third person, an orderly of sorts. Immediately opposite on the wooden benches sat the executive committee, other community members and the disputants whose cases were to be heard. No particular seating assignment existed. However, since disputants usually arrived either immediately before or during the meetings, they were often at the rear. This description is not meant to suggest that the organization of the NY141 meetings should be dismissed out of hand as *ad hoc* and as therefore somehow insignificant or less significant.

To begin, though neither removed nor detached, both the Secretary-scribe and Chair-facilitator were separated, by virtue of a table, from the rest of the participants at the meeting. The location of the Secretary illustrates the 'distanced gaze' invoked in documentary practices: the minutes were the recorded observations of someone whose presence was distanced enough to permit an 'accurate' account of the proceedings. And while the minutes were about the proceeding, they stood apart from it: the 'record' represents the entry of lived experience into documentary reality (see Smith 1987, 1991).

Like the Secretary, the Chair was also set off from others at the meeting. This separation signalled the oversight duty of the Chair. As one committee member put it: 'The Chair is a shepherd looking after his sheep. The Chair must have the confidence of the people' (interview 28 May 1998). The Chair exercised a kind of pastoral authority, guiding the meeting participants towards not absolute 'truth', but rather negotiated settlement. The Chair summed up individual contributions and the overall discussion, and identified fruitful areas for exploration and pitfalls to be avoided. And all of this was in order to get not at the 'truth', not to impose guilt and declare innocence, but to ensure the happiness, welfare and security of each and all. But here the shepherd analogy strains; the shepherd, in attending to the needs of each sheep, knows what specific pasture the flock should be heading to (for food, shelter etc.) and can correct any straying off course. In this sense, the shepherd stands above the flock, with a clear view of the telos of the journey (see the discussion of pastoralism in Foucault 1988, 57–85). The Chair of the disciplinary committee, on the other hand, led participants towards the generalized goal of reconciliation. But in terms of the particular conclusions to each dispute, the Chair submitted to the will of the collective: the Chair did not stand completely apart from the participants and had no foresight of the precise solutions to each case. In other words, the role of the Chair was not to take decisions for or on behalf of the disputants or the community. Rather, the Chair assembled residents together so that they could hear, debate and resolve cases collectively, rather than as individuals. The Chair highlighted and ensured the security of the community and of each member by creating the conditions under which everyone at the meeting could contribute to the deliberation about – and resolution of – cases.

The executive committee, disputants and other street residents sat together facing the Chair and Secretary. This inter-mixing suggested, first, that the role of the executive committee was that of peers: their authority derived in and through the 'community'. Secondly, it highlighted the importance of individual and collective experience rather than impersonal rules in the resolution of disputes: 'truth' and 'falsehood' were established in community. Thirdly, it announced that the disputants were not considered 'enemies of the people' (Foucault 1980), but remained an integral part of the community; their involvement in conflicts did not result in their exclusion from the community. And fourthly, it indicated that the objective was one of reconciliation and restitution.

The Meeting

At NY141's weekly two-hour evening meetings that I attended, the number of people present ranged from 10 to 30, with males generally outnumbering females. Street committees had a recognizable and highly structured process for receiving and resolving disputes between neighbours. Below I outline this mechanism of conflict resolution.

Disciplinary committee meetings opened (and closed) with a sung prayer during which all attendees stood. This replaced freedom songs that were used in the 1980s (Schärf, personal communication). The prayer functioned as a small, but effective, technique to foster inclusion and build cohesion among all in attendance. Following the opening prayer, the Secretary read out the minutes of the previous meeting. Prior to accepting the minutes, the Chair asked for any amendments or clarifications. The Chair then asked for any announcements or new cases to be reported. If there were no new cases, the meeting proceeded to consider the cases that had been postponed, carried over or scheduled for that day.

Entering Disputes into Record How did disputes between residents become registered as a 'case' with the street committee? How did issues – such as theft, robbery, property damage, physical assaults, child welfare concerns and contractual difficulties – come to the attention of the street committee? Generally, disputants could report a problem to any executive committee member. However, existing accounts suggest that where one or both parties to a dispute were considered to be 'youths' (in the cultural sense of the term) and where the case had already entered the criminal justice system, then the parents of either party could seek the involvement of the street committee (see Mncadi and Citabatwa 1996). Complainants did not, however, forego their right to proceed through the criminal justice system. In fact, this option was often kept open precisely to ensure the respondent's cooperation and compliance with the street committee (Nina 1995a).

Regardless of how the dispute entered the informal system, all complainants were eventually directed to the Secretary who recorded the 'case' and advised the individuals to attend the next meeting. The Secretary also notified defendants, in writing, of the case details along with the date of the meeting that they were to attend. If the hearing date presented difficulties for the defendant, the reasons for this were to be outlined in a letter to the Secretary together with an alternative date. This principle of documentation and defendant presence (and active participation, as we shall see shortly) meant that while a complainant could, in the first instance, approach the meeting directly to report an incident, this practice was discouraged; but however a complainant registered a problem, street committee involvement depended upon receipt of a complaint. In other words, the committee acted reactively. Its work was complaint-driven.

Procedure for Resolving Cases What was the procedure by which cases before the street committee were discussed and resolved? What powers and authorities were invoked? First, a due process principle operated: cases were not considered in the absence of either the complainant or defendant and both were provided with the opportunity to be heard. Failure to appear resulted in the committee dispatching 'errand boys/girls' (Ngcokoto 1997, 19) to ascertain the reasons for any absence and/or to accompany the errant party to the meeting. While pressure could be, and often was, brought to bear on the absent party to attend the meeting, it was generally accepted practice that participation was voluntary. Once both parties were present, the complainant was the first party given the opportunity to address the meeting. The complainant stated their case while standing and remained standing while committee members asked points of clarification. The defendant would then rise and put forward their position and answer any questions from the committee. Note that disputants represented themselves: no lawyers were involved. Witnesses before the committee then provided their accounts of the incident under consideration: these were witnesses of fact not of character (that is, not character witnesses for disputants). Discussion and deliberation on the nature and implementation of a sanction followed; this would begin with the Chair asking the complainant to suggest a solution to the problem experienced. Such deliberation was a collective endeavour, with all participants, including and especially the disputants, given a voice. The specifics of the solution – the when, where and how issues – were worked out and endorsed by the entire meeting. Most of the available sanctions involved some degree of service to the community, such as work on a brick project, restitutive fines (compensation for damages, reimbursement for medical costs attributable to the dispute, payment for work completed) or the imposition of a fine on families for the action of their children (Mncadi and Citabatwa 1996). More punitive sanctions included eviction of the defendant from their residence. Corporal punishment, for example whipping with a quirt (sjambok), prevalent during the mid-80s to early 90s (Schärf and Ngcokoto 1990), appeared to be no longer sanctioned by the street committee (Mncadi and Nina 1994; Nina 1994, 1995a; Ngcokoto 1997; but see Buur 2003; Seekings 1992a). On reaching a decision, the committee set in place some method for supervising the implementation of the decision: for example, the reporting back by a complainant or the reimbursement of a complainant in the presence of the committee. The case concluded with the Chair providing a summary of the problem and its resolution and thanking participants for their contributions.

The street committee sought throughout all dispute proceedings to mediate between the conflicting parties. This mediator role was signalled by the fact that the disputants, in presenting their cases, addressed the meeting not each other. Neither party was allowed to cross-examine the other party. Instead, questions and requests for clarifications emanated from the committee. The atmosphere created was not an adversarial one with disputants pitted against each other (Williams 1996). In stating their case, the parties focused less on rebutting, point for point, the other's account and more on contextualizing and personalizing the incident and its consequences. This indicates another role for the street committee: that of conciliator. The committee sought not to arbitrate between rights-bearing individuals, but to reconcile complainants and defendants who, after all, lived side by side. The social ordering practices of the street committee emphasized the significance of human bonds – familial ties, relations of fidelity and interpersonal trust and community-based networks of commercial exchange. Life in the township required a cooperative spirit and prolonged estrangement of neighbours negatively affected the individual disputants as well as the immediate community (Mncadi and Citabatwa 1996). Hence, the collective authority manifest in the committee's decision-making; and hence, the restorative aim of the meeting: it functioned to repair the harm done, to sustain and restore the relationship between disputants, and by extension, to prevent discordance at the community level. Hence, too, the restitutive and reintegrative character of sanctions: the defendant was not to be excluded from the community.

The determination of the 'facts' of the case featured importantly in this reconciliation project. In ascertaining who did what and to whom, the committee relied on two community sources: witnesses to the incident in question and committee members who had situated knowledge of each disputant as well as the relationship between disputants. More crucially, the committee also relied on the accounts provided by the parties in conflict. Indeed, the success of this fact-finding exercise depended on and demanded the active participation of both parties to a dispute; the due process principle and the requirement of self-representation make this clear.

Of particular interest is the defendant's position. Submission to the authority of the street committee required that the defendant freely admit culpability. Guilt could not be imposed nor could the defendant be coerced or compelled into accepting responsibility for an act. The establishment of guilt, or what Ncholo (1994) termed the 'fault principle', was not the primary mechanism for ordering at the community level. Rather, it was merely one aspect in a process aimed at restitution and reconciliation. And the factors that enabled the construction of a solution acceptable to both parties – factors such as willingness to compromise, self-critique and reflexivity – were the same elements involved in the voluntary admission of guilt. Thus, this statement by a committee member: 'If we can't make a person feel guilty in the street committee then it's over …' (interview February 1997). What this points to is the calculated use of shame as a kind of responsibilization technique, shaming as a 'route to freely chosen compliance' (Braithwaite 1989, 10) with a community's established order. The street committee operated a process of shaming, seeking to persuade the person to willingly acknowledge responsibility for the wrong done and in so doing, to take up the offer of reconciliation.

A Question of Legitimacy

As a 'bottom-up' approach to governing in the townships, street committees claimed to be representing the social body of the community – its norms, values, interests and concerns. But as Schärf (1989, 1991) and Schärf and Ngcokoto (1990) indicate, the specific basis for such a claim varied throughout the history of the street committees. Broadly speaking, in the mid-80s, the committees derived their legitimacy from their opposition to the apartheid state and its policies. They claimed authority on the basis of a specific political morality embodied in the anti-apartheid movements. By the early to mid-90s, street committees sought to legitimate themselves by reference to a particular vision of liberal democratic citizenship (Ditlhage nd): the good citizen as an individual with strong moral links to community networks; an individual who exercised a kind of responsibilized freedom in all aspects of life; an individual whose actions were governed not so much through command as through (not in spite of) their capacity to choose. Those who exercised authority (that is, committee members) and those over whom authority was exercised (that is, disputants), were seen to be actively involved in the management of their interpersonal relations, in fashioning their own individual lives and at the same time, actively involved in the betterment of the community. Thus, the individual and the community were not opposed. The street committee meeting afforded residents the opportunity to simultaneously meet their personal and civic responsibilities.

It is certainly true that street committees today continue to appeal to tradition for their legitimacy,[7] that is, to traditional notions of African justice – that body of customary norms and values held in common (Ncholo 1994; Pavlich 1992; Schärf 1991). Street committees deployed discourses and practices associated with the tribal chief's courts of pre-colonial times, in particular: the practices of *Makgotla, Iinkundla, Ibhunga* and *Imbizo*, involving collective decision-making; restorative and relational justice; and the philosophy of *ubuntu*, which promotes humanist values (Mncadi and Citabatwa 1996, 26–7). But even here the focus lies on the active role of the individual in customary regulatory practices.

> Looking at the african customary practice, one realises that ordering within communities was a function of the community as a whole. Each member of the community would take responsibility for the safety and security of such a community and all matters relating to a threat to this kind of ordering would then be dealt with by structures within such communities ... It is this notion which continues to inform the black community's sense of justice that ordering and justice are a *communal and individual responsibility*. [emphasis added].
>
> (Ncholo 1994, 6)

The individual, then, was not posited in opposition to history, with the former valiantly resisting the totalizing advances of the latter. Instead, appeals to tradition contained within them notions, such as freedom, choice and responsibility, in relation to the individual situated in history.

These forms of authority were supplemented by another form of authority. In his expert testimony in a regional (state) court case involving five members of the Thembalethu people's court in the Western Cape, Schärf (1991) argued that street committees were distinguishable from 'kangaroo courts' (see also Seekings 1992a). As a generic term, 'kangaroo courts' refers to 'impromptu forms of revenge, hooliganism and violence' (Schärf 1991, 1). By contrast, street committees were embedded in civic structures, conveying a sense of restraint, accountability and uniformity in form and content. The area, branch and local levels of SANCO formed an appeals system to which a case was referred should the street committee fail to resolve it or should either disputant remain unsatisfied with the process or the decision reached; though, in practice, cases rarely reached the branch or local levels (Schärf,

---

7 Appeals to tradition functions as a device to contrast state and non-state forms of justice. Such appeals also serve to set contemporary street committees apart from the youth-dominated courts of the mid-1980s; the youth had challenged the traditional lines of inter-generational authority by claiming the right to discipline elders and the courts they ran were often seen as dispensing brutal summary punishments (see Schärf and Ngcokoto 1990).

personal communication). Crucially, SANCO and the other civic associations that emerged in the 1990s were formally unaffiliated with any political party: 'Residents belonging to all shades of political opinion are welcome to join civic structures' (Schärf 1991, 47). As Schärf remarked, it is this separation of policing and ordering from party politics that sustains the committees' claims to represent the whole community rather than a narrow segment. I certainly agree with his observation that the authority of the street committees to intervene in conflicts between neighbours no longer appeared to be tied to a 'comrades code' of action and being. However, the street committees' claim to legitimate action was not based solely, or even mainly, on their non-partisanship. Something else was happening here. A clue might be found in the enthusiasm expressed by civic associations themselves for 'professionally-trained' street committees and other community mechanisms of dispute resolution, and the resultant multitude of training programmes and workshops for civic activists run by paralegals and the NGO sector as part of SANCO's self-regulatory project (Nina 1995a; Seekings 2001). The authority of street committees was based on their possession of local knowledge deemed relevant to the equitable and harmonious resolution of conflict in the community and increasingly such knowledge was rendered *technical* through certification, training and the like. Street committees were increasingly claiming legitimacy as anti-crime *technicians*.

Expertise, Liberal Rule and Community Crime Control

The governmentality literature has drawn attention to expertise as a key technology enabling 'action-at-a-distance' which it sees as characteristic of liberal governance (see the collection of articles in Barry *et al* 1996; also Rose 1993, 1994). On this view, experts – those whose authority rests on claims to competency in specialized skills and knowledge – provide a link between those who govern and those to be governed, promising to align the specific concerns and desires of the latter with the general objectives and interests of the former. Expertise here functions as a 'translation device' (Miller and Rose 1990), enabling individuals, populations and organizations to see the aspirations of various political authorities as commensurate with their own goals. Individuals, then, are to act in particular ways not out of fear or compulsion, but because they have come to feel it to be in their own personal interest to do so. Thus, experts enable political authorities to govern without the need for direct intervention, to rule at-a-distance without detracting from the freedom and autonomy of those to be governed. Indeed, it is through, rather than in spite of, the self-regulatory capacities of individuals that liberal rule occurs (Foucault 1979; Rose 1992, 1999). This expresses a key tension in liberal democratic rule: citizens and communities are recognized as operating their own internal logics and mechanisms of self-governance which can not be interdicted, yet must be rendered acceptable to ruling authorities.

In the new politics of security, individuals and communities were urged to assume responsibility for managing crime risks in partnership with volunteer associations, corporate entities and state agencies (DoSS 1996b; also O'Malley 1992; O'Malley and Palmer 1996; Garland 1996, 1997). The anti-crime practices of community-based structures were no longer categorically regarded as a form of political protest or as a reaction to inefficient and ineffective state policing in the townships. Instead, a space opened up for a more positive interpretation of local communities as self-governing in their own right, with street committees as a manifestation of the desire of township residents to raise safety and security standards at both a personal and community level (Ditlhage nd; Seekings 1992a). This, of course, was linked to the reconceptualization of crime as a 'social' issue, rather than as police 'property' (Christie 1978), the solutions to which lay within the local community itself thus necessitating the networking of resources and skills to promote individual and community participation in and control over localized security arrangements (see the discussion in Chapter 2). Van Zyl Smit (1999) identified a critical criminology, which came to the fore during the democratic transition (late 80s and early 90s) and exerted considerable influence in progressive academic circles and beyond – in the broader political field. This criminology emphasized individual and communal responsibility for crime control and the enlistment of voluntary agencies and community groups. As van Zyl Smit observed, such thinking has dominated in the post-apartheid period, with local autonomy in crime control at the centre of virtually all criminal justice policy debates. Discussion documents circulated through the Ministry of Justice – for example, proposals by the Assessor's Co-ordination Committee in 1996 and by the South African Law Commission in 1999 – provided broad support for informal community courts (including street committees), linking these to the development of active citizenship and notions of responsible self-governance (see Schärf 1997; Singh *et al* 1997; also Knox and Monaghan 2002 especially Chapter 6).

The acknowledgement that communities were self-ordering, that they were actively involved in addressing their own problems, gave rise to rationalized programmes for the governmentalization of street committees: a belief that these community-based anti-crime structures were governable and that in governing, one must know the nature of the street committees and its participants as this not only marked the limits of government, but was also 'an essential object, target, and resource for certain strategies, tactics, and procedures for regulation' (Rose 1999, 152; also Foucault 1979, 1997). In other words, the actions and decisions of street committees were to be rendered governable without destroying the capacity of their members for self-regulation.

Liberal projects to 'conduct the conduct' of street committee members did not seek to annex community structures or suppress individual freedom and autonomy as some commentators had feared (see Nina 1995a). Rather, committee members were to be persuaded to participate in managing crime risks and to do so in a manner commensurate with liberal democratic ideals of responsibility, choice and independence. Rule was ideally accomplished indirectly through the self-regulatory capacities of individuals.

The expertise exercised by various NGOs was of crucial significance. Throughout the early to mid-90s, NGOs working in the legal and policing fields forged alliances with government structures, civic associations and street committees (Mncadi and Nina 1994; Nina 1992, 1993, 1995a; Seekings 2001). To the political authorities, NGOs offered to shape the conduct of street committee members so that their anti-crime practices conformed to the emergent human rights discourse and rule of law. To civic leaders, they provided support for existing self-regulatory efforts, holding out the possibility of harmonizing street level practices with SANCO's regional and national objectives and enabling SANCO to engage on its own terms with the state and police in reformulating policing, without, that is, relinquishing its formal autonomy. To street committee members, NGOs promoted a technical approach to problems of theft, robbery, violence etc., entailing the coordination of resources and capacities for action; and they proposed to enhance the existing networking and ordering skills of committee members, promising to transform committee members into anti-crime technicians. Thus, the specific and independent concerns and values of the street committees, civic associations and political authorities were brought into temporary alignment: committee members, civic leaders and state agents came to perceive that 'their problems and goals [were] intrinsically linked, that their interests [were] consonant, that each [could] solve their difficulties or achieve their ends by joining forces or working along similar lines' (Miller and Rose 1990, 10). By mobilizing and promoting the responsibilized autonomy, freedom and choice of committee members, NGOs made it possible to govern street committees without the need to activate the state legal machinery. That is to say, street committees were ruled through their very capacity to manage local conflicts.

I wish to illustrate these remarks on the central role of NGO expertise in projects of indirect rule in liberal crime control by way of analyzing the NGO-sponsored training initiatives for civic activists that emerged in the early years of the 1990s, before the first democratic elections of 1994. During this period, the NGO sector provided training to, for example, SANCO's street committees and anti-crime committees in the Eastern Cape and the Western Cape. This section will focus on the training programmes conducted by one NGO[8] with Guguletu street committees, including NY141. In many important respects, this training was consistent with other projects operating elsewhere in the country (see Nina 1995a for an overview of some of these other training projects).

In 1993–94, a total of 32 committee members from all four sections of Guguletu attended a 32-hour course, run over three weekends (Mncadi and Nina 1994; Nina 1995a). The community policing/safety training simultaneously presupposed and constituted street committee members as active and responsible participants in community crime control mechanisms. The training manual introduced the programme and noted that: 'The first thing to acknowledge is that communities have been active in protecting their members from harm' (Manual, 1). The training programme aimed to enhance and consolidate the existing skills, practices and knowledges of these local governing bodies and authorities. It was 'designed to strengthen community skills in the administration of safety' (Manual, 2). But more than this, it also specified a particular kind of responsibilized freedom and regulated choice in relation to policing and security provision: in addressing conflicts between residents, committee members were not to rely on force and coercion, but were to negotiate and educate and apply paralegal and organizational skills (Guidelines).

8 All empirical material derives from the *Guidelines on Community Policing for Guguletu Street Committees* (in Nina 1995a), and the *Draft Community Policing Facilitator's Manual for Communities*. I will refer to these as the 'Guidelines' and the 'Manual' respectively, citing page references.

That is, the training was designed to instil in street committee members a respect for human rights and for rule of law: a form of 'democratization through crime'.

The street committees came to be seen as an ideal training ground for democratic citizenship. Committee members were taught to see the nascent Bill of Rights and other statutory legal provisions not as constraints on or impediments to the resolution of conflict, but as tools enabling the attainment of safety and security. They were taught to 'place [human rights] within the context of their daily experiences as members of the community and organisations' (Manual, 35). In their daily encounters with other community residents, as in the committees' work, street committee members embodied and promoted a human rights culture which included political tolerance, respect for individual difference and openness to debate and discussion. This emphasized that human rights was not a prohibitive code imposed from above – obedience to which was rooted in fear – but rather a core value shared by individuals as they sought to give shape to their own lives and to conduct relations with others. Nina (1995a) argued that it was this human rights training and not the threat of arrest and prosecution that effectively limited the use of corporal punishment by street committees in dispute resolution. This suggests that street committee members, as well as individuals appearing before the meetings, came to act in approved ways not under threat of compulsion, but because they were persuaded that their specific goals and objectives could be achieved in this way.

The goal of training was to inculcate a human rights approach to the management of crime and other security risks in the townships. This involved inscribing the cases that the street committees dealt with in human rights terms. The rape of a woman became a 'violent offence', a violation of human dignity and bodily integrity. The theft of a resident's car became a 'property offence', the unlawful deprivation of property. The beating of a youth by police became an 'abuse of police powers', an infringement on one's right to freedom and security of the person. But these problems were not so much understood to involve isolated individuals possessing inalienable rights, rather they were seen to involve individuals located in particular moral communities. From this perspective, conflict between neighbours not only affected those parties to a dispute, but also impacted on the communities of which they were members. Crime offended not only against the rights of the victim, but it also threatened the 'peace and stability of the community' more generally (Guidelines). The incidents that the street committees were called upon to resolve were therefore seen as 'community problems'.

The task of the street committees in responding to such collective concerns entailed assessing the appropriate resources and capacities of the community itself (for example, the family and street committees themselves) and of 'outside agencies' (for example, the police, social workers, ambulance services, fire brigade, Department of Education, municipal structures) (see the Guidelines). Street committees were trained in the direction of responsibilized networking with the police and other state agencies. The police did not occupy a privileged position in this security network. They were merely one of many service providers from which the community, as consumer, could choose when seeking to restore order. Cast in their traditional role as 'bandit catchers' (Brogden and Shearing 1993), the police nonetheless appeared as unique given their access to the legitimate use of force. But whereas once relations with the police were at best strained and at worst hostile (Mncadi and Nina 1994) – given that they often wielded force against township residents – the community was now empowered to engage with them on its own terms, without privileging either the police or reactive law-enforcement tools as essential to conflict resolution. As the NGO trainers put it, 'the community through its own organs of ordering, should keep control over the resources as well as the nature of the service to be provided in the area of policing' (Mncadi and Nina 1994, 19). Limited reliance on the police and other state agencies was encouraged and even normalized – not because the police were deemed inefficient or ineffective (though they might well have been), but because the successful management of crime risks required the mobilization of a wider range of service providers (both voluntary and commercial) and resources. Further, it was the community itself, through the street committees, that was tasked with coordinating and monitoring the multi-agency network of security provision. This involved the construction of a 'community profile' of available resources for safety and security, matching the capacity and competency of particular agencies and agents to the specific problem or case at hand. As this discussion makes clear, the training programme imparted new ways of construing both community problems and solutions.[9]

Street committee members were not passive recipients of instruction in such matters. Rather, the community policing/safety programme promoted an 'experiential model of learning' where the training techniques addressed committee representatives as active participants in the learning process. Consider, first, that a 'facilitator' and not an 'instructor' conducted the training. The facilitator was not to provide set answers or judge those responses provided, but was to enable participants to contribute to discussions by drawing on their experiences. The training manual reminded trainers that:

> [their] role [was] to listen to participants and facilitate discussions not to prescribe solutions. In most instances participants had through their experiences, dealt with many issues affecting their safety and … have the answers to issues that puzzle them … you help … [by] teasing out an understanding of policing as something they can/already participate in.
>
> (Manual, 5)

Experience became an invaluable resource for, and object of, training rather than an impediment to it; a move from 'forget all you've done before' to 'let's build on your experiences'. Consider, secondly, the various techniques to maximize the participation of participants. These ranged from limiting the input of facilitators (no more than five minutes per section), to small working groups (for mutual support), flipcharts (confirming the significance of individual contributions) and short, though regular, breaks (maintaining concentration and energy levels). Through these small

9 This strongly echoes the work of Goldstein (1979). Policing, for Goldstein, involved the management of 'a whole range of behavioral and social problems' on a collective, rather than individual, basis (Goldstein 1979, 242). But while Goldstein retained the police as central coordinating figures in the security network, the police were not given priority in the training programme.

and mundane techniques and tactics, the active involvement of committee members in the training process was ensured. Far from being breached, the autonomy and freedom of individuals actually constituted the mechanism through which training occurred.

Various elements of the training programme also laid emphasis on independence, responsibility and free choice in the operation of the street committees. Consider once more the Guidelines, which were designed to ensure a certain degree of uniformity in practices of community self-governance (Mncadi and Nina 1994, 23). These Guidelines were devised by programme participants themselves and adopted by SANCO Guguletu-Local in 1994. The Guidelines offered information on several areas: the definition of community policing/safety; the identification of community problems and solutions; the prioritization of community mechanisms in conflict resolution; the areas for the training of community representatives; educational campaigns to be undertaken by community structures; publicity mechanisms; and the establishment of a People's Forum. The relevant sections of the Guidelines did not set down rules to be rigidly obeyed in each and every situation; instead they outlined general principles, such as human rights and rule of law, that were to guide committee members in the exercise of their crime control responsibilities. The Guidelines thus left considerable scope for responsible choice on the part of committee members.

Consider, too, the new written forms developed for registering cases and notifying disputants of the hearing date (Mncadi and Nina 1994; Nina 1995a, 67). Record-keeping enjoined committee members to practise self-reflexion, making it possible to represent the Tuesday meetings as a *unified process* with a definite procedure for moving from beginning to end: the receipt of a complaint; the setting of a hearing date; the summary of the case details as presented to the meeting; the solutions proposed and accepted; and confirmation that the agreed upon solution had been satisfactorily implemented. The record-book also enabled information gathered on cases to be transported from the street level to the area, branch and local civic structures where decisions of the street committee were reviewed on appeal. In this way, the independent activities and judgments of individual street committees were rendered visible and subject to greater standardization and hence made amenable to comparison and evaluation. The record-book became a crucial tool of accountability, for SANCO required that all appeals and referrals to higher levels be accompanied by documented information on the nature of the 'case', on the reasons for appeal etc. As the NGO trainers remarked, the practice of documentation 'facilitate[d] a better understanding of the history of the case and help[ed] in follow-up situations. Fundamentally, it provide[d] greater legitimacy to the Street Committees: it symbolise[d] a greater level of seriousness and efficiency' (Mncadi and Nina 1994, 22–3). The new recording procedures, along with the Guidelines, appeared to have addressed a central concern about the street committees – the arbitrary and capricious exercise of authority. In all of this, the self-regulatory practices of township residents became the targets and resource of government.

Local Governing Authorities

The NGO interventions discussed above operated with the assumption of, and sought to constitute, individuals as active citizens who exercised 'an "economy" in their conduct of themselves ... striving to increase their quality of life' (Rose 1992, 4). Freedom, choice and responsibility were emphasized as crucial to projects of self-actualization. Personal as well as collective well-being was ensured through the self-regulatory capacities of individuals.

The training programmes also clearly projected an image of street committee members as possessing para-professional knowledge and as practising a kind of quasi-expertise in relation to other members of the community network. Consider, again, the Guidelines and the Manual. Training modules included first aid, negotiation skills, voter education, self-defence techniques, workshop organization and paralegal training. The training was to enable committee members to build 'capacity' to be able to settle conflicts between residents of the street. They were to be aware of the existent network of 'security' agencies – the street committee itself, families, police, social workers, ambulance service, fire brigade, Department of Education, municipal services – so that they could properly direct disputants to those structures best equipped to resolve each particular complaint. The training manual provided various scenarios of problem situations and asked participants where they would refer matters to and what role they perceived for themselves after the referral. It was not intended that participants put themselves in this or that problem situation and try to resolve it thus. Rather, they were asked to resolve a dispute to which they were not a direct party. Equipped with problem-solving techniques, paralegal training and an ethics and politics of rights and law, the street committee strove to shape, correct, manage and intervene in the conduct of disputants and street residents more generally, with the view of enhancing community cohesion and collective security.

Consider also the certification process marking the completion of the training course. The trainers anticipated that the certificate presented to trainees would be useful when a case before the street committee required the cooperation or involvement of state agencies: 'In a sense, the certificates provided documentary evidence of the trainee's capacity to intervene in problem-solving within the community and with the outside community' (Mncadi and Nina 1994, 22). The certificate, which outlined the training modules, confirmed the recipient's competency and technical skills in community crime control and 'help[ed] to improve the relations with the police, magistrates and City Council' (*ibid.*). The training certificate provided the basis for the right claimed by the street committee to take decisions on local safety and security matters. The work of the street committee was represented as rule-oriented and knowledge-based, rather than 'subjective' and driven by emotion or political allegiance. In the process, the relationship between the formal state apparatus and the street committees was transformed: it was not one between service provider and consumer, but among different service providers, both statutory and voluntary. Debates about the operations of street committees shifted from the normative ground – should they have a crime control role? – to the technical – that is, the quality of their training. Therefore, street committee members were not only to exercise self-mastery in terms of the management of their own crime risks. As *anti-crime technicians*, they were also to exercise a kind of localized crime control expertise in relation to other street residents with whom they were 'in community'.

The exercise of this authority was accompanied by a great deal of interest in the moral conduct of the street committees as defined and enacted within the community. Those wishing to become members of the street committee were required to demonstrate qualities of self-control and virtue. In Guguletu, as in other townships, they were to have and maintain a 'good reputation in the community' (the Guidelines); and in carrying out their crime control responsibilities, street committee members were obliged to be impartial, non-partisan, objective and free from the influence of alcohol and drugs (Nina 1995a). Therefore, certain moral attributes were seen to underpin the competencies and skills central to the exercise of crime control expertise. Authority came to be linked with morality in interesting ways.

The rise to prominence, especially in the established democracies of the West, of projects for 'governing through community' (Rose 1996a) – where community is understood as a voluntary network of agentive, expert and independent individuals – suggests that localized expertise, as discussed here, is likely to become increasingly prevalent. Stenson (1999) has described governmental projects initiated mainly outside the state, by an ethnic-religious minority, to secure local territory, enhance ethnic and religious identity, regulate leisure activities and manage perceived risks of victimization and criminal offending (see also Stenson and Factor 1996). Towards these ends, Jewish organizations set out to govern their youth through the activities of professionally trained Jewish street-youth workers and adult and youth volunteers who received psychological training in techniques of conflict avoidance and dispute resolution and classes in Jewish history and identity (Stenson and Factor 1994). Stenson's work aside, the specific forms of knowledge and expertise embedded in and emerging from local projects for governing 'from below' remain largely unexplored, despite the formal recognition among governmentality theorists that liberal democratic rule fosters a range of local governmental strategies beyond the state, for example in the voluntary sector (Stenson 1999; also O'Malley, Weir and Shearing 1997). Further attention certainly needs to be paid to what appears to be a new form of liberal citizenship: a kind of civic engagement in community groups and voluntary associations of civil society – as distinct from both public and commercial sectors – to provide for the security and other needs of communities and those within them.

Constraints on Governance

Sociological writings, in general, and the policing literature, in specific, typically treat the question of programme failure in terms of a problem of either theory or implementation. Failure appears as deviant, abnormal and therefore is to be eradicated. An alternative perspective – that of Foucault and those who have taken up and expanded on his notion of 'governmentality' – regards all those systematic attempts to intervene on and administer reality in relation to particular objectives, as 'congenitally failing' exercises (Miller and Rose 1990, 10).

> The world of programmes is heterogeneous and rivalrous, and the solutions for one programme tend to be the problems for another. 'Reality' always escapes the theories that

> inform programmes and the ambitions that underpin them; it is too unruly to be captured by any perfect knowledge. Technologies produce unexpected problems, are utilized for their own ends by those who are supposed to merely operate them, are hampered by underfunding, professional rivalries, and the impossibility of producing the technical conditions that would make them work – reliable statistics, efficient communication systems, clear lines of command, properly designed buildings, well framed regulations or whatever.
>
> (Miller and Rose 1990, 10–11)

In addition to this issue of programmatic failure, O'Malley, Weir and Shearing (1997) have drawn attention to the multivocality within rule itself, emphasizing the lines of struggle and contradiction among authorities. In such accounts, contestation and resistance appear as integral to practices of government. Thus, failure is to be examined not with an eye towards its elimination and control, nor necessarily with an eye towards evaluating policy (its operationalization or theoretical underpinnings); rather, it is to be investigated as part of the analysis of the practicability of governmental policy. Such an approach directs attention not to spectacular failures, but to the rather mundane factors, situations and occurrences that shape, constrain, prevent or redirect projects for the governance of individuals, populations and organizations. This section addresses two such factors that made difficult the governmentalization of street committees: concerns of a spatial nature and concerns of a temporal nature.

For a period of several months in 1997, the weekly meetings of NY141 street committee did not occur due to the lack of a public venue. Previously, the garage of an elderly male committee member had served as a meeting place. However, immediately following the Easter holidays (during which no meetings were held), this space was no longer available to the street committee. Two explanations for the sudden withdrawal of the garage as a meeting spot were in circulation. First, that the wife of the elderly committee member had grown impatient with these weekly sessions – perhaps it interfered with her business, a convenience store operating out of the house – and she had insisted that the street committee find an alternate location. Second, that a number of renovations to the house were to commence shortly thus rendering the garage unusable. Regardless, the first week of April 1997 marked the beginning of a series of cancelled Tuesday meetings. The committee Secretary hosted the occasional meeting at her home while negotiations for the use of a local school were underway. Generally though, during this period the committee convened 'on the spot' to deal with problems as they arose.

The difficulties in securing a public venue were tied to the lack of financial support – whether government, corporate or community – for street committees. Despite the rise to prominence of a liberal model of community crime control, there was little in the way of funding commitments towards enabling communities to assume primary responsibility for managing crime risks and/or to establish links with state criminal justice structures. Township communities often lacked basic amenities including, at times, permanent shelter, and spatial constraints were such that there were few facilities at the street level large enough to accommodate the public meetings of the street committees. In some townships across the country, though not in Guguletu, NGOs provided offices and trained mediators, therefore helping conflict resolution in the community. While these Justice Centres were linked to civic bodies, mediation was conducted in offices located at some distance from the street where the conflict occurred and involved only the disputants, and made no provision for community participation in the proceedings (Nina 1995a). The complainant and defendant were thus removed from the community, both geographically and relationally. They faced each other as isolated, abstracted entities and the 'dispute' achieved priority as that which linked them together.

In terms of strategies to govern the conduct of street committee members, the *ad hoc* gatherings of NY141 presented a challenge. For herein lay the possibility for individuals to act as individuals rather than as members of a community; to act certainly with autonomy and independence, but not in a responsibilized manner. As one committee member put it:

> There is a regular meeting so that the collective can solve problems. If there are no regular meetings then individuals must react as individuals.
>
> (interview May 1998)

Concrete concerns of accountability (through loosely structured rules), transparency (collective presence and participation) and justice (reconciliation and restitution) were all potentially jeopardized when the public meeting was replaced by a private one. Record-keeping, as a technique for documenting information necessary for the review and appeals process and as a technique that required and enabled committee members to engage in self-reflexive practices faltered. As the situation continued the likelihood increased that residents would perceive street committees not as anti-crime technicians but as renegades, or worse as vigilantes – even if this had little basis in reality – imposing a suspect order.

A second constraint on projects for the governmentalization of street committees concerned the enormous time demands on volunteers serving in community structures. For example, Monday evenings were usually reserved for the SANCO general meeting and Tuesday nights for the disciplinary committee meeting. In addition, on any other night the committee could be called upon to address special situations such as funerals, disputes involving residents of another street or 'sensitive' cases[10] deemed unsuitable for the Tuesday night public forum. Street committees were also actively engaged in a variety of other SANCO-sponsored anti-crime projects (see Tshehla 2002; also Baker 2002, 2004 for a survey of complementary and competing community-initiated policing structures). For example, during the research period, street committees in Guguletu and nearby areas, along with other township residents and with police support, regularly patrolled their different communities under the code name Operation *Kukulekani*,[11] in search of fugitives, illegal weapons and stolen

10 For instance, where a child or youth was the complainant and the family the defendant.

11 Translated as 'free the people from criminal activity'. The groups provided the police with information gathered on suspected crimes, confiscated weapons and stolen goods and made citizen arrests. They saw their role as assisting the police rather than performing their job for them. Similar operations were in place in the nearby townships of Langa and Crossroads (Jacobs 1997).

goods (Jacobs 1997). Unsurprisingly, street committee members felt that these myriad obligations impinged on the relatively little time available for their families and themselves. Township residents, when employed, usually worked considerable distances away in the city centres and suburbs and it was not unusual that 14 hours were spent outside the home, at work and going to and from work. While liberal models of community crime control required politically hyper-active citizens (Rose 1999), the practicalities of life made it difficult to achieve and sustain this hyper-active state (cf. Hirst 1994)

However, it was not only that time commitments were taxing – committee members also expressed frustration and possibly even resentment that they performed many of the safety and security functions that the new democratic government was expected and indeed promised to undertake. Street committees did not see themselves as 'police' or their activities as 'policing': 'I don't want to be police ... I don't want to search anyone', stressed a committee member (interview 3 February 1997). Instead, they referred to their role as one of solving 'problems' (Holtzman 1994). The committee's anti-crime practices represented not an appropriation or usurpation of police powers and authority, but a rational response to the very real problem of rampant crime, under-resourcing of police and under-policing in the townships, in a period where individuals were urged to be self-reliant. Figures supplied by the SAPS (Guguletu) in 1999 showed that, approximately 135,000 people lived in the 7-square-kilometres area of Guguletu which had one police station staffed by 150 members. The recorded crime rate for April 1997–March 1998 was 5,110 crimes of which violent crime constituted almost half (2,513). To township inhabitants lacking a powerful lobbying voice and purchasing power (Shearing 1994), the street committee appeared to offer the best solution to the crime and insecurity problems confronting them.

Government had indeed recognized the crime situation in poor, black townships and elsewhere as a serious social concern and committed itself, in the guise of various strategies and programmes, to fulfilling its safety and security obligations (see the discussion of the NCPS in Chapter 2). At the same time, the state had argued that *successful* crime prevention and control required a partnership approach, with the community (along with business and NGOs) assuming responsibility for managing its crime risks (*Cape Argus* 12 September 1995). In a 1995 interview, the (then) Minister of Safety and Security, Sydney Mufamadi, stressed that 'Crime is everybody's enemy and concern ... the police on their own cannot win the battle. To ensure that communities actively participate in the fight against crime, they should be empowered to take control over their own lives' (in *Imbizo* 1995, 30). The street committee could certainly be seen in terms of the community taking responsibility for its own security needs. However, the concentration and proliferation of these structures in poor, black communities, along with the great number and variety of cases that street committees dealt with, suggested something else: a persistent condition of inequality in the distribution of state policing resources between South Africa's rich and poor.[12]

12 The disparity in policing resources occurred both between regions and population groups. The historical context is important. First, 11 separate and distinct regional forces

When asked about resource distribution in the post-apartheid context, the Special Adviser at the time to the (then) Minister for Safety and Security (Western Cape) highlighted the need to redeploy personnel to assure adequate police representation throughout that province, especially in the townships (interview April 1997). He revealed that 40 'priority police stations' had been identified in the Western Cape as lacking properly trained personnel and key material resources such as computers. In a keynote address at a 1997 conference on security in the Western Cape, SAPS Director Viljoen also discussed the issue of disparity in resource allocation and explained that Reconciliation and Development Programme (RDP) and SAPS funds had been earmarked for the construction and/or upgrading of police stations in 'historically disadvantaged areas'. At national level, 'Project Lifeline', a partnership project involving the SAPS and business (McKinsey Inc. and BAC), identified the country's 100 'most needy' police stations (as detailed in Chapter 3). Interestingly, the Project aimed not to solicit more resources for these stations, but to enable police management to make better use of existing resources; but in many instances state policing resources in the townships were largely non-existent. Nearly three-quarters of the country's police stations were still concentrated in white suburbs and business districts (Pelser *et al* 2000); and those situated in the poor, black areas remained characterized by run-down buildings, understaffing, a shortage of police response vehicles and skilled personnel, a lack of electricity and limited access to phones and other telecommunication devices. Well-to-do communities continued to enjoy the benefits of decades of state investment in white areas, of police infrastructure and personnel, and this was supplemented through the purchase of private security in the form of guards and hardware, as discussed in Chapter 3. By contrast, township residents had no option, it seems, but to volunteer themselves as members of and participants in community structures like the street committee if their everyday safety and security needs were to be assured. Hence the common complaints of committee members: that the government had failed to meet its end of the partnership; that the SAPS had not provided even the minimum levels of safety and security in the townships; that the state had yet to convincingly redress the past imbalance with regard to police resource distribution. Street committees did not advocate for a state monopoly on crime control, but rather demanded that government deliver *basic* security at the community level and sought to influence the state in this regard. What emerges is 'the "reversibility" of relations of authority. What starts off as a norm to be implanted into citizens can be reposed as a demand which citizens can make of authorities' (Rose 1996b, 59). That is, government seeks to activate community and individual involvement in crime prevention and policing more generally (see various documents produced by the Technical Committee on Community Policing in 1995). It is in terms of this very notion of responsibilized citizenship and drawing on the nascent human rights discourse that poor communities agitated for a say in the construction of new police stations, for a say in the selection and de-selection of station commissioners and for much more (see Ferndale, Malekane and Schärf 1994; Schärf 2000).

---

operated before the 1994 creation of a single national police agency (the SAPS). Secondly, prior to 1990, state security forces sought primarily to police apartheid rather than combat 'ordinary crime' in the townships (Brewer 1994b).

Conclusion

Seekings (2001) argued that systematic evaluation of the street committees should include research on the attitude of township residents to these civic structures. In a similar vein, the following questions arise: were street committees successful in restoring relationships between feuding neighbours? Did the human rights training have any measurable impact on the use of coercion to ensure both attendance at meetings and acceptance of the committee's decisions? How effective were the committees in enforcing their decisions? I do not dispute the importance of these and similar issues; but as my discussion of the constraints on governance suggests, indicators of 'success' and 'failure' were themselves integral to and derived their specific content within projects for the government of the street committees. It is these projects that formed the focus of my inquiry in this chapter.

During the first half of the 1990s, both political and civic authorities acted on the street committee 'from a distance'. I have analyzed the forms of expertise that enabled such 'rule-at-a-distance' to occur and that emerged from it. I have highlighted the crucial role of NGOs as conduits between political authorities in the urban city centres, the township-wide, regional or national levels of the civics and residents of particular streets in the townships. NGOs promised to align the local governing practices and strategies of the street committees with the self-regulatory projects of the civics and specific political concerns with human rights and rule of law. In so doing, NGOs both mobilized and helped to constitute the independent, freely choosing, active individual who attended, in a responsibilized manner, to the crime problems confronting local communities.

I have also argued that street committee members were not only urged to exercise self-mastery or individualized responsibility, but also a kind of localized expertise. Committee members were to practice authority over others within a designated locality in order to settle interpersonal conflicts which, if left to fester, threatened to corrode the community network. Such localized expertise is best understood in the context where the roles and functions of various governing authorities were undergoing significant remodulation and revision. The emergent liberal models of crime control, which stressed the responsibility of the individual for managing their own crime risks as well as those of the community in which they are embedded, have yielded interesting consequences. The rich, as illustrated in Chapter 3, were likely to employ the market-based services of the private security industry that not only protected private property, but also patrolled public streets, maintaining a particular kind of order in those communities. The poor, on the other hand, invested a great deal of personal time in community-based structures. In so doing, they acquired and exercised a type of technical knowledge of the network of agencies and resources (within and without the community) that could be mobilized in local projects to resolve crime and other problems. Thus, while individuals were able to assume responsibility for crime control, the precise form that this took varied and must be established through empirical inquiry.

Chapter 6

Conclusion: Coercion, Crime Control and Governance

This concluding chapter explores the implications of this study for theorizing the role of coercion in contemporary practices of rule. In particular, it flags up the need to reconsider the place given by both the governmentality and policing literatures to techniques of compulsion. It calls for greater attention to the intersection of direct and indirect mechanisms of liberal rule in crime control and the conditions under which one comes to prominence over the other.

Contributions to the Policing Literature

That the activity of policing is not coterminous with the institution of the public police is by now a familiar enough observation in academic research. (In fact, this book is partly an experiment in writing about policing transformations without dedicated focus on the public police.) Policing thus involves a multiplicity of state and non-state entities explicitly organized around the management of perceived threats to order that have been variously defined. Bayley and Shearing (1996) use the term 'pluralization' to capture the extent to which government, commercial and voluntary sectors share policing responsibilities.

Statutory-, market- and community-based entities perform a wide range of tasks designed to promote and preserve safety and security considerations. Previous commentators have tended to emphasize policing problems other than crime, and resources other than law enforcement and coercive force, for addressing these problems. Private security, for instance, is often assumed to embody and reflect the same risk management/harm minimization/loss prevention logics that are prioritized by their employers (see Huey, Ericson and Haggerty 2005; Shearing and Stenning 1982, 1983). So, too, are the public police. Their primary role has been redefined as one of maintaining and defending localized order through 'problem-solving' (Goldstein 1979), community-building, partnerships and preventative strategies (see also Bayley 1994; Kelling and Stewart 1989; Moore and Trojanowicz 1988; Moore, Trojanowicz and Kelling 1988; Normandeau and Leighton 1990). Additionally, the public police have been described as 'information brokers' (Ericson and Haggerty 1997). They respond to the routine knowledge-demands of external institutions such as insurance agencies and educational organizations as these institutions seek, when managing subject populations, to identify risks and avert danger. Academic debate certainly exists over whether or not the police *should* prioritize crime control and law enforcement. Interestingly though, it is generally agreed that these practices nonetheless remain the business of the state and its criminal justice agencies. For even where commercial and community interests do express some concern about crime – and this is not often the case, according to existing accounts – the focus is on prevention through risk management (see Bayley and Shearing 1996). Thus, while recognizing that policing is no longer monopolized by the state, the literature nevertheless tends to regard crime control through applications of law and other punitive techniques as the preserve of the public police.

The analyses set out in the preceding chapters of this book demonstrate that neither crime control nor coercion are monopoly practices of the state and further that this fact has generated little public outcry. Crime has emerged as a primary and legitimate object and target of the regulatory strategies of statutory, commercial and community authorities alike. These authorities have turned to a range of security providers. These include civic structures and private security, both of which, today, are among the key performers in contemporary practices of crime control. In seeking to both prevent and respond to crime problems, policing actors of various stripes routinely operate coercive and punitive strategies – measures that impact directly on individual bodies. Sovereign and disciplinary controls of both the non-state and state variety receive massive support from 'below' (that is, from business and community interests) and 'above' (that is, from political and criminal justice officials). The privatization of the legitimate use of force does not necessarily undermine the strength of the central state, as feared by some commentators. As South (1997) has observed, following Ryan and Ward (1989), the state's claimed monopoly does not consist in owning the means of coercion, but rather concerns the power to authorize its use (this claim is underscored and reinforced in and through programmes to train citizens in the rule of law). The right to use force has been extended to large swathes of the South African population and the state has been experimenting with different regulatory regimes in this regard. For example, private security tends to be regulated through legal mechanisms with the public police occupying a key role while street committees are regulated more indirectly, through the expertise of NGOs.

In the conservative writings of policing analysts such as Klockars (1988) and Wilson and Kelling (1982), coercion provides the necessary basis for policing and consequently is/should be a state-owned resource. Such accounts tend to exaggerate the place of coercion in practices of control, seeing this as the essence of (public) policing. Thus, policing appears as an inherently repressive activity. In this book I have adopted a very different approach. This stresses the specificity of contemporary patterns of crime control, tracing through the fragmented conditions of their emergence. Attention centres on the contingent character of policing and crime control, seeing this as an ensemble of authorities, subjects, knowledges, techniques and materials, put together under definite historical circumstances to achieve quite pragmatic ends. If punitive measures come to be seen as appropriate solutions it is in relation to quite distinct and limited problems articulated within particular political programmes.

Coercion, as a workable technique, has been put to innovative and positive use, linked to the production and promotion of liberal democratic modes of citizenship. The conduct of individuals is managed directly, through interventions aimed at training the body, shaping morals and structuring the environment within which human beings make decisions and act. Relations of power operating within the field of crime control actually constitute the *ethically free subject* that acts responsibly in governing itself. The crime control initiatives of government, private enterprise and voluntary community networks not only target actual and potential offenders – held to be responsible for the consequences of their freely taken decisions – but are also increasingly directed towards actual and potential victims – deemed responsible in part for protecting themselves, their families and their communities from victimisation. Rather than power being principally encoded in prohibitions, repression and spectacles of terror, power is here accorded a more productive role in shaping, directing and managing the conduct of citizens (Foucault 1988). Strategies and systems of control certainly may be grounded in violence, and seek to negate or destroy the capacity for agency on the part of a certain individual or group. But liberal democratic practices of rule are precisely that – liberal democratic– in so far as they exhibit a concern to know and to observe the self-ordering and independent reality of that which is to be governed. The conduct of individuals may be governed through the issuance of commands or the imposition of a system of constraints – the legal code of a country, the moral code of a community or the employment code of a corporation – but these achieve their results not so much through fear, but because people themselves want to abide by these codes, finding it in their own best interests to act in approved ways. Speaking to the Johannesburg Press Club in February 1991, Nelson Mandela declared that a politically tolerant, just and democratic society is one governed by law, but that '[o]bedience to the law should not be based on fear, but rather on respect for the law as the expression of commonly held societal values and shared goals.'

Contributions to the Governmentality Literature

This book has demonstrated the utility of the conceptual framework of government – 'the conduct of conduct' – in analysing how the problem of crime is rendered intelligible and manageable in the context of profound political, economic and social transformations in contemporary South Africa. Beyond emphasizing the significance of this conceptual approach in anatomizing current practices of liberal crime control in non-Western environments, this text also seeks to make a modest contribution, at the theoretical level, to studies of governmentality more generally.

First, this study has provided implicit support for recent calls – from those within the 'governmentality school' (O'Malley, Weir and Shearing 1997; Stenson 1998, 1999, 2005) and those outside who are sympathetic to such work (Garland 1997) – for critical reflection on the principal objects and tools of analysis in govermentality work. I have pointed to the importance of attending to practical rationalities of governance at the local level, evidenced not only in textual and documentary forms, but also in oral and cultural discursive practices (cf. Stenson and Factor 1994, 1996; Stenson and Watt 1999). The myriad localized projects and agendas for managing crime problems are best regarded as governmental in their own right, rather than as mere instances of abstract political strategies formulated elsewhere, for instance by state or professional agents or agencies (cf. Gordon 1991). As Chapter 4 has made clear, political authorities have sought to enlist the active assistance of private enterprise in addressing white-collar crime and corruption, as well as in reducing overall levels of crime. Equally, corporate entities have sought to enrol criminal justice departments in specific anti-crime projects for their own particular corporate ends. Informal crime control programmes certainly do not have the character of the veridical discourses (for example, clinical medicine) examined by Foucault. Nonetheless, as I have maintained, it is possible to detect a certain rationality that is inscribed in these practices – a certain regularity in conceptions of the objects, subjects, tasks and limits of government. For example, in terms of the operation of the street committees discussed in Chapter 5, I have pointed to a certain prescriptive way of doing things – how incidents are entered into 'record' as 'cases' and presented to the disciplinary committee meetings, and how solutions are devised etc. I have also highlighted the reasons that exist that ground this particular way of doing things – a burgeoning human rights discourse, African customary tradition, etc. If governance is not to be equated with the functions of state officials, if practices of government are not simply 'imposed from above', then far greater attention needs to be paid to the heterogeneous, practical rationalities of those non-state bodies that seek to govern 'from below'.

Secondly, I have indicated the need to re-examine the now axiomatic interpretation of contemporary liberal governance as indirect rule. According to the governmentality literature, neo-liberal rule occurs 'at-a-distance' (Miller and Rose 1990; Rose and Miller 1992). By this is meant a shift in the locus of rule – the state retreats from centre stage – and a shift in the mechanisms of rule – the conduct of individuals and populations is regulated not through compulsion (acting on the individual, the issuance of commands) but through persuasion (acting through the individual's will and desires, the capacity for self-governance). Governing authorities, on this view, are spatially distant from the governed and rely primarily on compliance-based techniques that act indirectly on population categories to which individuals are linked, rather than directly targeting the individuals themselves. But as was shown, especially in Chapters 3 and 4, it is not at all assured that business organizations and voluntary associations, in taking on new and expanded regulatory functions such as the management of crime risks in domestic and commercial sectors, will not make either routine or selective use of more direct forms of intervention. Thus, we should look carefully at the intersection of indirect and direct mechanisms of liberal rule in crime control, as in other fields, and the conditions under which one comes to prominence over the other.

The governmentality literature, as Stenson (1999, 2005) argues, leaves largely unexplored the persistence of coercive and punitive techniques operated by the state and, similarly, if not more importantly, local governing authorities, as these seek to secure territory and manage populations. As documented in Chapters 2–5, coercive tactics are now prominently displayed in central business districts and relatively well-off residential neighbourhoods and efforts are well underway to equip the police with the latest technological innovations in order to boost their capacity for rapid response. Legal and punitive modes of intervention exist as a background threat in response to failures of the preferred responsibilization strategies. Those individuals who refuse or cannot be managed indirectly, from a distance, are subject to legal and other constraints. However, this book makes the further point that coercive and punitive interventions are not just limited to those on the margins – the recalcitrant, the excluded, the anti-citizens. Coercive controls are not simply mechanisms of last resort, where 'government at-a-distance' fails, but may also function as the preferred strategy – either by itself or in combination with indirect mechanisms of rule – to govern the everyday life of ordinary citizens. This book highlights the *routine* use of coercion in contemporary practices to shape and guide individual conduct. The exercise of legal and coercive authority is foregrounded, linked to prevention as much as control and both in turn may be tied to a model of individual responsibility. In the routine operation of coercive controls, the concern is not so much about the lack or absence of self-restraint, but rather the need to hold individuals to account for their freely chosen actions (see O'Malley 1994). In theory, if not in practice, all South Africans are potentially subject to coercive controls that now characterize daily existence in the 'new' South Africa.

The view of coercion as a viable and effective means of managing crime and securing order has mass support. In particular, there is significant public demand for a retooled, repressive criminal justice system operating with an explicit law and order mandate. It is not only the state, but also, and especially, private enterprise and civic bodies that are key drivers of the process wherein legal and punitive controls come to be regarded as appropriate and indeed desirable solutions to safety and security concerns. Statutory, commercial and voluntary sector actors play a crucial role in sustaining public images of human security as primarily organized around the problem of crime and manageable in large part through strategies for intervening directly and forcefully at the level of the individual. Through mechanisms of persuasion and techniques of translation, state and non-state authorities come to perceive that their own specific interests are somehow bound up with the extension of legal and coercive powers. The exercise of such powers is variously regarded as: a deterrent to crime; a resource for building cohesion and community; the foundational basis for the free play of interpersonal and market relations; and a symbol of the strength of the state, stimulating public and market confidence in the government's capacity to rule.

In highlighting the construction of this 'new' common sense of the necessity of legal and punitive controls, this book points to the possibility of thinking and acting otherwise, of questioning precisely such common-sense interpretations of the centrality of coercion in contemporary practices for governing. Coercion is not a universal or inevitable property of rule.

Bibliography

Africa Watch (1991), *The Killings in South Africa: The Role of the Security Forces and the Response of the State* (New York: Human Rights Watch).

African National Congress (ANC) (1994), The Reconstruction and Development Programme (Johannesburg: ANC).

African National Congress (ANC) (1996), The State and Social Transformation. Discussion Document, November <http://www.anc.org.za/ancdocs/policy/s&st.html>, accessed 01 June 2007.

Alonso, W. and Starr, P. (eds) (1987), *The Politics of Numbers* (New York: Russell Sage Foundation).

Amnesty International (1994), 'South Africa: Policing, Human Rights and the Prospects for Free and Fair Elections', Oral statement delivered to the 50th Session of the UN Commission on Human Rights, Geneva, Feb. 4.

Automobile Association of South Africa (1995), *Car Crime Campaign: A Survey of Motorist's Experiences as Victims of Car Crime*, August (South Africa: AA, RSA).

Baker, B. (2002), 'Living with Non-state Policing in South Africa: The Issues and Dilemmas', *Journal of Modern African Studies* 40:1, 28–53.

—— (2004), 'Protection from Crime: What is on Offer for Africans?', *Journal of Contemporary African Studies* 22:2, 165–188.

Ballock, J. and May, M. (eds) (1996), *Social Policy Review* No. 7 (London: Social Policy Association).

Barnes, L. (1998), 'Business set to tackle crime', *The Cape Argus*, 20 April.

Barrow, O. (ed.) (1996), *Criminal Procedure Act 51 of 1977*, 8th Edition. (Cape Town: Juta & Co. Ltd).

Barry, A, Osborne, T., and Rose, N. (eds) (1996), *Foucault and Political Reason: Liberalism, Neo-Liberalism and Rationalities of Government* (London: UCL Press).

Bayley, D. (1994), *Police for the Future* (US: Oxford University Press).

—— (1995), 'A Foreign Policy for Democratic Policing', *Policing and Society* 5:2, 79–93.

Bayley, D. and Shearing, C. (1996), 'The Future of Policing', *Law and Society Review* 30: 3, 585–606.

Beck, U. (1992), 'Modern Society as a Risk Society', in N. Stehr and R. Ericson (eds).

Berg, J. (2004), 'Challenges to a Formal Private Security-SAPS Partnership: Lessons from the Western Cape', *Society in Transition* 35:1, 105–124.

Bohannan, P. (ed.) (1967), *Law and Warfare: Studies in the Anthropology of Conflict* (USA: Doubleday & Company Inc.).

Braithwaite, J. (1989), *Crime, Shame and Reintegration* (Cambridge: Cambridge University Press).

Brewer, J.D. (1990), 'Policing', in H. Giliomee and J. Gagiano (eds).

—— (1994a), 'Some Observations on Policing and Politics: A South African Case Study', *Policing and Society* 4, 175–183.

—— (1994b), *Black and Blue: Policing in South Africa* (Oxford: Claredon Press).

Brewer, J.D., Guelke, A., Hume, I., Moxon-Browne, E. and Wilford, R. (1996), *The Police, Public Order and the State: Policing in Great Britain, Northern Ireland, the Irish Republic, the USA, Israel, South Africa and China*, 2nd Edition. (London: Macmillan Press).

Brogden, M. (1994), 'Reforming Police Powers in South Africa', *Police Studies* 17:1, 25–44.

Brogden, M. and Shearing, C. (1993), *Policing For a New South Africa* (London: Routledge).

Burchell, D. (1995), 'The Attributes of Citizens: Virtues, Manners and the Activity of Citizenship', *Economy and Society* 24:4, 540–58.

Burchell, G. (1993), 'Liberal Government and the Technologies of the Self', *Economy and Society*, 22, 267–82.

—— (1996), 'Liberal Government and Techniques of the Self', in A. Barry, T. Osbourne and N. Rose (eds).

Burchell, G., Gordon, C., Miller, P. (1991), *The Foucault Effect: Studies in Governmentality* (Chicago: University of Chicago Press).

Burman, S. and Schärf, W. (1990), 'Creating People's Justice: Street Committees and People's Courts in a South African City', *Law and Society Review* 24:3, 693–744.

Business Against Crime (BAC) (circa 1996), *The Time for Action is Now!* (Auckland Park: BAC).

Buur, L. (2003), 'Crime and Punishment on the Margins of the Postapartheid State', *Anthropology and Humanism* 28:1, 23–42.

Canadian Center for Justice Statistics (2004), 'Private Security and Public Policing in Canada, 2001', *Juristat* 24:7 (Ottawa: Statistics Canada).

Canguilhem, G. (1978), *On the Normal and the Pathological* (Dordrecht: Reidel).

Cape Argus (1998),'City blitz zeroes in on crime and grime', 24 August.

Cape Argus (1995),'Police can't do it alone, Omar tells workshop', 12 September.

Cape Times (1998),'Progress by June or I'll quit – Kahn', 18 February.

Castel, R. (1991), 'From Dangerousness to Risk', in G. Burchell, C. Gordon and P. Miller (eds).

Cawthra, G. (1992), *South Africa's Police: From Police State to Democratic Policing?* (London: Catholic Institute for International Relations).

—— (1993), *Policing South Africa: the South African Police and the Transition from Apartheid* (London: Zed Books Ltd.).

Chick, D. (1998), 'Board has inspection rights, says high court', *Business Day*, 18 August.

Christie, N. (1978), 'Conflicts as Property' in C. Reasons and R. Rich (eds).

Cilliers, J. (1997), 'Tentative Remarks on Security Scenario's For South Africa', unpublished Paper, Institute for Security Studies, South Africa.

Cock, J. and Mckenzie, P. (eds) (1998), *From Defence to Development: Redirecting Military Resources in South Africa* (Cape Town: David Philip).

Cohen, S. (1985), *Visions of Social Control: Crime, Punishment and Classification* (Cambridge: Polity).

Comaroff, J and Comaroff, J.L. (2006), 'Figuring Crime: Quantifacts and the Production of the Un/real', *Public Culture* 18:1, 209–246.

Cooley, D. (ed.) (2005), *Re-imagining Policing in Canada* (Toronto: University of Toronto Press).

Crais, C. (1998), 'Of Men, Magic and Law: Popular Justice and the Political Imagination in South Africa', *Journal of Social History* 32:1, 49–72.

Crawford, A. (1994), 'The Partnership Approach to Community Crime Prevention: Corporatism at the Local Level?', *Social and Legal Studies* 3, 497–519.

—— (1998), *Crime Prevention and Community Safety: Politics, Policies and Practices* (Harlow: Addison Wesley Longman Ltd.).

—— (2006), 'Policing and Security as 'Club Goods': The New Enclosures', in J. Wood and B. Dupont (eds).

Crehan, K. and Shapiro, J. (Nd), 'Masking Reality: NGOs and the Concept of Community in the New South Africa', unpublished paper, New York University.

Cunningham, W.C., Strauchs, J.J. and Van Meter, C. (1991), 'The Hallcrest Report II: Private Security Trends 1970 to 2000', *Journal of Security Administration* 14:2, 3–22.

Cunningham, W.C. and Taylor, T. (1985), *Private Security and Police in America* (*The Hallcrest Report*) (Portland: Chancellor Press).

Davis, M. (1990), *City of Quartz: Excavating the Future in Los Angeles* (London: Verso).

—— (1992), *Beyond Blade Runner: Excavating the Future of Los Angeles* (London: Verso).

Democratic Party (DP) (1996), *Winning the War Against Crime: Practical Solutions*, 16 November.

Dempster, C. (2003), 'Xenophobia in South Africa', *BBC News Online*, 15 August <https://news.bbc.co.uk/2/hi/africa/3153461.stm>, accessed 12 January.

Department of Correctional Services (DoCS) (1988), *The Battle Against Crime!* Pamphlet.

—— (2004), *Draft White Paper on Corrections in South Africa* (Pretoria: DoCS).

—— (2005), *Strategic Plan 2005/6-2009/10* (Pretoria: DOCS).

Department of Justice and Constitutional Development (DOJC) (2003), *Annual Report 2002/3* (Pretoria: DOJC).

Department of Public Service and Administration (DPSA) (1997), *Batho Pele White Paper* (The White Paper on Transforming Public Service Delivery) (Pretoria: DPSA).

Department of Safety and Security (DoSS) (1996a), *Annual Plan of the South African Police Service 1996/97* (Pretoria: National Standards and Management Services, South Africa Police Service).

—— (1996b), *National Crime Prevention Strategy* (NCPS) (Pretoria: DoSS).

—— (1998), '*In Service of Safety 1999–2004: White Paper on Safety and Security*'(Pretoria: DoSS).

Dingwall, G. and Moody, S. (eds) (1999), *In the Countryside* (Cardiff: University of Wales Press).

Ditlhage, G. (Nd), 'Associations, Path-Dependency and Democratic Governance: A Case Study of Street Committees in South Africa', Politics Department, University of Witwatersrand.

Dixon, B. (2004), 'Cosmetic Crime Prevention', in B. Dixon and E. van Der Spuy (eds).

—— (2006), 'Development, Crime Prevention and Social Policy in Post-apartheid South Africa', *Critical Social Policy* 26:1, 16–191.

Dixon, B and van Der Spuy, E. (eds) (2004), *Justice Gained?:Crime and Crime Control in South Africa's Transition* (Cape Town: University of Cape Town Press).

Dolling, D. and Feltes, T. (eds) (1992), *Community Policing* (Holzkirchen: Feliz-Verlag).

Doob, A and Greenspan, E. (eds) (1984), *Perspectives in Criminal* Law (Toronto: Canada Law Book).

Dupont, B., Grabosky, P. and Shearing, C. (2003), 'The Governance of Security in Weak and Failing States', *Criminal Justice* 3:4, 331–49.

du Rand, P. (2005), 'Towards an Integrated Justice System', Paper presented at the 'Criminal Justice Conference', Center for the Study of Violence and Reconciliation.

Durrheim, K. and Foster, D. (1999), 'Technologies of Social Control: Crowd Management in Liberal Democracy', *Economy and Society* 28:1, 56–74.

du Toit, A., Lt-col. (1993), 'Community Supported Policing in South Africa – A New Approach', Issued by the Institute for Strategic Studies, University of Pretoria.

du Toit, E. et al. (1993), *Commentary on the Criminal Procedure Act* (Cape Town: Juta & Co. Ltd.).

Ebrahim, H. (2003), 'The Integrated Justice System: How Far We've Come', *Service Delivery Review* 2:3, 46–49.

The Economist (1996), 'South Africa: How wrong is it going?', 12–18 October.

Edmunds, M., (1998), 'Human Rights Abuses Still Widespread', *The Mail & Guardian* 20 March <http://www.mg.co.za > [home page], accessed 01 June 2007.

Ericson, R. and Haggerty, K. (1997), *Policing the Risk Society* (Oxford: Oxford University Press).

Ero, C. (2000), 'Vigilantes, Civil Defence Force and Militia Groups: The Other Side of the Privatisation of Security in Africa', *Conflict Trends* 1, 25–9.

Eskom (1997), Extract from Eskom's Submission to the TRC's Business Sector Hearing (available at <www.saha.org.za/research/publications/SAHA_guidebook_06.pdf>, accessed 01 June 2007).

Eveleth, A. (1997), 'Calls for Private Policing', *The Mail & Guardian*, 12 September <http://www.mg.co.za> [home page], accessed 01 June 2007.

F&T Weekly (1997), Business Against Crime Supplement, 17 October.

Feeley, M. and Simon, J. (1994), 'Actuarial Justice: the Emerging New Criminal Law', in D. Nelken (ed.).

Felson, M. and Clarke, R. (eds) (1997), *Business and Crime Prevention* (Monsey, New York: Criminal Justice Press).

Ferndale, C., Malekane, L. Schärf, W. (1994), 'From Police Station to Community Peace Centre: A New Vision for South African Policing', *Imbizo: Initiatives on Community Policing* 2, 31–38 (Cape Town: Community Peace Foundation).

Fielding, N. (1995), *Community Policing* (Oxford: Clarendon Press).

The Financial Mail, (1997), 'Cashing in on the Crime Dividend', Economy and Business Section, 7 November.

Fine, D. (1989), 'Kitskonstables: A Case Study in Black on Black Policing', *Acta Juridica* 44–85.

Fisher, B. (1991), '"Neighbourhood Business Proprietors" Reactions to Crime [in Minnesota]', *Journal of Security Administration* 14:2, 23–54.

Fisher, G. and Friedman, L. (eds) (1997), *The Crime Conundrum: Essays on Criminal Justice* (New York: Westview Press).

Foucault, M. (1970), 'The Order of Discourse', Inaugural lecture delivered at the College de France.

—— (1972a), *The Archaeology of Knowledge* (London: Tavistock Publications).

—— (1972b), 'Orders of Discourse', translated by R. Swyer, *Social Science Information*, 10, 7–30.

—— (1977), *Discipline and Punish: The Birth of the Prison*, translated by A. Sheridan (London: Allen Lane).

—— (1979), 'Governmentality', *Ideology and Consciousness* 6: 5–21.

—— (1980), 'On Popular Justice: A Discussion with Maoists', in C. Gordon (ed.).

—— (1988), *Politics, Philosophy, Culture: Interviews and Other Writings 1977–1984*, edited by L. Kritzman, translated by Alan Seridan and others (London and New York: Routledge).

—— (1997), *Ethics, Subjectivity and Truth*, edited by P. Rabinow (New York: The New Press).

Foucault, M., Lotringer, S. (ed.) (1989), *Foucault Live: Interviews, 1961–1984*, translated by L. Hochroth and J. Johnston (New York: Semiotext).

Fourie, A. and Mhangwana, V. (1995), *The Prevention and Management of the High Levels of Crime and Violence in South Africa* (South Africa: National Business Initiative).

—— (1996), 'Business Against Crime', *Crime and Conflict* 5, 6–8.

Francis, P., Davies, D., Jupp, V. (eds) (1997), *Policing Futures: The Police, Law Enforcement and the Twenty-First Century* (Great Britain: MacMillan Press Ltd.).

Frankel, P., Pines, N. and Swilling, M. (eds) (1988), *State, Resistance and Change in South Africa* (Great Britain: Belling & Songs Ltd.).

Garland, D. (1996), 'The Limits of the Sovereign State', *The British Journal of Criminology* 36:4, 445–471.

—— (1997) '"Governmentality" and the Problem of Crime: Foucault, Criminology, Sociology', *Theoretical Criminology* 1:2, 173–214.

—— (1999), '"Governmentality and the Problem of Crime', in R. Smandych (ed.).

—— (2000), 'The Culture of High Crime Societies', *British Journal of Criminology* 40:3, 347–75.

Garson, P. (1996), 'Security Firms Linked to Violence', *Weekly Mail & Guardian,* 22 March <http://www.mg.co.za> [home page], accessed 01 June 2007.

Gastrow, P. (1997), *Rapid Transformation and its Impact on Crime*. Address at UCT Summer School (Jan. 28/97) – Crime and Punishment.

Giddens, A. (1990), *The Consequences of Modernity* (Stanford, Stanford University Press).

Gifford, G. (1997), 'Crime Fear as Soldiers sit Idle', *The Star*, 15 December.

Giliomee, H. and Gagiano, J. (eds) (1990), *The Elusive Search for Peace: South Africa, Israel and Northern Ireland* (New York: Oxford University Press).

Gilligan, G. and Pratt, J. (eds) (2004), *Crime, Truth and Justice: Official Inquiry, Discourse and Knowledge* (Cullompton: Willan Publishing).

Glantz, L. (1995), 'Recent Crime Trends in South Africa', *Imbizo: Crime, Security and Human Rights* 3/4, 28–33 (Cape Town: Community Peace Foundation).

Goffman, E. (1959), The Presentation of Self in Everyday Life (New York: Doubleday).

—— (1961), *Asylums* (London: Penguin Books).

Goldstein, H. (1979), 'Policing: A Problem-Oriented Approach', *Crime and Delinquency* 25, 236–58.

Goldstone Commission (1992), *2nd Interim Report*, 29 April <http://www.anc.org.za/ancdocs/history/transition>, accessed 01 June 2007.

Gordon, C. (ed.). (1980), *Power/Knowledge* (Brighton: Harvester).

—— (1991), 'Governmental Rationality: An Introduction', in G. Burchell et al. (eds).

Gould, C. and Lamb, G. (2004), *Hide and Seek: Taking Account of Small Arms in Southern Africa* (Pretoria: Institute for Security Studies).

Grant, E. (1989), 'Private Policing', *Acta Juridica* (Cape Town: Juta & Co).

Greene, J. and Mastrofski, J. (eds) (1988), *Community Policing: Rhetoric or Reality* (New York: Praeger).

Hacking, I. (1975), *Why does Language Matter to Philosophy?* (UK: Cambridge University Press).

Hadland, A. (1997), 'Forgotten by their leaders, former soldiers turn to a life of crime', *Sunday Independent*, 2 November.

Haggerty, K. (2001), *Making Crime Count* (Toronto: University of Toronto Press).

Haggerty, K. and Ericson, R. (2000), 'The Surveillant Assemblage', *British Journal of Sociology* 51:4, 605–22.

—— (2001), 'The Military Technostructures of Policing', in P. Kraska (ed.).

Hammerschick, W. (ed.) (1995), *Jahrubuch fur Rechts und Kriminalsoziologie* (Baden: Nomos).

Hannah-Moffat, K. (1999), 'Moral Agent or Actuarial Subject', *Theoretical Criminology* 3:1, 71–94.

—— (2001), Punishment in Disguise: Penal Governance and Federal Imprisonment of Women in Canada (Toronto: University of Toronto Press).

Hansard (1990) (Cape Town: Government Printers).

Hansson, D. and van Zyl Smit, D. (eds) (1990), *Towards Justice? Crime and State Control in South Africa* (Cape Town: Oxford University Press).

Harris, B. (2002), 'Xenophobia: A New Pathology for a New South Africa?', in D. Hook and G. Eagle (eds).

Haysom, F. (nd.), Policing the Transition: Transforming the Police. Discussion Paper on Policing commissioned by the Department of Information and Publicity *South Africa: African National Congress) www.anc.org.za/ancdocs/policy/policing.html, accessed 01 June 2007.

Hermer, J. and Mosher, J. (eds) (2002), *Disorderly People: Law and the Politics of Exclusion in Ontario* (Halifax: Fernwood Publishing).

Hills, A. (1996), 'Towards a Critique of policing and National Development in Africa', *The Journal of Modern African Studies* 34:2, 271–91.

Hirst, P. (1994), *Associative Democracy* (Cambridge: Polity Press).

Holtzman, Z. (1994), 'Policing in South Africa: Guguletu A Case Study', in P. Ncholo (ed.).

Hook, D. and Eagle, G. (eds) (2002), *Psychopathology and Social Prejudice* (Cape Town: University of Cape Town Press).

Hudson, B. (2001), 'Punishments, Rights and Difference: Defending Justice in the Risk Society', in K. Stenson and R. Sullivan (eds).

Huey, L., Ericson, R. and Haggerty, K. (2005), 'Policing Fantasy City' in D. Cooley (ed.).

Huffajee, F. and Hess, S. (1998), 'Making a killing in the business world', *The Mail & Guardian*, 31 July <http://www.mg.co.za/mg/new/98jul2/31jul-security.html>, accessed 01 June 2007.

Human Rights Watch/Africa (1995), *South Africa: Threats to a New Democracy* (New York: Human Rights Watch).

Hunt, Alan and Wickham, G. (1994), *Foucault and Law*. (London: Pluto Press).

Ibbotson, J. (1994), 'Repositioning the security industry in a changing South Africa', Paper presented to the South African Security Association Annual Conference, 22–23 September.

Independent Online (2001), 'Legal Challenges to Crime-Stats Moratorium', 7 February <http//www.iol.co.za/index.php?set_id=1&click_id=13&crt_id=qw981553021995B265.html>, accessed 01 June 2007.

Institute for Security Studies (ISS), (1997), *Safer by Design: Towards Effective Crime Prevention Through Environmental Design in South Africa*, ISS Monograph Series No. 16 (November) (Pretoria: Institute for Security Studies).

—— (2004), *National Victims of Crime Survey: South Africa 2003*, ISS Monograph Series No. 101 (Pretoria: Institute for Security Studies).

Institute of Criminology (1990), *Kitskonstables in Crisis: A Closer Look at Black on Black Policing* (Cape Town: University of Cape Town).

Irish, J. (1999), *Policing for Profit: The Future of South Africa's Private Security Industry,* ISS Monograph Series No. 39 (August) (Pretoria: Institute for Security Studies).

Jacobs, J. (1997), 'People of Guguletu join forces with police to drive criminals out', *The Cape Argus*, 28–29 June.

Johnston, L. (1992), *The Rebirth of Private Policing* (London: Routledge).

—— (1997), 'Policing Communities of Risk', in P. Francis, P. Davies and V. Jupp (eds).

—— (2000), 'Transnational Private Policing: The Impact of Global Commercial Security' in J. Sheptycki (ed.).
—— (2006), 'Transnational Security Governance' in J. Wood and B. Dupont (ed.).
Jones, T. and Newburn, T. (1995), 'How Big is the Private Security Sector?', *Policing and Society* 5: 221–232.
Jones, T., Newburn, T. and Smith D. (1996), 'Policing and the Idea of Democracy', *British Journal of Criminology* 36:2, 182–98.
Kelling, G. and Stewart, J.K. (1989), 'Neighborhoods and Police: The Maintenance of Civil Authority', *Perspectives on Policing,* No.10: May, (Washington, D.C.: National Institute of Justice and Harvard University).
Kelling, G. and Moore, M. (1988), 'The Evolving Strategy of Policing', *Perspectives on Policing,* No. 4 (Washington, D.C.: National Institute of Justice and Harvard University).
Kempa, M. and Shearing, C. (2002), 'Microscopic and Macroscopic Responses to Inequalities in the Governance of Security: Respective Experiments in South Africa and Northern Ireland', *Transformation: Critical Perspectives on Southern Africa* (Special Issue on Crime and Policing in Transition) 29:2, 54–5.
Kinnes, I. (2000), *From Urban Street Gangs to Criminal Empires: The Changing Face of Gangs in the Western Cape*, ISS Monograph Series No. 48 (Pretoria: Institute for Security Studies).
Klockars, C. (1988), 'The Rhetoric of Community Policing', in J. Greene and S. Mastrofski (eds).
Knox, C. and Monaghan, R. (2002), *Informal Justice in Divided Societies: Northern Ireland and South Africa* (New York: Palgrave MacMillan).
Kobese, F. (1996), 'Anti-Crime Committees and Community Courts in the Eastern Cape', *Imbizo: Non-State and Private Policing,* 3 (Cape Town: Community Peace Foundation), 35–39 .
Kraska, P. (ed.) (2001), *Militarizing the American Criminal Justice System* (Boston: Northeastern University Press).
Lacey, N. (1994), 'Government as Manager, Citizen as Consumer', *The Modern Law Review* 57:4, 534–554.
Leighton, B. (1991), 'Visions of Community Policing: Rhetoric and Reality in Canada' *Canadian Journal of Criminology*, July–October: 485–522.
Leman-Langlois, S. and Shearing, C. (2004), 'Repairing the Future: The South African Truth and Reconciliation Commission at Work', in G. Gilligan and J. Pratt (eds).
Lessing, C. (1996), 'Crime cost SA R 31-b last year; Country 'giving up the fight', *Pretoria News*, 12 June.
Loader, I. (1994), 'Democracy, Justice and the Limits of Policing: Rethinking Police Accountability', *Social & Legal Studies* 3, 521–44.
Lochrenberg, M. and Stanton, S. (eds) (1995), Interim Report of the Workshop 'Confronting Crime: Innovating for Safety', Cape Town, September 9–13.
Lue-Dugmore, M. (2003), Paper Commissioned by the Committee on the Administration of Justice, Northern Ireland, (Cape Town: Institute of Criminology, UCT).

MacFarlen, R. (1994), 'The Private Security Industry in South Africa', *African Defence Review* 19.

Maharaj, G. (ed.) (1999), *Between Unity and Diversity: Essays on Nation-Building in Post-Apartheid South Africa* (Cape Town: David Philip Publishers).

Malan, M. (1997), 'The Future of Private Security – Regulation or Castration?' *Security Today* Oct/Nov: 28–31.

Mandela, N. (1993), *Nelson Mandela Speaks: Forging a Democratic, Non-racial South Africa*, edited by S. Clarke (New York: Pathfinder Press).

Manganyi, C. and du Toit, A. (eds) (1990), *Political Violence and the Struggle in South Africa* (London: MacMillan).

Marks, M. and Mckenzie, P. (1998), 'Militarised Youth: Political Pawns or Social Agents?', in J. Cock and P. Mckenzie (eds).

—— (2001), 'Alternative Policing Structures? A Look at Youth Defence Structures in Gauteng', in W. Schärf and D. Nina (eds).

Mattes, R. (2006), 'Good News and Bad: Public Perceptions of Crime, Corruption and Government', *South African Crime Quarterly* 18.

Mbhela, W. (1998), 'Chauke's arrest is immanent, say police', *The Mail* & G*uardian*, 13 –19 February <http:www.mg.co.za> [home page], accessed 01 June 2007.

McLaughlin, E. and Murji, K. (1997), 'The Future Lasts a Long Time: Public Policework and the Managerialist Paradox', in P. Francis, P. Davies and V. Jupp (eds).

—— (2001), 'Lost Connections and New Directions: Neo-Liberalism, New Public Managerialism, and the "Modernization" of the British Police', in K. Stenson and R. Sullivan (eds).

Mguire, K. (1997), 'Policing the New South Africa: Law, Order and the Dynamics of Self-Sustaining Violence', *The Police Journal* LXX: 1 (Jan–March), 11–18.

Miller, P. and Rose, N. (1990), 'Governing Economic Life', *Economy and Society* 19:1, 1–31.

Minnaar, A. (1999), 'The New Vigilantism in Post-April 1994 South Africa: Crime Prevention or an Expression of Lawlessness?', Paper presented to CRIMSA Conference in East London, May 25–28.

Minnaar, A. and Mistry, D. (2004), 'Outsourcing and the South African Police Service' in M. Schonteich, A. Minnaar, D. Mistry and K.C. Goyer (eds).

Mncadi, M. and Citabatwa, S, (1996), 'Justice, Safety and Correction: An Urban Indigenous Model?', *Imbizo: Exploring Community Justice* 1, 25–29 (Cape Town: Community Peace Foundation).

Mncadi, M. and Nina, D. (1994), 'A Year After: A Training Programme in Guguletu on Community Policing', *Imbizo:Initiatives on Community Policing* 2, 18–24 (Cape Town: Community Peace Foundation).

Moka, J. and Stoehner, T. (1995), 'Private Security Arches over St. Louis', *Security Management* (September), 94–5.

Moore, M. and Trojanowicz, R. (1988), 'Corporate Strategies for Policing', *Perspectives on Policing* 6: November (Washington, D.C.: National Institute of Justice and Harvard University).

Moore, M., Trojanowicz, R. and Kelling, G. (1988), 'Crime and Policing', *Perspectives on Policing,* 2 (Washington, D.C.: National Institute of Justice and Harvard University).
Moss, G. and Obery, I. (eds) (1992), *South African Review 6: From 'Red Friday' to Codesa* (Johannesburg: Ravan Press).
Nathan, L. (1992), 'Beyond Arms and Armed Forces: A New Approach to Security' *South African Defence Review* 4.
Naudé, B. (2000), 'The South African National Crime Prevention Strategy: A Critique', *Acta Criminologica* 13:2, 1–4.
National Secretariat for Safety and Security (1997), *NCPS News*, 1:1 (July), 1–4 (Pretoria: DoSS).
Ncholo, P. (1994), 'Alternate Ordering Mechanisms and Alternate Justice: Myth and Reality', *Imbizo: Rethinking Policing* 1 (Cape Town: Community Peace Foundation).
Ncholo, P. (ed.). (1994), *Towards Democratic Policing* (Cape Town: Community Peace Foundation).
NCPS News (1997), 'Nedcor ISS Crime Index', *Crime Prevention Co-ordination Newsletter* 1:1, July.
Nedcor Project on Crime, Violence and Investment (1995), Briefing Paper delivered at the Business Initiative Against Crime and Corruption (August).
—— (1995) 'Stop Crime' (Johannesburg: Nedcor), December.
—— (1996), Newsletter No. 7 (Johannesburg: Nedcor), February.
—— (1996), *Final Report* (Johannesburg: Nedcor), April. Nedcor/ISS (1997), *Crime Index* (Midrand: Criminal Justice Information Centre).
—— (1998), 'Crime and Policing: Perceptions and Fears', *Crime Index* 2:1 (Pretoria: Institute for Security Studies).
—— (2000), 'Crime and Confidence: Voters' Perceptions of Crime', *Crime Index* 4:2 (Pretoria: Institute for Security Studies).
Nelken, D. (ed.) (1994), *The Futures of Criminology* (London: Sage).
Network of Independent Monitors (NIM) (1996), Untitled Report on Private Security in South Africa, March.
Newburn, T. and Sparks, R. (eds) (2004), *Criminal Justice and Political Cultures: Naitonal and International Dimensions of Crime Control* (Cullompton: Willan Publishing).
Ngcokoto, B. (1997), 'Street Committees in Guguletu Section 3:1982–1995', Occasional Paper No. 1, Community Peace Foundation, Cape Town.
Nina, D. (1992), 'Popular Justice in a 'New South Africa': From People's Courts to Community Courts in Alexandra', Occasional Paper 15, Centre for Applied Legal Studies, University of the Witwatersrand, Johannesburg.
—— (1993), '(Re)Making Justice in South Africa: Popular Justice in Transition', Working Paper No. 8, Centre for Social Development Studies, University of Natal, Durban.
—— (1994), 'Reorganising People's Power in the "New" South Africa: Working on Peace, Safety and Justice with a Guguletu Street Committee', *Imbizo: Rethinking Policing* 1 (Cape Town: Community Peace Foundation).

—— (1995a), *Re-thinking Popular Justice: Self-regulation and Civil Society in South Africa* (Cape Town: Community Peace Foundation).

—— (1995b), 'Reflections on the Role of State Justice and Popular Justice in post-Apartheid South Africa.' *Imbizo:Crime, Security and Human Rights* 3, 7–14 (Cape Town: Community Peace Foundation).

Nina, D. and Russell, S. (1997), 'Policing "by any means necessary": Reflections on Privatisation, Human Rights and Police Issues – Considerations for Australia and South Africa', *Australian Journal of Human Rights* 3:2,157–182.

Normandeau, A. and Leighton, B. (1990), *A Vision of the Future of Policing in Canada: Police Challenge 2000*. Background Document (Ottawa: Solicitor General).

Nunn, S. (2003), 'Seeking Tools for the War on Terror', *Policing: An International Journal of Police Strategies and Management* 26:3, 454–72.

O'Malley, P. (1992), 'Risk, Power and Crime Prevention', *Economy and Society* 21, 252–275.

—— (1994), 'Penalising Crime in Advanced Liberalism', Paper presented to the American Society of Criminology Annual Meeting, November.

—— (1996a), 'Post-Social Criminologies: Some Implications of Current Political Trends for Criminological Theory and Practice', *Current Issues in Criminal Justice* 8: 26–39.

—— (1996b), 'Risk and Responsibility', in A. Barry, T. Osborne and N. Rose (eds).

—— (2001), 'Policing Crime Risks in the Neo-Liberal Era', in K. Stenson and R. Sullivan (eds).

O'Malley, P. and Palmer, D. (1996), "Post-Keynesian policing," *Economy and Society* 25:2, 137–155.

O'Malley, P., Weir, L., and Shearing, C. (1997), 'Governmentality, Criticism, Politics', *Economy and Society* 26:4, 501–517.

O'Neill, M., Marks, M. and Singh, A.-M. (eds) (2007), *Police Occupational Culture: New Debates and Directions* (London: Elsevier).

Parnell, S. and Mabin, A. (1995), 'Rethinking Urban South Africa', *Journal of Southern African Studies* 21:1, 39–61.

Pavlich, G. (1992), 'People's Courts, Postmodern Difference and Socialist Justice in South Africa', *Social Justice* 19:3, 29–45.

Pelser, E., Louws, A. and Ntuli, S. (2000), *Poor Safety and Policing in South Africa's Rural Areas*, ISS Monograph Series No. 39 (Pretoria: Institute for Strategic Studies).

Phosa, M. (1993), 'The Role of the Police in the Transitional Period', Speech at the SA Top Management Course. Silverton, Pretoria, 25 October.

Plasket, C. (1989), 'Sub-Contracting the Dirty Work', *Acta Juridica* 165–88.

Powell, I. (1999), '"Apartheid Army" Still in Charge', *Mail & Guardian,* 20 August.

Pratt, J. (1999), 'Governmentality, Neo-Liberalism and Dangerousness', in R. Smandych (ed.).

Pretoria News (1996), 'R1.2-b Earmarked for Criminal Justice System', 13 December.

Price, R.M. (1991), *The Apartheid State in Crisis: Political Transformations in South Africa, 1975–1990* (New York: Oxford University Press).

Prior, A. (1989), 'The South African Police and the Counter-Revolution of 1985–87', *Acta Juridica* 189–205.

Prinsloo, J. (1998), 'Crime Prevention in South Africa Utilising Indigenous Practices', *Acta Criminologica* 11:2, 72–79.

Private Security Industry Regulatory Authority (PSIRA) (2006), *Annual Report 2005–6* <http://www.psira.co.za/pdfs/annualreport_2005_06_pdf>, accessed 02 June 2007.

Rauch, J. (2001), 'The 1996 National Crime Prevention Strategy'http://www.csvr.org.za/papers/papncps3.html, accessed 01 June 2007.

Reichman, N. (1986), 'Managing Crime Risks: Towards an Insurance Based Model of Social Control', *Research in Law and Social Control* 8, 151–72.

Reiner, R. and Cross, M. (eds) (1991), *Beyond Law & Order: Criminal Justice Policy and Politics into the 1990s* (London: Macmillan Academic and Professional Ltd.).

Reiss, A. (1987), 'The Legitimacy of Intrusion into Private Space', in C. Shearing and P. Stenning (eds).

Rigakos, G. (2002), *The New Parapolice* (Toronto: University of Toronto Press).

Robertshaw, R., Louw, A., Shaw, M., Mashiyane, M. and Brettell, S. (2001), *Reducing Crime in Durban: A Victim Survey and Safer City Strategy*, ISS Monograph Series No. 58 (Pretoria: Institute for Security Studies).

Roche, D. (2002), 'Restorative Justice and the Regulatory State in South African Townships', *British Journal of Criminology* 42: 514–533.

Rorty, R. (1980), *Philosophy and the Mirror of Nature* (New Jersey: Princeton University Press).

Rose, N. (1991), 'Governing by Numbers: Figuring Out Democracy', *Accounting, Organization and Society* 16:7, 673–92.

—— (1992), 'Towards a Critical Sociology of Freedom', Inaugural Lecture, Goldsmiths College, University of London.

—— (1993), 'Government, Authority and Expertise in Advanced Liberalism', *Economy and Society* 22:3, 283–99.

—— (1994), "Expertise and the Government of Conduct", *Studies in Law, Politics and Society* 14: 359–97.

—— (1996a), 'The Death of the Social?: Re-Figuring the Territory of Government', *Economy and Society* 25:3, 376–356.

—— (1996b), 'Governing "Advanced" Liberal Democracies', in A. Barry, T. Osborne and N. Rose (eds).

—— (1999), *Powers of Freedom: Reframing Political Thought* (Cambridge: Cambridge University Press).

Rose, N. and Miller, P. (1992), 'Political Power Beyond the State: Problematics of Government', *British Journal of Sociology* 43:2, 173–205.

Samara, T. (2003), 'State Security in Transition: The War on Crime in Post-Apartheid South Africa', *Social Identities* 9:2, 277–312.

Sarre, R. (1997), 'Community Policing: Themes for South Africa', *Acta Criminologica* 10:1, 5–10.

Schärf, W. (1989), 'Community Policing in South Africa', in *Acta Juridica*, (Cape Town: Juta & Co.).

—— (1991), 'Report to the George Regional Court in the State vs. Sipati and 4 Others'.

——(1997), 'Specialist Courts and Community Courts', Position Paper Commissioned by the Planning Unit, Ministry of Justice, South Africa, May.

—— (2000), 'Community Justice and Community Policing in Post Apartheid South Africa: How Appropriate are the Justice Systems of Africa?, *IDS Bulletin* 34, 74–82.

Schärf, W. and Artz, L. (1996), *Government Responses to the Current Crime Wave Crime Prevention Policies and Programmes of Central Government.*

Commissioned Report for the Nedcor Project on Crime, Violence and Investment.

Schärf, W. and Ngcokoto, B. (1990), 'Images of Punishment in the People's Courts of Cape Town, 1985–7: From Prefigurative Justice to Populist Violence' in C. Manganyi and A. du Toit (eds).

Schärf, W. and Nina, D. (eds) (2001), *The Other Law: Non-State Ordering in South Africa* (Lansdowne: JUTA Law).

Schönteich, M. (2002), '2001 Crime Trends: A Turning Point', *South Africa Crime Quarterly* No. 1 July.

Schonteich, M., Minnaar, A., Mistry, D. and Goyer, K. (eds) (2004), *Private Muscle: Outsourcing the Provision of Criminal Justice Services*, ISS Monograph Series No. 93 (Pretoria: Institute for Security Studies).

Seamon, T. (1995), 'Private Forces for Public Good', *Security Management* (September), 92–7.

Security Focus (1997), Sept/Oct/Nov. (South Africa: Primedia Publishing).

Security Today (1997), Oct/Nov. (South Africa: Security Publications S.A. (Pty) Ltd.).

Seekings, J. (1991), 'Township Resistance in the 1980s," in M. Swilling, R. Humphries and K. Shubane (eds).

—— (1992a), 'The Revival of "People's Court": Informal Justice in Transitional South Africa' in G. Moss and I. Obery (eds).

—— (1992b), 'Civic Organisations in South African Townships', in G. Moss and I. Obery (eds).

—— (2001), 'Social Ordering in the African Townships of South Africa: An Historical Overview of Extra-State Initiatives from the 1940s to the 1990s,' in W. Schärf and D. Nina (eds).

Shaw, M. (1995), *Partners in Crime? Crime, Political Transition and Changing Forms of Policing Control,* Research Report No. 39, June (South Africa: Centre for Policy Studies).

—— (1996), 'South Africa: Crime in Transition', Unpublished Paper, Institute for Security Studies.

—— (1997), 'Crime in Transition', in *Policing the Transformation: Further Issues in South Africa's Crime Debate*, ISS Monograph Series No. 12 (Pretoria: Institute for Security Studies).

—— (2001), 'Profitable Policing? The Growth of South Africa's Private Security Industry', in W. Schärf and D. Nina (eds).

—— (2002), *Crime and Policing in Post-Apartheid South Africa: Transforming Under Fire* (Bloomington: Indiana University Press).

Shaw, M. and Shearing, C. (1998), 'Reshaping Security: An Examination of the Governance of Security in South Africa', *African Security Review* 7:3, 3–12.

Shearing, C. (1992), 'The Relation Between Public and Private Policing', in M. Tonry and N. Morris (eds).

—— (1994), 'Reinventing Policing: Policing as Governance' *Imbizo: Rethinking Policing 1,* 1–12 (Cape Town: Community Peace Foundation).

—— (1997), 'The Unrecognized Origins of the New Policing: Linkages between Public and Private Policing', in M. Felson and R. Clarke (eds).

—— (2006), 'Reflections on the Refusal to Acknowledge Private Governments', in J. Wood and B. Dupont (eds).

Shearing, C. and Stenning, P. (1982), *Private Security and Private Justice* (Ottawa: The Institute for Research on Public Policy).

—— (1983), 'Private Security: Implications for Social Control', *Social Problems* 30:5, 493–506.

—— (1984), 'From the Panopticon to Disney World: the Development of Discipline', in A. Doob and E. Greenspan (eds).

—— (eds) (1987), *Private Policing* (USA: Sage Publications).

Shearing, C., Farnell, M. and Stenning, P. (1980), *Contract Security in Ontario* (Toronto: Centre of Criminology, University of Toronto).

Sheptycki, J. (ed.) (2000), *Issues in Transnational Policing* (London: Routledge).

Simon, J. (1997), 'Governing Through Crime', in G. Fisher and L. Friedman (eds).

—— (2001), 'Entitlement to Cruelty: neo-liberalism and the punitive mentality in the United States', in K. Stenson and R. Sullivan (eds).

Simpson, G. and Rauch, J. (1999), 'Reflections on the National Crime Prevention Strategy', in Maharaj, G. (ed).

Singh, A.-M. and Kempa, M. (2007), 'Reflections on the Study of Private Policing Culture: Early Leads and Key Themes', in M. O'Neill, M. Marks and A.-M. Singh (eds).

Singh, A.-M, Frank, C., McClain,C., Schärf, C. and Seekings, J. (1997), Popular Participation in the Administration of Justice, Position Paper Commissioned by the Planning Unit, Ministry of Justice, South Africa, May.

Smandych, R. (ed.) (1999), *Governable Places: Readings on Governmentality and Crime Control* (Aldershot: Darmouth).

Smith, D. (1987), *The Everyday World as Problematic: A Feminist Sociology* (Toronto: University of Toronto Press).

—— (1991), *The Conceptual Practices of Power: A Feminist Sociology* (Toronto: University of Toronto Press).

South African Foundation (1996), *Growth for All: An Economic Strategy for South Africa* (Johannesburg: The South African Foundation).

South African Police Service (SAPS) (1996), *Status Report: Transformation of the South African Police Service.* Report by the National Commissioner J.G. Fivaz (Pretoria: SAPS).

—— (1996), *SAPS Transformation Workshop* (Pretoria: National Support Services, SAPS).

—— (2002), *Strategic Plan 2002–5* (Pretoria: SAPS).

South, N. (1988), *Policing for Profit: The Private Security Sector* (London: Sage).

—— (1997), 'Control, Crime and the "End of Century Criminology"', in P. Francis, P. Davies and V. Jupp (eds).

The Sowetan (1998), 'Mercenaries still helping rebels', 18 August.

Starr, P. and Corson, R. (1987), 'Who will have the numbers?: the rise of statistical services industry and the politics of public data', in W. Alonso and P. Starr (eds)

Stehr, N. and Ericson, R. (eds) (1992), *The Culture and Power of Knowledge* (Berline and New York: de Gruyter).

Stenson, K. (1993), 'Community Policing as a Governmental Technology', *Economy and Society* 22, 373–389.

—— (1995), 'Communal Security as Government – The British Experience', in W. Hammerschick (ed.).

—— (1998), 'Beyond Histories of the Present', *Economy and Society* 27:4, 333–352.

—— (1999), 'Crime Control, Governmentality and Sovereignty', in R. Smandych (ed).

—— (2005), 'Sovereignty, Biopolitics and the Local Government of Crime in Britain', *Theoretical Criminology* 9:3, 265–87.

Stenson, K. and Factor, F. (1994), 'Youth Work, Risk and Crime Prevention', *Youth and Policy* 45:1, 1–15.

—— (1996), 'Governing Youth: New Directions for the Youth Service', in J. Ballock and M. May (eds).

Stenson, K. and Watt, P. (1999), 'Crime, Risk and Governance in a Southern English Village', in G. Dingwall and S. Moody (eds).

Stenson, K. and Sullivan, R. (eds) (2001), *Crime, Risk and Justice* (Cullompton: Willan Publishing).

Steytler, Nico. (1993), 'Policing Political Opponents: Death Squads in South Africa', in Mark Findlay and Ugljesa Zvekic (eds).

Storer, D. (1996), 'From South Africa to Chicago: International Conference Blasts Police Abuse', *Copwatch Report*, Winter: 2 (California: COPWATCH).

Streek, B. (2001), '"Unreliable" crime stats released to SA', *The Mail & Guardian*, 01 June <http://www.mg.co.za > [home page], accessed 01 June 2007.

Swilling, M., Humphries R., and Shubane, K. (eds) (1991), *Apartheid City in Transition* (Cape Town: Oxford University Press).

Taylor, I. and Vale, P. (2000), 'South Africa's Transition Revisted: Globalisation as Vision and Virtue', *Global Society* 14:3, 399–414.

Technical Committee (Community Policing) (1995), *Work Document on Community-Police Forums* (Pretoria: Department of Safety and Security).

Tonry, M. and Morris, N. (eds) (1992), *Modern Policing* (Chicago: University of Chicago Press).

Tshehla, B. (2002), 'Non-State Justice in Post-Apartheid South Africa: A Scan of Khayelitsha', *African Sociological Review* 6:2, 47–70.

Valji, N., Harris, B. and Simpson, S. (2004), 'Crime, Security and Fear of the Other' *SA Reconciliation Barometer* 2:1 (South Africa: Center for the Study of Violence and Reconciliation).

Valverde, M. (1990), 'The Rhetoric of Reform: Tropes and the Moral Subject', *International Journal of the Sociology of Law* 18, 61–73.

van der Spuy, E. (1989), 'Literature on the Police in South Africa: An Historical Perspective', *Acta Juridica* (Cape Town: Juta & Co.).

—— (1990), 'Political Discourse and the History of the South African Police', in D. Hansson and D. van Zyl Smit (eds).

—— (2000), 'Foreign Donor Assistance and Policing Reform in South Africa', *Policing and Society* 10, 342–66.

—— (2004), 'South African Policing Studies in the Making', in B. Dixon and E. van der Spuy (eds).

van der Spuy, E., Geerlings, J., and Singh, A.-M. (1998), Donor Assistance to Crime Prevention and Criminal Justice Reform in South Africa, 1994–1998. Report commissioned by the National Crime Prevention Secretariat (Cape Town: Institute of Criminology, University of Cape Town).

van Zyl Smit, D. (1989), 'Adopting and Adapting Criminological Ideas: Criminology and Afrikaner Nationalism in South Africa', *Contemporary Crises* 13, 227–251.

—— (1999), 'Criminological Ideas and the South African Transition', *British Journal of Criminology* 39:2, 198–215.

van Zyl Smit, D. and van der Spuy, E. (2004), 'Importing Criminological Ideas in a New Democracy: Recent South African Experiences', in T. Newburn and R. Sparks (eds).

Waddington, P.A.J. (1994), "Policing South Africa: The View From Biopatong', *Policing and Society* 4, 83–95.

Wainstein, P. (1997), 'Security – A South African perspective', edited extract of paper presented at the International Security Conference, New York.

Weir, L. (1996), 'Recent Developments in the Government of Pregnancy', *Economy and Society* 25:3, 372–92.

Williams, D. (1996), 'Popular Justice: Lateral Thinking and Believing the Impossible', *Imbizo Issue: Exploring Community Justice* 1, 4–9 (Cape Town: Community Peace Foundation).

Williams, J. (2005), 'Reflections on Private Versus Public Policing of Economic Crime', *British Journal of Criminology*, 45, 316–339.

Wilson, J. Q. and Kelling, G. (1982), 'Broken Windows', *The Atlantic Monthly* 249:3, 29–38.

Wood, J. and Dupont B. (eds) (2006), *Democracy, Society and the Governance of Security* (Cambridge: Cambridge University Press).

Wright, J. (1995), 'Crime and its Effects on the Short Term Insurance Industry', Paper presented at the 1995 Annual Conference of the Security Association of South Africa (Durban, 4 July 1995).

Index